Crime prevention

Crime prevention

Theory, policy and politics

Daniel Gilling
University of Plymouth

First published in 1997 by UCL Press

UCL Press Limited
1 Gunpowder Square
London EC4A 3DE
UK

and

1900 Frost Road, Suite 101
Bristol
Pennsylvania 19007-1598
USA

The name of University College London (UCL) is a registered
trade mark used by UCL Press with the consent of the owner.

British Library Cataloguing-in-Publication Data
A catalogue record for this book is available from the British Library.

Library of Congress Cataloging-in-Publication Data are available.

ISBNs:1-85728-490-9 HB
1-85728-491-7 PB

Typeset in Palatino by Kate Williams, London.
Printed and bound in Great Britain by
T.J. International Ltd., Padstow, Cornwall.

To Karen

Contents

Preface and acknowledgements

Crime prevention is a difficult beast to tame. It has always been taken as an implicit purpose of any deliberate strategy of crime control pursued by state or private agencies, but more recently it has been employed to describe a disparate set of practices that may be contrasted with more traditional approaches to crime control. It is the latter sense that this book explores, although inevitably the line between the two is at times blurred and hard to define.

The rise of crime prevention as a distinct set of practices in contrast to traditional criminal justice policy is an international phenomenon of the latter half of the twentieth century, which ironically presages the return of certain pre-modern forms of crime control. Its contemporary ascendancy has fed off the inexorable rise in officially recorded rates of crime in this period, and it has profited from the apparent exhaustion of the capacity of traditional criminal justice agencies to control crime and the widespread fear and concern that comes in its wake. But it also owes a great deal to broader paradigmatic changes in the nature of the relationship between the state and its citizens, as well as between state agencies themselves.

In contrast to its more established alternatives, and especially because of its lack of a strong professional constituency, crime prevention is relatively new and still has to prove itself. As a consequence, the overwhelming majority of its growing literature is, with a few notable exceptions, of a practical and scientific nature, seeking to ascertain whether, and if so how, it works. Much of the literature is therefore, not surprisingly, inward-looking, self-contained, and rather dry. This book takes the luxury of casting most of the technical questions aside, and focusing instead upon issues that, whilst frequently impinging upon the matter of effectiveness, frame crime prevention upon a much broader canvas. Crime prevention thus becomes a part of an overall strategy of governance, the political and practical implications of which are explored in the pages that follow.

The first chapter considers the difficulties in defining crime prevention, which present political opportunities for the concept to be employed in pursuit of a number of objectives that may serve purposes beyond only the control of crime. The second and third chapters project these difficulties on to the enterprise of criminological theorizing, enabling different theories to be differentially interpreted in terms of their crime preventive implications. The third chapter also introduces the contemporary theories that have formed the bedrock of modern crime prevention practice, the unfolding of which, in the English policy context, is explored at length in Chapter 4. In Chapters 5 and 6, the political and practical dimensions of this are explored at the organizational and institutional levels through a review of the different elements of the mixed economy of crime prevention.

Chapter 7 sharpens the focus further, exploring the micro-level problems of interagency collaboration, and contextualizing them also within mezzo- and macro-levels of analysis. The political and practical consequences of the flexible meaning of crime prevention run through these chapters, but are returned to more centrally in the final Chapter 8, which explores the reasons for the change from crime prevention to community safety, and reflects upon the implications of this significant paradigmatic shift in this aspect of criminal justice policy.

The book assumes no prior knowledge of crime prevention, and in this regard is intended as an introductory text, providing a resource through which this much neglected aspect of criminal justice can be brought into the academic mainstream. As the previous paragraph suggests, there is a thread of an argument running through the book, which looks more at the political manipulation of crime prevention than its practical application. However, the chapters also stand alone and may be read in isolation from one another.

This is my first book, and it has taken longer than I had anticipated. For that, I have to thank a busy timetable, and the arrival of my son

Jack, whose first year of interrupted sleep has left his father feeling older, but not wiser, except for an intimate knowledge of those small hours that I once slept through. He has, however, been a beautiful distraction, and I would not be without him. For their academic support, I would like to thank those people whose constructive comments on my earlier work have kept the fire alight; whilst for their help with specific queries for this book I am indebted to Gloria Laycock, Ken Pease, and David Walton for their kind assistance. I have nobody but myself to thank for the typing, which is another reason why this has taken longer than expected. I must also thank all those at UCL Press who have helped to see the project through to its fruition. Finally, for her long-suffering support and encouragement, I hope Karen finds it all worthwhile. Together we cracked it!

CHAPTER 1

The concept of prevention

Introduction

It can hardly have escaped the attention of those with a professional or academic interest in crime that there has been a great deal more attention devoted to the concept of crime prevention in recent years, although any criminologist with a sense of history would rightfully question the extent to which the phenomenon is indeed a recent one. There may be more talk about the prevention of crime today, with the concept being used as a contrast with more traditional criminal justice system approaches to crime control, but as a principle and objective crime prevention has always lain at the heart of criminal justice policy in the modern period, and the practice itself is much older. Hence, as Reith (1956) points out, the prevention of crime has been "the principal object" of the police since their establishment on a permanent footing in England in 1829, while the codification of the criminal law in the nineteenth century, the rationalization of penal policy around the central institution of the prison, and the eventual extension of penal discourses and practices into the community in the early twentieth century have all been similarly justified in the name of crime prevention.

Consequently, the modern use of the term to refer to contemporary developments in crime control, sometimes complementary and some times in opposition to more traditional institutional responses (police, probation and prisons), is in fact somewhat misleading, and fails to capture the essence of the changes currently taking place in crime control policies both in England and Wales, and across much of the world. Crime prevention, then, is too vague and broad a term on which to hang a study such as this, and requires further elaboration, for as it stands it has a catch-all nature that defies disciplining, enabling it to embrace a range of areas that would by themselves be worthy of study in their own right. Crime prevention incorporates not only the practices of the entire criminal justice system, but also those of many other social and public policies, as well as those of private citizens and private enterprise. The situation is further complicated when one considers that the prevention of crime is often not the primary rationale for practices that do, nevertheless, have a crime preventive effect.

If we were to unpack the concept of crime prevention, we would immediately recognize that crime itself is by no means a precise term, covering a host of qualitatively and quantitatively different acts that, as befits social constructs, vary across time and space. But the real problem lies with the word prevention, which Billis (1981: 368) succinctly and accurately describes as "slippery", and certainly difficult to contain. Freeman (1992) explores the reasons for this by breaking the word down into two constituent parts, namely prediction and intervention. That is to say that in order to prevent the occurrence of something one must first be able to predict where it is likely to occur, and then apply appropriate intervention at this predicted point. Prediction is, however, literally a risky business. It depends upon a theory of causality, and when applied to social constructs such as crime and criminality it is very uncertain, drawing as it does upon social scientific knowledge and understanding that has historically proved to be "more successful at predicting the experience of populations than of individuals." (Freeman 1992: 36). Social science, as Graham (1990: 11) observes, "is not an exact science. It deals largely with probabilities and correlates rather than certainties and causes."

The prediction of crime and criminality is mainly the province of criminology, a multidisciplinary domain comprising a broad church drawn mainly from other social sciences, principally sociology, psychology, politics and economics, with some geography, philosophy and biology thrown in for good measure. A diverse array of theories of causality and prediction emanate from this scientific melting pot, some focusing upon specific categories of crime (for example, expressive or acquisitive crimes), others focusing upon specific types of criminal, or simply criminality in general (Eysenck 1977). Such theoretical diversity spawns equally diverse preventive prognoses, none of which when applied in practice has proved to be spectacularly successful in turning the tide of generally and universally rising rates of officially recorded crime in the post-war period.

This is where intervention, the second constituent element of prevention, comes in. Different theories imply different modes of intervention, relying on different agents (such as criminal justice professionals, or the general public) and different techniques, applied at different stages in the genesis of crime, and at different sites. Even in the unlikely event that the theoretical prognoses were wholly accurate, moreover, it does not follow automatically that the correct form of intervention would be selected, or even if it were, that it would work. This is because the gap between prediction and intervention is filled by the very human process of implementation, in which the politics of policy-making is encountered, where intended and unintended consequences collide, and where unanticipated barriers manifest themselves. Invariably this is very rough terrain, although in a more optimistic scenario it is equally possible to envisage interventions working without actually knowing the reasons why, more a consequence of chance than design.

Typologies of prevention

Prevention is an uncertain business, then, and through its sheer diversity an extraordinarily unhelpful word. Brantingham & Faust do not overstep the mark when they describe crime prevention as "probably the most overworked and least understood concept in contemporary criminology" (1976: 284), although some progress has been made since they wrote these words, and a number of attempts have been made to make the term more manageable and useful by fitting it into a conceptual framework that discriminates between forms of prevention. One such approach is that of the National Crime Prevention Institute (1986) in the USA, which distinguishes between direct crime prevention controls, which proactively address opportunities for crime, and indirect controls, which are supposed to cover everything else. In contrast, Johnson (1987) refers to a distinction between correc-

3

tive prevention, which seeks to address the causes of crime, and punitive prevention, which seeks to deter through the force of the criminal justice system. Elsewhere, Forrester and his colleagues (1988) distinguish victim-focused crime prevention from its offender-focused equivalent.

These distinctions all serve to illustrate points of difference between approaches to crime prevention, reflecting differences in forms of intervention, techniques (correction or deterrence), developmental stages (proactive or reactive) and sites (offenders or victims). While in some ways useful, however, they are by no means conceptually watertight, principally because one finds an inevitable grey area between such binary distinctions, and because some approaches can be made to fit different categories, so that, for example, many offender-focused interventions are also victim-focused in so far as they perform a surveillance or incapacitation function for them. Such distinctions, therefore, often fail to allow for the difference between intention and outcome. Moreover, given that crime prevention covers such a vast area of activities, a binary distinction is never likely to serve as a major feat of elucidation.

An alternative, and by far the most commonly employed approach is that which borrows from the literature on medical epidemiology in making a three-way distinction between primary, secondary, and tertiary prevention. The distinction is ultimately attributable to Brantingham & Faust (1976), who identified the site of primary prevention as the general public or environment; the site of secondary prevention as those regarded as being "at risk" of offending or criminal victimization; and the site of tertiary prevention as those who have already succumbed to either criminality or criminal victimization. Primary interventions are regarded by Brantingham & Faust as "the ideal objective" (ibid.: 292) in so far as they seek to secure the elimination of criminogenic conditions in society, thus being truly proactive, while tertiary interventions are the least satisfactory, but conversely constitute the main business of the criminal justice system and its correctional interventions into offenders' lives. Secondary interventions, meanwhile, absorb the main energies of scientific criminological research in the identification and treatment of those who might be predicted to be "at risk" of crime. This may have been so in the mid-1970s, but is less true today, notwithstanding the contribution of criminal career researchers (Farrington 1992).

This primary to tertiary distinction represents an advance upon binary approaches, if only because it increases the number of categories within a typology from two to six, given that at each of the three stages there is a further distinction between victim- and offender-focused initiatives. There are still difficulties, however, for the same approaches can still be placed in different categories: correctional practices, for example, are both individually deterrent (tertiary prevention), and generally deterrent (primary prevention) in their exemplary status. Consequently, while at least this distinction separates out the different developmental stages and sites of intervention, it is hard to disagree with Graham's (1990: 11) warning that crime prevention risks being a broad and potentially "meaningless phrase".

In the last decade or so another distinction has emerged and claimed a common currency within the crime prevention literature, although it too suffers the same shortcomings mentioned above. This is the distinction between situational crime prevention (sometimes referred to as opportunity reduction, or designing out crime), and social crime prevention (sometimes labelled the social problem approach). South (1987: 42) proffers the following definition of situational crime prevention:

> Situational crime prevention focuses on the management, design and manipulation of the built physical environment, in order to reduce the opportunity to commit crime and increase the risk of detection if deterrence fails.

The key words here are probably opportunity and physical environment: it seeks to change the structure of criminal opportunities that are perceived to lie in phenomena located within the physical environment. It aims to do this principally either by physical security measures, which rely to a great extent upon technology supported by publicity and incentives to use it; or by measures which increase the costs of crime (by increasing the risk of apprehension) and reduce the benefits (for example, by property-marking) (Graham 1990).

By contrast, social crime prevention seeks to change criminal motivations, which are perceived to lie in people rather than things, in the social environment. As Sutton (1994: 10) says, "social prevention now embraces almost any program that can claim to affect the pattern of behaviour, values and the self-disciplines of groups seen as having potential to offend". It seeks to achieve this via social policy-type measures such as housing policies; health treatment and education in respect of drugs and alcohol; family and educational policy; youth work; and employment policy (Graham 1990). This covers a very broad range of interventions, but children and youth are the principal focus, closely followed by some other politically and economically marginalized groups. In part because of this breadth, Tonry & Farrington (1995) prefer to subdivide social crime prevention into developmental crime prevention, which seeks to prevent the development of criminal potential within individuals, and community crime prevention (discussed below), which seeks to do likewise in residential communities by changing their social conditions.

Given that there are so many different possible forms or distinctions of crime prevention, used across an international stage, it is not surprising to find occasional confusion in the use of the terminology, and the reader is urged to beware of this. For example, some writers (e.g. Harris 1992) have taken the term social crime prevention to refer to collective means of crime prevention, as distinct from individual means of prevention, and as such these social approaches can focus upon either motivations or opportunities. Furthermore, as van Dijk (1990) reports, the Dutch tend to use the term social crime prevention to refer to approaches that depend not on the actions of criminal justice agencies, but rather on the actions of the general public or other public officials, which again might be focused on opportunities or motivations. There is nothing essentially wrong with the use of the label social crime prevention to cover these activities, but such a usage of the term does not correspond to the sense in which it is normally and widely used, certainly in England and among most practitioners, and thus it is not the sense in which social crime prevention will be used throughout this book.

In a definitive typology drawn up for the benefit of the United Nations, Graham (1990) offers a different label for what van Dijk calls social crime prevention, namely community crime prevention. This essentially comprises a mix of social and situational approaches, pursued either by individuals or groups. Its distinctiveness stems from the fact that it is developed by agencies outside of the traditional criminal justice system: the community element comes from the fact that it is very much a bottom-up, participatory approach, relying upon partnership across a range of non-criminal justice agencies and groups (Rosenbaum 1988).

Graham and Rosenbaum, however, are both guilty of exceeding the boundaries of their definitions of community crime prevention, for both ultimately include community policing within its purview. This shows how hard it is to fix definitional boundaries and exclude moments of arbitrariness: no typology is watertight. In this case, including community policing clearly breaks the rule about the exclusion of criminal justice agencies, but such an infraction appears justified since community policing employs crime prevention techniques that rely heavily upon localism and community participation, while simultaneously conjuring up the same rosy ideological image. However, once the definitional rules are broken the floodgates may be opened, and if community policing is included, then why not also community probation, or community punishments, and virtually anything else with the community prefix that distinguishes it from erstwhile forbears of, presumably, noncommunity crime prevention?

Graham argues that community crime prevention may constitute both social and situational crime prevention, but in doing so it "creates a whole greater than the sum of its two parts" (1990: 2). Yet he does not clarify exactly how this is so, and thus risks falling for the ideological appeal of community, which is often more presentational than practical. Nevertheless, the term has become popularized in recent years, and in England in the 1990s it has now become further refined as simply "community safety" (Home Office 1991).

The various attempts that have been made to provide a typology for crime prevention, or to distinguish one form from another, ultimately fail to achieve what they set out to do, and their scientific inexactitude does little to challenge the claim that it is still "a rather vague and ill-defined concept" (Graham 1990: 10), or as Sutton (1994: 7) observes, "a diffuse set of theories and practices." There is no common currency to which all theories or practices are ultimately reducible, and hence the definitional difficulties should be fully expected. Nevertheless, what the distinctions do manage to achieve is a demonstration of the broad nature of paradigmatic shifts that have occurred in crime prevention, thereby qualifying our perception of the growth of interest in crime prevention in recent years. That is to say that it is not so much that crime prevention is new, but rather that its character has changed by means of the paradigmatic shifts picked up in the definitions discussed above.

Crime prevention, then, is a constant with a changing character. Once mainly the responsibility of private citizens, in the last two centuries it has gradually been taken over by the criminal justice system, but since the 1970s there has been a discernible shift of emphasis and responsibility from this system to those outside of it, either the general public, or other public and private agencies. This shift has become so marked now that van Dijk (1990: 205) feels justified in defining crime prevention as

> the total of all policies, measures and techniques, outside the boundaries of the criminal justice, aiming at the reduction of the various kinds of damage caused by acts defined as criminal by the state.

By the same token, while Graham (1990) recognizes that the criminal justice system does have a crime preventive role, principally in terms of tertiary prevention, he nevertheless elects to exclude tertiary prevention, and thus the main business of the criminal justice system, from his definitive crime prevention guide. This is a largely pragmatic decision, taken to make the subject matter altogether more discrete and manageable. But something else lies behind the decision too, and it is this that alerts us to the wider significance of crime prevention as a label worth fighting for.

Crime prevention is nothing if not a good idea: as Freeman says of the concept in general, being for prevention is akin to being against sin, and "the rhetorical power of prevention is felt across the political spectrum" (1992: 40). Crime prevention is a worthy end to aspire to, and anything that can be so labelled by implication carries a good deal of favour. Because of this, however, it is also a label that may be jealously guarded: many practices may aspire to being crime preventive, but not all are necessarily regarded as such. This is the vital difference between the objective meaning of crime prevention, which applies to a vast array of practices, and the subjective reality, where the label is effectively reserved for those practices that have had their causes championed within the political arena, and have gained their rewards in the shape of considerable public investment. This point will become clearer as the story of crime prevention is gradually unfolded in this and subsequent chapters.

For now, the important point is that the acts of selective interpretation of crime prevention discussed above may be partly pragmatic, but they are also inherently political. Van Dijk's definition, for example, could be read as inferring an expressed preference for activities that take place outside of the criminal justice system, and so could Graham's. Similarly, having bemoaned the fact that "the phrase crime prevention has been loosely applied to any kind of effort aimed at controlling criminal behaviour", the National Crime Prevention Institute (1986: 2) goes on to highlight the preferability of what it calls direct crime prevention, as a "pragmatic, scientifically-based management approach to before-the-fact crime reduction" (ibid.: 11). The implication is that direct crime prevention is better because it is direct – before-the-fact rather than after-the-fact, proactive rather than reactive. This is a distinction that has a weak scientific basis, however, for as Tuck (1987: 5) points out, "No clear analytic distinction can be made between future orientated and past orientated actions against crime." Direct crime prevention may be preferred, then, but it is not necessarily any more scientific, and indeed any criminological claim to a pure scientific status rests on shaky foundations. The point is that the question of whether one approach is more crime preventive, or more deserving of the title, than another will always be politically contentious, at least in part.

Nevertheless, the fact that crime prevention lends itself to this sort of politics is itself of considerable interest, and points to an important quality of the concept that merits further inquiry.

The political appeal of prevention and preventionism

As the previous section has made apparent, prevention as a concept possesses something of an elastic quality that enables it to cover a broad range of theoretical premises and practical interventions. This breadth renders the term scientifically problematic, but what is scientifically problematic may conversely be politically useful, for the concept can serve as an empty vessel into which may be poured any potent brew intended to satisfy thirsts that extend well beyond the pragmatic or technical.

The promise to prevent a social problem such as crime is likely to attract considerable popular support, and is thus a means by which those who aspire to govern in democratic states may stake a claim to

9

legitimacy: that is why crime is a hot political issue, as the British Labour Party found to its cost in 1979 as the Conservatives fought and won the general election of that year in large part because of the law and order platform they adopted. The flexibility of the concept of prevention, moreover, means that it can be cut to the cloths of either political constituency: as Freeman (1992) observes, prevention can equally fit left wing ambitions of benign interventionist social engineering or right wing ambitions of market solutions and individual responsibility. The fact that prevention can be used in this way, even if the term itself is not explicit, infers that it is an instrumental part of the process by which social problems are socially constructed for ends that are as much political or ideological as practical.

Manning (1985), who takes this constructionist view of social problems, suggests that if things are going to be accepted as social problems that require some sort of institutional response, they must needs be discrete, moral and technical. That is to say that they must be worthy of public attention, and they must be seen as something about which something can actually be done – again, a conception that relies as much upon ideology as science. The concept of prevention is a means by which this can be achieved, and thus one may read the development of criminal justice policy not so much as a series of scientific innovations, but rather as the development of a series of assertions and counter-assertions about the ways in which crime can be prevented.

However, because of the breadth of the concept, and the weakness of criminology and other theorizing about crime as pure science (see Ch. 2), all of these assertions or counter-assertions are likely to have some claim to theoretical plausibility, no matter how bizarre they may appear to be – and many criminological theories and control programmes have been very bizarre. It is clearly not possible to invest in all these programmes, and thus what is in vogue at any one time is largely a matter of the combination of such factors as economic constraint; political, cultural and ideological appeal; and criminological validity as demonstrated by the latest research. Thus there is potentially an ever-widening pool of crime preventive ideas that become superimposed one upon the other, and a filtering process that selects the most favoured at any particular historical moment. While it may not be certain which ideas or practices will be selected, it is at least certain that some will – there is always a demand, regardless of how effective the practices are. Billis (1981: 375) attributes this to what he calls preventionism, which consists of "the belief that social problems can be prevented rather than resolved."

This belief is generated from within the political arena, establishing a sort of market in which promises are traded for votes. In this case, however, it is the supply from such promises that helps create its own demand (Billis ibid.: 368), for once the preventionist belief is implanted "The logic of 'preventive work' seems so clear-cut, so uncontroversial, that any criticism runs the risk of appearing short-sighted and reactionary". The phenomenon of preventionism, therefore, lends itself also to interventionist expansionism:

> Since it is difficult to object to the apparent logic of preventive activity, it is consequently difficult to contain the steady encroachment of public agencies into areas of life that might more appropriately be left to other public or voluntary organisations, to the private sector, or to the individual and his (sic) family. (Billis ibid.: 379)

This interventionist expansionism can come despite, and quite possibly because of, diminishing returns in terms of effective outcomes, prompting Billis to complain (ibid.: 369) of the field of his inquiry that "prevention in social welfare has spread to the point where culling is required." However, so long as the concept has this enduring political appeal, specifically in terms of its promise to eliminate social problems, it is unlikely to be culled in the way Billis envisages, although economic constraints can certainly limit reliance on some forms of preventive intervention.

Given the political utility of preventionism, it is essential that we ask who benefits. It is evidently unlikely to be the apparently intended beneficiaries, the public, for preventionism's persistence depends ultimately upon its continued failure to succeed in its stated objectives. There would appear to be two main beneficiaries; first, those who profess to have the knowledge and expertise to intervene in order to prevent – the professions. According to Wilding (1982), professions in social welfare, and by implication in criminal justice, depend upon being able to identify areas of intervention over which they can attain both occupational control and social closure, thereby maximizing their own rewards and status. The concept of prevention affords these professions the opportunity to do this because it can be used instrumentally, "to capture and control demand for professional services" (Freeman 1992: 42), in turn because this demand is brokered through the executive arm of the state, which uses the prevention of social problems as a source of its own legitimacy, and which constitutes the second main beneficiary of preventionism.

The prevention of social problems, therefore, justifies a profession's existence, while also providing a means of understanding the nature of their means of intervention. Hence, if prevention is a source of legitimacy, but that legitimacy also depends upon the persistence of the problem, then there may well be a natural tendency for the means of professional intervention to gravitate towards after-the-fact tertiary prevention – preventing recurrence rather than occurrence, and symptoms rather than causes. But while tertiary prevention is the natural home of the profession, drip-feeding its life blood, the scope for expansionism is not ruled out, for professions can always seek to increase the value of their stock by promising to be still more preventive, via earlier intervention. Hence, as Freeman (1992: 42) observes "preventive programmes increase the number of points of access to the individual". Cohen (1985) refers to this as "the anticipatory syndrome".

Indeed it is curious how short the collective professional memory can be: programmes originally justified as preventive may suddenly be recast as reactive (but nevertheless necessary), while new programmes are superimposed upon them through appeal once more to the logic of prevention. Hence, for example, residential care is dropped in favour of community care; prisons are dropped in favour of community sanctions; and detection is dropped in favour of targeted patrolling. In each case, the old gives way to the new, which then assumes the preventive mantle.

Billis (1981) identifies some of the means by which professions achieve these conceptual leaps. Pride of place seemingly goes to the secondary category of prevention, which seeks to identify those "at risk". If professions start by dealing with those who already have the problem they can attempt to expand their domain by claiming a refinement in their knowledge base to a point at which they now claim to be able to identify those who are "at risk" of succumbing to that problem, but do not yet have it. This is where occupational closure comes into its own, for it can have the effect of obviating close scrutiny of the nature of these claims by outsiders, which is just as well for they often entail "an assumptive leap from *associating* particular problems with some conditions to *explaining* these problems as *caused* by those conditions." (Billis ibid.: 372, emphasis in original). So, notwithstanding the very shaky foundations of professional knowledge bases, overlooked because of the useful role they perform for the state in managing populations (Wilding 1982, Hugman 1992), the concept of "at risk" opens up a whole new area for professional intervention.

Another way in which professions can seek to extend their preventive orientation is by intervening across a broader canvas, particularly by means of better co-ordination with other agencies and services (Billis 1981). In this way a more holistic package is offered to those who may be experiencing or may be at risk of a problem, the package being sold on the basis of its being more preventive by means of its being more effective. This may be a fall-back strategy for professions that have come under fire for alleged ineffectiveness; a means of preserving their own position by uniting with those who are not under such assault, and it may well be that this is a strong motivation behind a number of inter-agency or multi-agency initiatives in crime prevention and elsewhere, which have taken root since the 1980s (see Chs 5, 6 and 7). The resultant corporate strategy is, however, a risky one, for while it may help to preserve preventive integrity, it does so only at the expense of a potential dilution of their power and control, which may be relocated from an individual profession to a corporate entity. That is why it is likely to be a fall-back, a last ditch effort when other avenues of escape, such as the concept of at risk, have been exhausted. This is an issue to which we shall return in the final chapter.

Professions are not completely free to expand their empires, and there are certain obvious constraints that help to determine how far preventionism can be made to work for them. First, since preventionism depends upon interventionism, boundaries are set by the wider socio-economic milieu within which they operate, which determines the resources available for preventive intervention, while also shaping the nature of ideological support for it. Secondly, professional usefulness depends upon the continuation of the problems they have been established and sanctioned to tackle, and so there is a natural hesitancy to venture too far down the preventive road if that road is likely to lead to any significant elimination of the problem.

Hence, for example, where police establishment levels are determined by formulae that rest in part on a calculation of the crime rate there may be a reluctance to invest too heavily in anything that might significantly reduce this.

Thirdly, there is a danger in venturing too far down the prevention road because a point is reached where the prevention of a problem changes from being a matter of professional intervention to a matter of public responsibility – the point where secondary prevention becomes primary prevention, where non-specialist action is requisite. Consequently, as with the second point, there is hesitancy to take preventionism too far, especially among patronage professions (Johnson 1972) that cannot exist without state support, for in the wrong socio-economic and ideological conditions it can end up undermining the rationale for professional intervention altogether. Rather, a balance must be struck here, because while primary prevention risks limiting the scope for professional intervention it at least has the merit, for professions, of relocating the responsibility for the persistence of social problems from their failed interventions to the public's own inattentiveness. A fine line must be trodden, therefore, between victim-finding and victim-blaming.

The preventive credentials of many public service professions have come under increasing attack in recent years, although their failure to deliver what they promise, ". . . continual failure is a condition for [professional] survival" (Cohen 1985: 173), is essentially nothing new. Their tendency to create dependency and disable (Illich 1977) has left them vulnerable in an unsupportive socio-economic milieu, and this is one key reason why, in crime prevention, the major paradigmatic shift has been, as noted above, away from the criminal justice professions and towards either the general public (primary prevention), or the sharing of responsibility with other public sector professions (the partnership approach). According to some, though, professions have a fall-back position that makes any talk of their demise both unwise and premature. This position stems from the fact that some element of intervention will always be needed to tackle social problems whose ultimate causes, once one transcends the obfuscation of professional discourse, are structural rather than individual. Consequently, primary prevention will always have its limits and, in so far as it is essential that governments are seen to be doing something to tackle the problem, there will always be room for the professions in secondary or tertiary modes of preventive intervention. This preventionism obscures the point that prevention will only really succeed if it takes the form of structural change, and thus Billis's (1981: 379) call for "the abandonment of pseudo-prevention" is a vain hope indeed.

Preventionism is as important for the state as it is for the professions, because it affords the opportunity to manage social problems without eliminating them, and in so doing removing its source of legitimacy. Freeman (1992) makes this point well, arguing that prevention is essentially a strategy of governance. The security of the state is threatened if social problems give the appearance of running out of control, and it is the concern generated by this threat that motivates the state to invest in preventive strategies, particularly and self-evidently at times of crisis, but also at other times, for the commitment to prevention is something of an uncontrollable addiction. The difficulty, however, is that while the problem must be contained, it must not be eliminated altogether, and so this makes prevention risky. It must appear to be working, without working that well, and hence the management of this balancing act entails the state walking "a tightrope between action and inaction, between promising and pretending." (Freeman ibid.: 46).

This would seem to infer that policies require continuous monitoring and adjustment in the light of their impact on social problems, although this hardly corresponds to the general mode of policy-making to which we are used. Yet this is not so, for another advantage of prevention is that it can serve to insulate the state from criticism by deflecting it elsewhere. In the case of primary prevention, citizens themselves may be co-opted into managing the problem, with their failure to do so being regarded as their own fault. This, however, is potentially risky, for it simultaneously renders more visible the structural sources of problems should primary strategies fail to any significant degree. Secondary and tertiary forms of prevention may be safer, for they entail not only an element of co-opting individuals into their own treatment, but also a buffer zone of professional intervention, where blame for any deterioration in the social problems can be attributed to professional deficiencies.

In summary, then, it can be seen that the concept of prevention can be made to serve a number of useful purposes for governments, professions, and ultimately for the state itself. This is because of the inherent and self-evident appeal of prevention in association with social problems, and because of the flexible interpretation of the word, which enables it to be stretched in a number of possible directions, for a number of possible reasons and motives, only some of which are practical. There is a sense in all of this that the concept is manipulated and corrupted from its purely scientific meaning and purpose by the almost conspiratorial actions and processes of other agencies and structures. This assumes that prevention does have a scientific base in the first place: scientific prediction of risk supported by precise scientific intervention. Notwithstanding the aspirations of many criminologists, however, this assumption is deeply questionable, and a deeper analysis of the concept will serve to show its essentially political nature.

Prevention and governance

In many ways prevention lies at the heart of the business of the modern state, the institutions and machinery of which are geared to the prevention of a host of social ills and problems, such as wars and epidemics, economic decline, unemployment and inflation, poverty, and of course crime itself. But exactly on what basis is such a preventive role justified? Who is it that decides which problems must be prevented, and which can be tolerated? The search for answers to such questions inevitably takes us into the realms of utilitarian thought, where the concept of prevention holds a special place.

According to Sen & Williams (1982), utilitarian governmental action hinges on two things, namely consequentiality, which holds that the choice of action should be predicated upon a full consideration of its consequences; and welfarism, which holds that the choice of action should be oriented towards the selection of the option that secures the greatest happiness. Together, these two considerations lead us to Jeremy Bentham's famous utilitarian maxim, which sought to dissociate government from any partisan influence and instead arrive at a scientific and democratic rationale for any governmental action, namely the greatest good for the greatest number. It has often been assumed that Bentham's ideas were immensely influential on the nascent Victorian British state, and very much set the pattern for modern government, although Roberts (1982) suggests that Bentham was actually only one of several thinkers ploughing a similar furrow at much the same time.

Hence, we may also bring in Foucault's (1991) genealogy of "governmentality" in which he traces a paradigmatic shift from a Machiavellian style, where the principal object of government is the sovereign's self-preservation, to a more recognizable modern style, where the principal object becomes, similar to the utilitarian maxim, the wellbeing of the entire population. In this transformation, which started around the period of the emergence of the mercantile state, Foucault argues that the sovereign is no longer separate from the people, but is part of them, leading by example via a natural progression through government of the self (morality), one's family (economy), and the state (politics). Bentham's utilitarianism makes a similar connection between the actions of individuals (the pursuit of pleasure and the avoidance of pain) and of the state (the greatest happiness).

The key question for both Foucault's genealogy and Bentham's theory is how the wellbeing of the population, or the greatest happiness, may actually be secured. The belief that it can be at all is largely a product of Enlightenment thought, and humankind's new self-belief and reluctance to accede solely to divine providence (Gamble 1981). Moreover, it was the concept of prevention that was the key to understanding the proper role government should play.

For Bentham, prevention was the means by which consequentialist and welfarist objectives could best be met, and the concept recurs throughout Bentham's work, not only with regard to criminal justice, but with regard to government in general. Bentham believed that under general conditions of security individuals could be relied upon to act rationally, maximizing pleasure and minimizing pain. This belief demonstrates his adherence to the *laissez faire* tradition of political economy, which aimed not so much to do nothing (Adam Smith's list of permitted interventions in the *Wealth of Nations* is long indeed), but rather to preserve those conditions under which the market performed at its best. It was only because these conditions could not be taken for granted that intervention was ever justified. As Dinwiddy (1989) observes, this essentially translates to an equation whereby happiness, the object of government action and the ideal state, is the sum of pleasure (individual rational actions) plus security, the occasionally missing ingredient that government should have to supply.

The key to security was the absence of those conditions including the unrestrained egoism of some that threatened it. The government's task, therefore, was to see that they remained absent – that their occurrence or presence was prevented. This can be seen very clearly in Bentham's Constitutional Code, which was published posthumously in 1841. The Code identified a number of ways in which government action could serve to maintain security, stressing the value of what Bentham called "indirect" means, especially the law (an aspect of sovereignty in Foucault's terms), which was a deterrent guide to conduct that also possessed the considerable utilitarian virtue of economy. In other words, happiness would be so much the greater if security could be achieved without undue expense, which ultimately fell on the public in the painful form of taxation. This was the preventive ideal.

In addition to this ideal, however, Bentham recognized the need and ultimately also the justification for more proactive measures to avert potential problems that defied simple general deterrence. Consequently, among the 13 ministries that he proposed in his Code was a Ministry for Preventive Services, intended to take action among other things to avert epidemics by public health measures (something eventually taken forward by his secretary and "disciple" Edwin Chadwick); to avert floods by building flood defences; and to avoid food shortages by storing food surpluses (Dinwiddy 1989). The same emphasis on prevention permeated his proposals for other ministries, and notably his proposals in the criminal justice field, which are considered in more detail in the following chapter.

Bentham's utilitarian prescription in the Constitutional Code was very clear on what could or should be done, but less explicit about exactly when governments would be able to know that security was under threat, when they should act and how they should act. An answer to such questions may, however, be found within Foucault's work on governmentality, which addresses the vein of thought of which Bentham's contribution was typical. Foucault claims that it was the "invention" of statistics that was instrumental in transforming governed populations from an unknown mass to a known assemblage of data covering numerous dimensions of security in relation to such factors as mortality, morbidity, marriage, birth, and of course crime rates. Manning (1985) supports this point when he draws attention to the pivotal role played by statistical societies and quasi-scientific journalists in drawing attention to, and thereby constructing, social problems in the nineteenth century. These statistics were used to determine the extent to which families were not coping with events around them, and the extent, therefore, to which security was under threat. Consequently, families were gradually transformed from erstwhile models of good government to instruments of governance, through which data could be collected (to aid the prediction element of prevention) and problems addressed (the intervention element). Addressing these problems was the business of what Foucault termed "the disciplines" – a variety of power-knowledge discourses employed to control, in yet finer and finer detail, the lives and activities of the governed, under apparently benign welfarist intentions. These are the modern welfare professions, whose preventive role already has been considered above.

Historians have debated for some time over the extent to which Bentham was an adherent to *laissez faire* or interventionist principles (Dinwiddy 1989), but if we consider the central role of prevention within his work we can throw clearer light on the issue. In essence, the question becomes not whether Bentham was for or against interventionism, but rather which form of prevention he was willing to support. Prevention, then, is a key dimension of the politics of the state. Bentham's ideal was deterrent legislation, or primary prevention from a minimalist state intent on laying down the rules of human conduct. However, he clearly recognized the limitations of this ideal in the real world, and so many of his proposals in the Constitutional Code show an increased level of support for more interventionist forms of secondary and tertiary prevention (increasingly disciplinary in Foucault's terms), opening up new areas for colonization by the disciplines, and starting a dynamic that has a certain inevitability to it.

The important point is that Bentham's utilitarianism facilitates an interventionist momentum not because of the flexibility of prevention, but because of the uncertainty of what it is that is to be prevented, for things that threaten security, and social problems, are ultimately clothed in political subjectivity. Security is an extremely vague concept, and impossibly difficult to define objectively, much like a social problem such as poverty.

An example of this difficulty, and thus of the onward march of preventionism, may be found in the field of social welfare reform, and specifically the Webbs' ambition to reform the Poor Law at the beginning of the twentieth century. Squires (1990) describes how the structure of welfare was changed from deterrence and coercion (sovereignty) to a much more ambitious blueprint of social administration, incorporating many more deeply interventionist measures, such as family visiting, labour camps and labour training (discipline). The proposed changes were justified by an appeal for a more preventive orientation, for as Squires (ibid.: 110) observes, "the Webbs drew attention to the fact that in a truly 'preventative' social policy the state must not wait for poverty and distress to reveal itself but must anticipate its appearance".

The flexibility of prevention made such an assertion justifiable, but the real genius came in the reconception of what it was that was to be prevented. Thus, while poverty and pauperism had been regarded as the social problem that threatened security in the nineteenth century, the Webbs tried to turn the twentieth century equivalent to simply being "in need", a term so incredibly vague that it widened the scope for preventive intervention immeasurably, incorporating anything that failed to conform to the normative standards and judgements of the great social reformers. This reconception, in turn, was built upon a new theory of causality of social problems: the prediction element of prevention changed from fecklessness to being in need. The theory was built at least as much upon political concern as any scientific analysis, and in the end facilitated the emergence of another strategy of governance or prevention, based upon actuarialism, or the insurance principle.

In the foregoing analysis, one could easily substitute poverty for crime, and being in need to being at risk. The character of crime prevention has changed as our understanding of the crime problem has altered, as the immediately following two chapters will demonstrate. The key point, moreover, is that the dynamic behind this change is only in a small way attributable to any scientific advances with regard to questions of causality and appropriate intervention. Far more important has been the potential of prevention to fit in with different political strategies of governance: the essential criterion has been political utility rather than effectiveness.

Summary

A recent paper by Ekblom confirms the message of this chapter, that crime prevention is, conceptually speaking, in something of a mess. His solution (1994: 4) is to employ a bland definition of crime prevention as "intervention in mechanisms that cause criminal events ". This is a definition that draws attention to the two core elements of cause and intervention that are discussed in this chapter and that constitute the two main themes of the remaining chapters in this book.

From this bland definition, Ekblom expresses his preference that crime prevention should be constructed into a discipline, employing a common vocabulary that specifies the exact causes of crime to be tackled, and the precise specification and mechanism of the intended intervention. He fixes upon the term "proximal causes", and proposes (ibid.: 13) that

> The focus on proximal causes will hopefully act as a source of discipline, requiring the more complex theories of crime and crime prevention to come down to earth at some point to define their essential processes in terms of immediate behavioural and ecological realities – or at least make them connect up.

Ekblom articulates the worthy and laudable ambitions of the scientist, but this chapter has sought to demonstrate that crime prevention is far too important to leave to the scientist, because it is too instrumental a part of the armoury of governmentality and the legitimacy of the state and state agencies. Ekblom's hope for a scientific discipline is partly informed by such an awareness, for he ends with the suggestion that if crime prevention were a *bona fide* scientific discipline it would give its researchers more professional credibility or clout, in the policy process, over others' crime preventive folkways, which remain deeply entrenched. This chapter suggests, however, that for the present this hope may be forlorn, as scientific rationality continues to play second fiddle to its political equivalent, and later chapters illustrate this point further.

CHAPTER 2

Theories of crime prevention I

Introduction

This chapter examines the first constituent part of prevention, namely prediction. As noted in Chapter 1, prediction is predicated upon a theory of causality. In the case of crime prevention, a distinction must be made here between theories of crime, which is an event and a legal category, and theories of criminality, which is the manifestation of an assumed motivation for behaviour which fits such a category. The distinction is an important one, not only because the causes of these two phenomena may be different, as the thing to be explained may be in dispute, but also because in different historical epochs one or other of these approaches has tended to be dominant, although the contemporary emphasis is towards integration.

In the main, theorizing about crime (or criminality – crime is used hereafter as a shorthand for both) has been conducted through the medium of the discipline of criminology. As Garland (1994) observes, this discipline was born in the last decades of the nineteenth century, and is in fact less discipline than multidisciplinary, constructed out of the applied interests of an array of professions, from doctors and lawyers to psychiatrists, psychologists and statisticians. Yet theorizing on crime is not the preserve of criminology. Preceding criminology, and accompanying its onward march, has been a number of folk explanations of crime that pass as common sense, and that receive a regular airing at Conservative Party annual conferences, for example. In addition, scientific explanations preceded criminology in the shape of the classical school, which rose to prominence in the late eighteenth century in Europe; and marched parallel to criminology in the shape of the more liberal sociology of deviance, which was at its most vibrant in America and in Europe in the 1960s. Thereafter, according to Sumner (1994) the sociology of deviance self-destructed and died a death in the 1970s, although continued interest in the subject suggests that reports of its demise may be seriously premature.

Between the three "scientific" areas of classicism, criminology and the sociology of deviance, a massive amount of theory and empirical detail has been generated, but here is not the place for a detailed review, because space prohibits it, and there are anyway numerous other texts that more than adequately cover these areas. The purpose here is more an illustrative one, to demonstrate how different preventive interventions, of the primary, secondary and tertiary kinds identified in Chapter 1, have their origins in different theories of crime. This is not to imply that there is a simple correlation between theory and practice, however, for between the two lie many political, ideological and socioeconomic variables, which must first be negotiated. The intention is to show that one reason why there is space for so many discourses of prevention is that there is no agreed conception, let alone explanation, of the crime problem that has widespread empirical validity. This chapter will also seek to show, therefore, the tenuous nature of some of the theories which have been generated. This makes for a lively politics of crime prevention, which is explored at the national level in Chapter 4, and at the organizational and interorganizational levels in Chapters 5, 6 and 7.

The idea of prevention, it ought to be noted, presupposes a certain moral stance. In the case of crime, it relates to the supposition that crime is something necessarily bad and injurious, and in so far as this relates to criminals, it conveys an underpinning correctionalism or reformism. Cohen (1988) identifies correctionalism as a key characteristic of criminological endeavour, which entails either the recommendation of a plan of intervention, or at the very least an acceptance of definitions of crime by official agencies seeking such a plan. However, it is important to acknowledge that not all theorists of crime share such an objective. As Downes & Rock (1995) observe, sociological theories in particular often have objectives beyond that of practical application, such as the functionalist analysis of crime as a means of maintaining social order, and other accounts that see crime as a feature of the social structure that may not actually be amenable to change.

The important point is that not all theories of crime are also theories of crime prevention, at least not in original intent. It is possible, however, that despite the best intentions of theorists to remain detached from the correctionalist logic, they can nevertheless be interpreted by others in this light. Thus, as Cohen (1981) reports, much of the more radical sociology of deviance of the 1960s was incorporated into the more mainstream criminology of the 1970s without necessarily shaking its foundations or diverting it from its correctionalist course. A good example of this may be found in the case of the labelling perspective, which despite its radical edge could be co-opted into a utilitarian, correctionalist criminological project via an ironic and contradictory state-managed preventive programme of non-intervention.

Finally, before embarking upon our theoretical tour, it is worth echoing another observation made by Downes & Rock (1995), which is that the theoretical enterprise has been continually dogged by the difficulty of acquiring valid and reliable data about crime. Criminals rarely announce themselves or broadcast their deeds, whilst the criminal justice system's knowledge is dependent upon its effectiveness, as well as vice versa. Other sources of information are equally problematic, so theorists of crime are effectively left with snippets from which to construct their tentative contributions. These, then, tend inevitably to be partial, and as Downes & Rock (1995) observe of different schools of thought, "Each group will preclude certain kinds of knowledge and deliver certain truths."

Classical theory

The publication of Cesare Beccaria's *Dei Delitti e Delle Pene* in 1764 marks the origins of the classical school. The work was translated into the English language in 1767, and had a significant impact (Roshier 1989: 5) as "a comprehensive, coherent treatise on the iniquities of the contemporary European criminal justice systems, and offering a systematic alternative".

25

Up until this time, and for some while after, these criminal just-ice systems were characterized by an array of cruel and unusual punishments, often for the most minor of transgressions, typified in England by the Black Act of the 1720s, which infamously brought more than 200 capital offences on to the statute book (Hostettler 1992). The preventive logic of these punishments, on the face of it, was one of general deterrence, based upon the threat of terror, backed by a rather final and potentially messy incapacitation for those who failed to heed the message. Beneath the surface terror, however, revisionist historians such as Hay (1975) have argued that by facilitating displays of mercy through the commutation of severe sentences, these punish-ments, or more properly the threat of them, made England more gov-ernable by means of class control.

Nevertheless, contemporaries of Beccaria were persuaded to see only the inefficiency of such systems of punishment, for despite the terror of the occasional public spectacle, there was a perception that many offenders were not deterred, because the enforcement machin-ery was patchy, selective and inefficient; and the punishment was uncertain because it was rarely carried out. The rational man of classi-cal and utilitarian theory was wheeled in to demonstrate that in such circumstances, the prospect of pain through apprehension and pun-ishment was much dimmer than the prospect of pleasure gained from the rewards of the criminal act.

Consequently, Beccaria proposed an alternative, whilst remaining within an essentially punitive and deterrent paradigm. Foucault (1977: 93) captures the essence of the proposed reforms very well when he notes that "the prevention that was expected as a result of the punishment and its spectacle – and therefore of its excess – tended now to become the principle of its economy and the measure of its just proportions". In place of a barbaric threat, Beccaria proposed a more measured response, employing the utilitarian calculus in order to construct a penal tariff where, at each stage, the pain threatened by the punishment just exceeded the anticipated pleasure from the com-mission of the act. The aim was to establish a scale of proportionality, where the more serious the crime was, the more severe the punish-ment became. The proposal's effect was therefore to humanize the penal system, and Beccaria's liberalism endowed him with a degree of humanitarianism and a desire to curtail excessive state power. As ever, though, the humanizing effect was arrived at through practical rather than principled reasoning: excessive punishment for minor crimes had the potential to escalate them into more serious ones, as the offender had nothing to lose.

Translating this plan from theory into practice required a number of major criminal justice reforms that did indeed take place across much of Europe, although England was more resistant to change than most. Establishing a scale of proportionality between offence and penalty, and getting this to work in a generally deterrent way, required that the criminal law be codified and well publicized, rather than being made up largely after the event, and shrouded in mystification. If the threat was to be taken seriously, moreover, it had to be genuine, so that potential offenders would be persuaded of the certainty of their apprehension and punishment. This meant an efficient and consistent enforcement machinery, which given the absence of a permanent police force until 1829, and a largely privatized prosecution process, were not characteristics of the criminal justice system in the eighteenth century. However, in the course of the nineteenth century these things, along with the codification of the criminal law, were addressed, and in time the criminal justice system came to take on a certain classical form.

Classical theory, however, was not without its difficulties. It was not based upon an empirically informed notion of crime. Instead, it was armchair theorizing, in which the criminal was represented by the rational man of utilitarian thought and legal individualism. This detaches the subject from the wider social and environmental context, and in this way classicism was never interested in the causes of crime, beyond seeing it as a hedonistic choice. But this wider context affects the circumstances of the offender, and may endow them with an altogether different rationality, or a bounded one in so far as they may be constrained by virtue of such factors as age, education or mental health. We do not all think or act like the rational man of utilitarian thought, and therefore we are not all equally responsive to the deterrent messages of criminal laws and punishments. Consequently, any preventive structure built upon such premisses is bound to be weak and fragile.

Another difficulty with classical theory, which raises a similar point, concerns the notion of proportionality. Proportionality assumes in this context the greater the reward, the harsher the punishment. However, the harshest punishments are reserved for crimes such as murder which do not necessarily bring great reward to the offender. Utilitarian theory tends to view crime in instrumentalist terms, but punishments are related more to questions of seriousness, which emanate from moral and political considerations. Seriousness and instrumentality are therefore not equivalents, and cannot be measured on the same scale. This poses further problems for classical theory, because Beccaria believed that the notion of proportionality would only work if it was considered to be legitimate by liberal sensibilities. If proportionality cannot be established because seriousness is a political and moral concept, then nor can full legitimacy, for some will always find the scale unjust. This moreover, damages preventive efficiency, which depends upon such prior legitimacy.

On balance, classical theory finds it difficult to escape its class origins. The rational man or *Homo penalis* (Pasquino 1991) which it employed displays a flawed logic, but clearly made political sense at a time when a rising bourgeoisie demanded limits on arbitrary royal and aristocratic power, and sought the establishment of a nominally equal criminal law as the foundation stone of civil society. It also reflected a bourgeois morality, and a bourgeois anxiety, for as Hostettler (1992: 116) observes, "What they all wanted was a better protection of their property and more efficient laws."

Despite its logical inconsistencies, but because of the rising political power of the bourgeoisie, the English criminal justice system gradually took on a classical shape in the course of the first half of the nineteenth century – the origin of our modern system. The utilitarian Jeremy Bentham was a key instigator of the reforms that eventually took place, although many of them only reached fruition after his death. Interestingly, however, in his work we find some of the contradictions of classicism, and in his ideas we see the beginnings of a path that led away from classicism and towards neoclassicism (Taylor et al. 1973), which Roshier (1989: 13) claims 'has dominated most Western criminal justice systems".

In police and criminal law reform, Bentham was a true disciple of Beccaria's classicism, but when it came to penal policy, one notices a clear divergence. Classicism's principal preventive strategy was based upon general deterrence, and was intended to work mainly at the symbolic level, through the threat rather than the actuality of punishment. Beccaria was not very clear about the form of punishment for those who should fail to heed this symbolic threat, beyond recommending "perpetual servitude" for those committing the most serious of crimes (Roshier 1989). He did not necessarily mean imprisonment by this: in his day, certainly in England, prisons were used mainly as holding places, rather than as punishments. Bentham, however, took a much greater interest in the subject, and clearly showed an interest in the causes of offending and how they might be addressed. He still employed the classical utilitarian notion of rational man, but evidently believed that for some people the pull of hedonism was much stronger than for others. This could be tackled at the predelinquent and delinquent stages. In the case of the former, for example, in an essay on preventive legislation (Dinwiddy 1989: 91) he proposed a number of schemes, including employment and education, "to divert the current of the desires from objects in the pursuit of which men are more apt to be led into the tract of delinquency". On another occasion (Atkinson 1969: 143) he wrote that "We must seek to eliminate . . . the criminal propensities of the individual, to introduce and encourage habits of thought alien from crime." He did not write whom he meant by 'the individual', yet it was evident that he was not referring to himself or those of his class.

For delinquents, Bentham had in mind something else – the *Panopticon*. The *Panopticon* demonstrated how two modes of prevention, namely deterrence and reform, could be made to work side-by-side. It was generally deterrent by virtue of the fact that it was to be sited within the community as an awesome structure that the public might be persuaded to visit in order to witness the conditions of less eligibility contained therein. The austere regime, combined with a design feature – the inspection principle – which ensured that inmates felt under constant threat of surveillance from the gaoler, was intended to ensure individual deterrence. The *Panopticon* was intended to be a place to which offenders would have no wish to return. However, there was also a concession to the object of reform, to be achieved by three means. First, solitary confinement, for Bentham (1791: 39) was convinced that "solitude is in its nature subservient to the purpose of reformation". In addition, religious instruction and hard productive labour were intended to bring about the same effect, with the latter helping to make a nice little profit on the side – always important for Bentham's utilitarian sensibilities.

Bentham's interest in reformation was not strictly classical, but it was shared by some of his contemporaries, such as Colquhoun (1969).

Colquhoun did not see classicism as being in any way inconsistent with his own thoughts on tackling the causes of offending ("public crimes"), which he saw as lying in various forms of immorality ("private offences"), which were inevitably concentrated among the working-class unrespectables. He believed this immorality could be tackled as one of the functions of a permanent police, performing a quasi-social work role which resonates with some contemporary notions of community policing. For delinquents, however, penitentiaries provided the answer, mixing deterrence and reform in much the same way as envisaged by Bentham, in a pattern which had actually been set many centuries before in Elizabethan Houses of Correction. John Howard showed a similar interest in reform, particularly through productive labour and religious instruction, within the context of a more healthy and less corrupt prison environment.

The kind of reformation envisaged in all these contributions was not entirely kindly: the emphasis was disciplinary (Foucault 1977), intended above all to socialize the recalcitrant into the virtues of the nascent capitalist work ethic. But it was nevertheless reform, and it marked a corruption of classicism in order to address one of the latter's deficiencies, namely its failure to take the circumstances of the offender into account, although these circumstances were viewed through a bourgeois morality. Bentham's plan for his *Panopticon* never saw the light of day in England, but many of Howard's proposals were adopted, and they contributed to a major debate that accompanied the rise of the prison as the principal penal disposal by the latter half of the nineteenth century. The debate concerned the relative merits of reform and deterrence, and policy see-sawed between the two until the end of the century, by which time the latter had been vanquished as the 1895 Gladstone Committee recommended reform as the primary purpose of imprisonment, although looking through modern eyes the distinction between the two seems rather blurred anyway.

Neoclassicism represented a very crude means of interpreting the causes of crime, based more upon conjecture and fear of the "dangerous classes" than scientific observation. It may, however, be regarded as a step towards a more scientific understanding of the causes and treatment of crime, which was eventually brought into being as the positivist criminological project, to which we now turn.

In the latter half of the nineteenth century there was a growing concern that the neoclassical criminal justice system had failed at the practical level, as crime rates continued to rise across continental Europe, despite (and quite possible because of) the criminal justice reforms which had been effected (Pasquino 1991, Brantingham 1979). England had escaped the same excessive rises as elsewhere by virtue of its policy of transportation, but this had ground to a halt by the 1860s, as prisons contained increasing numbers of domestic offenders, and concern grew over the fate of discharged prisoners. This climate of concern provided fertile soil for the emergence of an alternative paradigm of prevention, with the promise of greater effectiveness.

Positivism

The fertility of the soil was enhanced by the technological progress of early capitalism, which had found a new religion in positive science, which sought to replace metaphysical and conjectural accounts of human action and indeed of the physical world, with empirically observed, documented and classified explanation. Scientific explanation therefore had a revered status, and as it entered the field of criminal justice it left its mark by replacing rational man – classicism's *Homo penalis* – with the criminal type, or positivism's *Homo criminalis* (Pasquino 1991).

The theoretical underpinnings of positivist criminology can be found in the dominant human science of the nineteenth century, namely Darwinism. Backed up by an anthropological methodology, this supported the politically conservative notion that some societies, "races" and individuals were inferior: they were more primitive and less evolved than others. It was a short step to apply the same scientific logic to criminals, for the anthropologists and missionaries who went abroad carried the same ideological and moral baggage as those who started their investigations closer to home, in the study of England's equivalent dangerous places and dangerous classes. These amoral and asocial people were deemed to be as different to the English norm as the primitive cultures, and this notion of difference, or more specifically deficient difference, was in large part responsible for undermining the universalist underpinnings of classicism, and for the declining faith in the potential of classical deterrence to work on such people.

Where classicism was confined to armchair theorizing, positivism's scientific spirit of discovery was aided by the ready availability of criminals to observe in this period of the great confinement in prisons and other institutions of containment. The possibility that institutionalized offenders were not representative of all offenders, or that the experience of institutionalization affected those the scientists observed, was not generally recognized.

Although there were a number of pseudo-sciences applied to the study of crime, like physiognomy and phrenology, which sought to deduce psychological characteristics from physical constitution, positivist criminology itself took off in Italy with the publication of Cesare Lombroso's *L'Uomo Delinquente* in 1876. He revised his theory over the course of a number of editions, and in response to criticisms, but his basic position held throughout. This was that scientific observation could be employed to identify a classification of distinct criminal types, the most important of which was the born criminal, who was essentially a biological throwback to an earlier asocial stage of human evolution. Other types included the insane criminal, the occasional criminal, and the criminal of passion, whilst Ferri, a follower of Lombroso and founder of the Italian Positive School, added the habitual criminal and the involuntary criminal to this list. The born criminal was the most biologically determinist type within the classification, whilst the others represented a variable mix of biology and psychology, with a few social characteristics thrown in.

In terms of crime prevention, positivist criminology did not so much replace neoclassicism as add a number of alternatives to its repertoire, which by this stage included general and individual deterrence, and reformism. Pasquino (1991: 238) neatly summarizes the entirety of the new repertoire as "social hygiene", oriented to clearing up what he imaginatively calls "the excrement of the social body". He describes it (1991: 242) thus:

> between the two extremes of residual intimidation for delinquents and neutralization (tending towards physical liquidation) for hardened criminals . . . [lies] a vast domain of intervention . . . designed to act as a preventive clean-up of the social breeding grounds for crime.

This entailed a further departure from the discourse of due process and legal equality underpinning classicism, implying the transformation of the criminal justice process into a massive diagnostic operation dominated by scientists rather than lawyers. It did not have to wait for an infringement of the criminal law to be set in motion, moreover. The positivist Garofalo, for example, followed Colquhoun's notion of "private offences" in his rejection of legalistic categories of crime, in favour of a more practical and universal category of "natural crime". Natural criminals could be plucked from the population and subjected to all sorts of unpleasant preventive interventions, according to this paradigm, which had very strong Darwinian and eugenic overtones.

Positivist criminology of this sort had profound implications for a criminal justice system built upon the principles of neoclassicism, especially politically, since it implied a subordinate role for legalism, and a dominant role for the scientist. Unsurprisingly, therefore, there was no fundamental conversion of the criminal justice system to the positivist cause, although that is not to suggest that the latter was not without influence.

Positivist criminology opened up a search for the causes of crime which itself positively blossomed in the twentieth century. As befits its scientific credo, the many different forms of positivism – biological, psychological, sociological or a particular combination of these – all shared a basic determinism, that there were certain factors which effectively disposed certain individuals or groups towards crime. But the precise nature of these factors varies from theory to theory in such a way that it would be impossible for the criminal justice system to incorporate them into a viable preventive strategy, even if it had been receptive to the idea of so-doing. Early positivist theories tended to agree that criminals were degenerate and deficient, but they disagreed over the nature of the cause. Thus, for example, Lombroso's theory might have set a paradigm, but it was not itself very influential in practical terms, especially after in England Goring found that the "criminal stigmata" of the supposed born criminal were just as common among university students and the armed forces (Garland 1994).

In England, then, there was considerable scientific scepticism regarding general theories of crime such as Lombroso's, and official mistrust for preventive interventions or technologies which strayed too far from the neoclassical orthodoxy which dominated the period. Nevertheless, the notion of the incorrigible criminal must have held some currency in the establishment of a containment-oriented sentence of preventive detention at the beginning of the twentieth century, although it was rarely used. In other countries, meanwhile, the neo-Lombrosian view of crime being attributed to biologically inherited low intelligence held more influence, and contributed to preventive policies such as sterilization and laws which forbade interracial marriage (Lilly et al. 1995).

In England, the dominant form of positivism was not Lombrosian, but rather that of the psychiatric profession, which was more pragmatic, and more moderate in terms of its capacity not to clash too fundamentally with the principle of due process. This was important, and quite probably peculiarly English, where, as Garland (1994: 54) observes, "the central purpose of scientific research was not the construction of explanatory theory but instead the more immediate end of aiding the policy-making process". In this regard, psychiatric diagnosed problems could be clinically treated within the existing reformist regime of the prison. The only good criminology was useful criminology, and to an extent criminology has always compromised its science by accepting official definitions of crime as its starting point.

In addition to psychiatric positivism, in the course of the twentieth century psychological positivism also grew in influence, itself being influenced by Freudian psychoanalysis. Again, it fitted wider developments in criminal justice and social policy. Cyril Burt's focus on family problems in "The Young Delinquent", for example, fitted the predelinquent interventions made possible by the appearance of child guidance clinics from the 1930s. In the same decade, the fledgling probation service increasingly arranged for the training of its officers in psychoanalytic methods, as diagnostic treatment and rehabilitation moved outside of the prison and into the community, and this scientific basis of the new probation work justified its professionalizing status, in place of its erstwhile reformist philanthropy.

The problem with this psychoanalytic theory, however, was that it was impossible to verify or refute objectively, because the alleged causal mechanism was buried within the subject's unconscious, and diagnosed only by the expert. In addition, like other contemporary forms of positivism it derived its theory from a rather limited sample. As Glaser (1979: 208) notes:

These clinicians are asked for advice primarily on the cases most puzzling to others, or on those from homes affluent enough to pay for private psychological services; consequently, their generalizations about crime tend to be based on an atypical sampling of offenders.

Psychological and biological theories, which essentially seek to explain how certain individuals remain undersocialized, have continued to be developed in the twentieth century, and have recently tended to merge over the search for genetic causes to attitudes and behaviours which may be conducive to criminality. But these theories have difficulty in reaching a wider audience and being translated into preventive interventions, because as Jeffery (1990) observes, their effectiveness and utility depends upon early diagnosis, often using neurological procedures, yet such an approach remains incompatible with neoclassical legalism.

Psychological positivism remained dominant in England in the middle decades of the twentieth century, until damning research meant that the individual treatment paradigm largely fell into disrepute; but elsewhere, and notably in America, the focus switched to sociological positivism. The first serious sociological analysis of crime was conducted within Europe by Durkheim, but his identification of the functionality and normality of crime clearly set him apart from the criminological enterprise. His correctionalism was confined to limiting the excesses of capitalist individualism: beyond that, crime was a social fact which could not be prevented. Sumner's (1994) account of 1920s America implies that this should have been the conclusion reached by those writing for the Chicago School, not least because the pervasiveness of organized crime made it very difficult to hold on to the contemporary criminological tenet of individual pathology.

However, this is not what happened. Instead, the criminological contribution of the Chicago School was to shift the focus from individual pathology to group pathology, underpinned by a more liberal sensibility which was characteristic of the closer inter-connection between criminal justice and social policy in this period (Garland 1985). Employing Burgess's neo-Darwinist ecological theory of urban development through concentric zones, Shaw & McKay, in the best remembered of the Chicago studies, plotted the residence of known delinquents. They found them congregated, along with other social problems, in the "zone of transition", sandwiched between the central business district and more affluent and comfortable residential districts. The zone of transition was occupied mainly by new immigrant workers: but not necessarily the same ones, as the rates of delinquency showed a constant pattern over time despite population turnover, and similar patterns were found in 20 other American cities (Baldwin 1979).

Shaw & McKay sought to explain this phenomenon by reference to a value-laden notion of social disorganization, in which the "normal" controls of "normal" communities were absent. The process, they argued, resulted from the squeeze exerted over the zone of transition from the central business district, which made it an undesirable place to live. Those who could escape from it did so, migrating to the outer zones, and leaving behind an area with rapid population turnover and low property prices, which in turn encouraged an influx of new poor migrant workers. The process militated against the development of stable informal social controls from parents, relatives and neighbours, and in such conditions crime flourished. This was evidenced by supporting ethnographic studies of delinquent subcultures, which demonstrated how these were transmitted among juveniles, successfully beating off the challenge of whatever conventional values existed in such areas.

The causes of crime in this theory, therefore, were seen to lie in the territorial area, from where they were picked up by the people living there in a sort of process of criminal osmosis. This, as many critics have since pointed out, is the ecological fallacy, with all the hallmarks of determinism in positivist criminology. The fallacy was perpetuated, moreover, by the use of official statistics, and the failure to distinguish offence from offender rates. Nevertheless, despite these weaknesses which were replicated in a number of sociological studies up until the 1960s, the work was popular, fitting an often racist notion of (immigrant) undesirables, a generally negative view of twentieth-century urbanization, and a political ideology prepared to embark upon programmes of social intervention in the name of crime prevention.

In terms of crime prevention, the practical implications of the theory were clear: if communities were disorganized, they needed organization. This meant providing white middle-class surrogate informal social controls, something which was eventually done via the Chicago Area Project, which entailed, among other things, the provision of legitimate recreational activities, outreach youth work, and resident participation in community development. It was still social hygiene in Pasquino's (1991) terms, but a more liberal strain of it.

In fact, these crime preventive implications were only clear because the assumptions underpinning the theory were equally transparent. Others have correctly pointed out that different readings are equally plausible. Smith (1986a) suggests that the ecological process is primarily responsible – in other words, the unchecked movements of a capitalist political economy, which might therefore require intervention at the social structural level. Sumner (1994), on a similar theme, observes that the delinquency was not so much a product of social disorganization as a consequence of the individualistic culture having been learned too well: again, the fault lies with capitalism. This demonstrates the important point that the link between theory and practice is not always unilinear, particularly in the case of sociological positivism. The practical implications of theories are more politically deduced that scientifically deduced.

The longevity of the Chicago Area Project bears testimony to the enduring appeal of the idea of social disorganization as a rationale for crime prevention, despite the fact that the theory has not tended to travel well. Baldwin (1979) shows that the post-war growth of municipal suburban housing made the concentric ring ecological theory particularly unsuitable in England, whilst the work of Anthony Bottoms and his various colleagues in Sheffield has demonstrated that in these municipal areas it is the allocations policies of the housing authorities which have the key role in determining the criminal profile of an area. Nevertheless, despite these differences the common theme is often that of the existence of a criminal subculture of some description, and the policy implications have tended to be similar. Thus the targeted urban policy initiatives from the 1960s onwards in England, often focused upon youth, betray a core similarity with the Chicagoan community-oriented approach (Hope & Shaw 1988).

Although it would be misleading to portray a unilinear sequence of theoretical development, the Chicago School was undoubtedly the progenitor of a number of other sociological studies of crime which sought or served to refine or amend some of its basic propositions. They all shared a basic sociological position which saw crime as a product of criminal or delinquent values, which meant that their crime preventive implications were often quite similar, or at least could be so interpreted, given that this is largely a matter of political preference anyway.

37

Robert Merton employed Durkheim's concept of anomie to explain the deviant and sometimes criminal responses of those socialized into the ends of the "American Dream", but denied access to the legitimate means of attaining it. The poor fit between means and ends prompted a strain which could be resolved for some by criminal means to financial success and status. The cause of crime, then, was not so much the individual or group as the culture of society itself, which became embedded in individual personalities (Sumner 1994), but which produced an unconscious strain when it proved unattainable. One might have surmised that the solution to this strain, and thus the preventive implications of the theory, lay in providing more opportunities for those who aspired to the American Dream. But Merton took a more conservative view, holding that the New Deal had provided many new opportunities as it reasonably could, and that the best way forward was to expose the Dream as a myth, and make it more realistic.

Merton identified a number of different deviant modes of adaptation to the strain, only some of which were criminal. Thereafter, however, he set in train a number of other "subculture" studies which sought more empirically informed typologies of these adaptations. In particular, they focused upon juvenile delinquency. Merton's pessimistic view of the American culture had been born in the wake of the Depression and Prohibition years, but those writing in the 1950s were generally more optimistic, seeing juvenile delinquency as "the last remaining block on a copybook whose dirty reality had been largely erased by the new utopia" (Sumner 1994: 173). Albert Cohen, for example, documented the way that delinquent boys effectively inverted the cultural norm and replaced it with a culture of violence and destructiveness, rather than conformity, as a path to success.

The crime preventive implications of these theories varied according to their political interpretation. Since they remained within Merton's basic model of strain, conservatives were inclined to think that such theories excused deviance and sought liberal solutions, but Sumner disagrees and identifies within them a basic tendency to relocate the responsibility for crime from the social structure to the delinquent subculture. In his view (1994: 1181) the concept of the latter "measured the depth of the ideological need to believe that there was an enemy within that could subvert the drive to consensus". The enemy could be defeated by the liberal means of preventing the strain, or by the not so liberal means of preventing the translation of the strain into actual crime.

A major problem with these sociological theories concerns their general acceptance of official portrayals of the crime problem: their theories were overwhelmingly based upon the working-class street criminal, and were thus limited in much the same way as early biological and psychological positivism was by its focus upon convicted criminals. Also, they made much the same kinds of assumptions as Bentham and other neoclassicals about middle-class culture being the (law-abiding) norm from which criminals deviated.

The Chicagoan theory of social disorganization assumed that crime resulted from an absence of "normal" controls, and subculture and strain theories sought to explain the reasons for this absence, in terms of the motivation resulting from the possible reactions to the dominant culture and its fit with one's life chances and situation. However, these theories represent only one genealogical line from Chicago theory. Another lies in the area of control theory, which is a generic term capturing a range of criminological contributions, the most representative and complete of which is probably found in the work of Travis Hirschi, who first came to prominence in the 1960s.

The control theory side of Chicago theory – that crime was the consequence of a lack of controls – was generally overlooked within mainstream sociology because it was obvious and common sense. Essentially, it failed to hold much scientific interest (Downes & Rock 1995). However, as disquiet grew among both conservatives and radicals about the deterministic excesses of subcultural motivational theories, so space inevitably opened up for alternative lines of enquiry. Control theory sought to make explicit what remained implicit in the positivist theories: that most of us were held back from criminality because of the power of controls imposed through the socialization process. It took this as its central problematic, and in so doing resurrected the older classical notion of *Homo penalis*. Hirschi's contribution was to identify, via an extensive self-report survey, a typology of four social bonds which kept *Homo penalis* on the straight and narrow, namely attachment, commitment, involvement and belief. When these are strong, people had a strong stake in conformity, but when they are weak, the chances of criminality are increased.

The crime preventive implications of this position depend very much upon how this is interpreted. Since control theory is a theory of why criminality does not occur, it does not necessarily follow that the absence or weakness of social bonds directly leads to crime. Rather, absence makes it more possible, whereas the presence of the bonds makes it extremely unlikely. This leads on to two possible approaches to crime prevention. Without the bonds, Hirschi's potential criminal takes on the same character as classicism's *Homo penalis*, whose utilitarian logic is expected to respond to deterrence, either of a general or situational (see Ch. 3) nature. However, an alternative and equally plausible preventive approach, supported less by the theory's more conservative adherents, would be to strengthen the bonds to significant others through home, school, work and so forth through a range of social policy-type interventions. This is an essentially Chicagoan liberal solution, and ironically ends up placing control theory in the same practical category as its sociological theoretical antecedents, which Hirschi quite deliberately sought to distance himself from.

Control theory, and especially David Matza's version of it, served the purpose of countering sociological positivism's pathologizing tendency with a view of offenders being not especially different from so-called normal others. Hirschi's research seemed to confirm this, finding, for example, that his data showed no association between delinquency and social class, although the limited response rate of the self-report study, and concern about the validity of the replies, serve to cast some doubt on this point. Nevertheless, in terms of the wider development of criminological thought, control theory at least set a marker for a paradigmatic shift in thinking about crime, which arrived in the 1960s with the rise of the labelling perspective.

In identifying the offender as basically normal, or at least not inherently pathological, control theory helped to shift the focus away from the criminal and towards the crime, as the phenomenon in need of explanation. This had been an element of an emergent sociology of deviance in 1930s America, seen initially in the work of Tannenbaum and Mills. It harped back to classicism's focus upon the criminal justice system rather than the offender, but whilst for classical theory the system was seen as the solution to crime, for labelling it was seen as the problem.

The emergent sociology of deviance from the 1930s failed to materialize until the 1960s because of the impact of McCarthyism on American radicalism in the intervening period (Sumner 1994). However, as the climate became more receptive so labelling demonstrated its utility as a means of explaining the treatment by state agencies of a number of new social movements, from antiwar and nuclear arms protesters to gay liberation, the counterculture, and those advancing the causes of other oppressed minorities. Labelling essentially drew attention to the fact that what passed for deviance was a product of cultural conflict, and that it was formal social control which reinforced this, as a process of moral censure by the powerful over the powerless.

It was Lemert who outlined the labelling perspective in the most articulate way, although it was popularized by Howard Becker in the 1960s. The essence of it was that whatever the reason for the initial deviant or criminal act, and there was no special reason since similar acts were often not so labelled, it was the societal reaction, and especially the reaction of social control agencies, which served to reinforce the label, construct a deviant self-image, and bring about the phenomenon of secondary deviance in a self-fulfilling prophecy. Importantly, this was done in discriminatory ways, a point which rendered official criminal statistics useless other than as indices of these same ways. In turn, this meant that theories based upon such indices were badly misled and misleading, contributing to very partial accounts of crime.

The labelling perspective focuses more on deviance than crime, and its stance is more appreciative than correctionalist, since its symbolic interactionist underpinnings make it more interested in understanding than explanation and recommendation. Inevitably, however, criminology looks for its practical utility, and even those writing from within the perspective occasionally do so: thus, for example, Lemert recommends that social control agencies should adopt a position of greater tolerance, in order to minimize the detrimental impact of the attentions of official control agencies such as the police. The liberal crime preventive case, then, is for non-intervention, but this can actually be taken to quite radical degrees. In the context of the 1960s, then, calls for decriminalization and decarceration were interpreted this way by an establishment which was effectively being blamed for causing the very social problems it purported to be preventing. Labelling was easily entwined in the more radical demands of the new social movements. The one exception to this was in the field of youth justice, where non-intervention could be presented in a more liberal, reasoned light, in the 1969 Children and Young Persons Act. Even here, however, the changed climate of the 1970s brought a hurried withdrawal from some of its key principles.

The labelling perspective was in an impossible position for a number of reasons. Its liberal adherents recognized the impracticality of doing nothing about crime, and thus ended up merely proposing the exchange of the state's hard machine of social control for its soft machine, with the latter not necessarily being any less stigmatizing, discriminatory or damaging. In so doing, however, it brought the politics of crime control to the fore, both between social control agencies themselves, and at the broader macro-level (the care versus control debate). Finally, having begun its assault on the edifice of the criminal justice system, it found it difficult to resist the attention of more structurally informed critical analyses, which sought to finish the job by locating the particularistic social and historical origins of the morality which framed the system's purpose.

Unsurprisingly, therefore, the advent of the labelling perspective and its distillation into a more radical critique coincided with the growth of official scepticism with the sociological positivist branch of criminology which now seemed to be blaming apparently normal and consensual cultural processes for generating crime. The soft defence for the underdog which had been a characteristic of the work of Becker gave way to a harsher critique of the criminal justice system, and eventually to the idealist promotion of the deviant or the criminal as a proto-revolutionary. In the case of crime, though, this was patently absurd, transforming the project of crime prevention, at least in any form which required formal intervention and in the context of no fundamental social change, from potential solution to potential problem. This did not square with common perceptions or experiences of crime, and suggested that in some quarters at least, theorizing about crime was getting badly out of hand.

Summary

The intention in this chapter has not been to suggest some kind of unilinear development to theorizing about crime, where one theory is replaced by another in a rational process like natural selection. Rather, the purpose has been to demonstrate, in an albeit limited way, some of the breadth and diversity of theorizing about crime from the late eighteenth century through to the recent past. Theories have been developed from within a particular cultural context, as have the crime preventive practices which they have spawned, although the latter have not followed directly from the theories so much as having been deduced from the theories within a particular political context. As a consequence, the theories and practices have tended to come in and out of favour. The overall effect is of a superimposition of one theory–practice coupling upon another, with the result being the melange which is characteristic of our modern approach to crime.

The limitations of the theories have been hinted at in this section, deriving mainly from their narrow conceptions of human nature, or the generally poor quality of the information upon which they are based. These limitations, however, have not prevented the employment of the theories to justify certain preventive approaches, and in this regard their scientific utility is considerably less important than their political utility. However, the perceived post-war rise in crime has damaged their political utility, and has rendered the recycling of traditional theories and criminal justice practices more problematic. There has been increased political and scientific dissatisfaction: "nothing works" refers as much to the theory as it does to the practice, even if it is an exaggeration. Consequently, there has been an increased receptiveness towards alternative ways of conceiving of the crime problem, and alternative ways of addressing it. Chapter 3 undertakes an exploration of these.

CHAPTER 3

Theories of crime prevention II

Introduction

In common with the previous chapter, this chapter adopts a broad chronological structure, picking up the story of theoretical developments from the 1960s onwards, at a time when mainstream theorizing about crime was beginning to look rather limited in its usefulness and applicability. This was either because its practice had failed to deliver the expected reduction in crime, or because the practical implications of the theorizing were in fact highly impractical. The decline in the practical utility of scientific theorizing about crime might have created a space for new approaches to the study of crime, but it was a space that criminology was not that well placed to exploit at this time.

In Britain, the positivist paradigm held a vicelike grip over the discipline of criminology in part because of the influence exerted by the criminal justice policy community over research, the vast majority of which was expected to have a correctionalist stance (Roshier 1989). In the context of the period between the mid-1950s and mid-1960s, this meant subscription to the treatment paradigm. For example, the government White Paper *Penal Practice in a Changing Society* (1959) urged future policy to be grounded more fully in criminological research, while simultaneously assuming that such research would aid the identification of criminal personality types, which might then be made use of in assessment units at court centres, that ultimately never saw the light of day. The main focus continued to be the criminal and not the crime: the first series of Home Office research publications was entitled *Studies in the Causes of Delinquency and the Treatment of Offenders*, only in 1969 changed to the more neutral *Home Office Research Studies*.

It was not the case, as Clarke & Felson (1993) somewhat harshly imply, that there was no criminological interest in the phenomenology of crime. Rather, the practical influence of the system itself ensured that it was those aspects of theories that had something to say about criminals that were given greater precedence, and attracted greater interest and investment. Hence, as Brantingham & Jeffery observe in their account of early disinterest in the spatial characteristics of crime, "spatial patterns became the *method* by which the sources of individual behaviour were to be discovered, rather than independent dimensions of the criminal event" (1991: 234). In Britain, the main spatial criminological contribution, from the Chicago school, could be largely disregarded anyway, for as noted in Chapter 2, the pattern of post-war municipal housing development ensured that the concentric ring model never really fitted (Baldwin 1979).

However, while criminology continued its obsessive search for dispositional factors that separated the criminal from the law-abiding, others had to live with the consequences of its spectacular failure to make inroads into steadily climbing rates of crime when translated into preventive programmes of either the old faithful neoclassical deterrence, or the treatment paradigm. Put simply, rising crime, and the repercussions felt from rising crime increasingly became a problem for others besides criminologists and the agencies of the criminal justice system. Consequently, in retrospect it is hardly surprising that different ways of thinking about crime eventually emanated from sources outside of mainstream criminology, which eventually directed a fresh breath of air through the discipline itself. In the period between the early 1960s and 1970s, the key influences were Jane Jacobs and Oscar Newman, whose refreshingly different perspective combined a number of contemporary concerns about urban change into a powerful momentum for change in theory and practice.

Jane Jacobs: *The death and life of great American cities*

Jane Jacobs was an architectural journalist rather than a criminologist, whose book, first published in the USA in 1961, represented a stinging attack upon planning orthodoxy that had, in her view, done so much to destroy the city's soul through its crass and over-sentimentalised pursuit of nature in urban design. Planners had failed to understand that cities were organic, living things, constituting a myriad of every-day social and economic interactions, and thus their designs – particularly the *bête noire* high rise – frequently rode roughshod over such processes, leading, among other things, to "city districts that are custom made for crime" (UK edition 1965: 41). In essence, planning orthodoxy had been responsible for making cities unsafe places, where vandals, robbers and other street criminals could ply their unnatural trades without fear of apprehension.

The city, however, was not beyond salvation, for contemporary planning orthodoxy had not penetrated everywhere, and vestiges of hope remained in a number of models of urban safety from some older city quarters, from which valuable lessons could be learned, "to strengthen whatever workable forces for maintaining safety and civi-lisation do exist – in the cities we do have" (1965: 41).

The "workable forces", in Jacobs' eyes translated as the replication and re-creation of diversity in land use patterns, which helped to keep older urban quarters safe, and which had been lost in the artificial compartmentalization of activities that accompanied modern zoning. This diversity would, of itself, constrain the opportunities for crime on the streets, the focus of her criminological attention. In particular, diversity of use would bring more "eyes onto the street" by encourag-ing more widespread and continuous use of the streets and parks as places of leisure, play and commerce, and by clearly demarcating public and private space. This could be reinforced, moreover, by designing buildings in order to maximize their surveillance potential, which was far preferable to attempting to ensure safety by building physical barriers that encouraged a socially divisive "fortress mental-ity" and an aggressive "turf" attitude, not so dissimilar to that held by delinquent gangs.

Jacobs' approach to crime prevention, then, was straightforward and practical, bringing into the criminological limelight ideas and activities that people outside of the criminal justice system were bringing to bear on the crime problem. However, the straightforward-ness of her approach was a weakness as well as a strength, for the study lacked the methodological rigour that characterized criminology's scientific pretensions, which, as Reppetto (1976) points out, makes little allowance for "brilliant insights" that might characterize fields such as architecture and planning. Thus it could be dismissed as mere anecdote or polemic. In a male-dominated field such as criminology, moreover, it could not have helped that she was a woman, oversimplifying a problem that apparently greater male minds had struggled with for decades. Indeed, Jacobs herself was mindful of her recommendations being taken as any kind of panacea, pointing out that, ultimately, "deep and complicated social ills must lie behind delinquency and crime" (1965: 41), and thereby paying reverence to the orthodoxies of the day.

There were other good reasons why the criminal justice community should be hostile towards Jacobs: her proposals did not require their participation, and the implication "that the public rather than the police are the crucial element in crime control" (Davidson 1981: 82) was little short of heretical at the time. By the same token, the planning community had much the same response, for she went against the orthodoxies of the day inspired by Howard and Le Corbusier, and in Britain such proposals were unlikely to make headway against established planning principles of low housing density and land-use zoning (Clarke 1983). Even the public had good reason to be sceptical, for as Reppetto (1976) points out, support for diversity of use is generally conditional upon such diversity occurring within the parameters of cultural homogeneity, and yet such parameters have become increasingly rare in modern urban life. Furthermore, as Henry Mayhew's graphic accounts of life in the rookeries of Victorian London suggest, Jacobs' nostalgia for the apparent safety of pre-modern urban designs may have been misplaced. Indeed, as both Clarke (1983) and Mayhew (1991) observe, increased street activity may not of itself create safer communities, and may in fact create more opportunities for crime.

Jacobs' work, then, was far from being without its limitations, but its impact should perhaps be seen less in terms of its intrinsic value, and more in terms of its contribution towards the reorientation of criminology's field of study.

Oscar Newman: *Defensible space*

There can be little doubt that, despite limited reference to her work, Oscar Newman owed a great deal to Jacobs' pioneering study (Mawby 1977), although his work reached a much wider and more receptive audience (Baldwin 1979). Coleman (1990) identifies one reason for this in the British context, in the fact that high rise had yet to make an appearance at the time of the publication of Jacobs' work, but by the early 1970s had become well established, and, in places, equally well hated. Hope, furthermore, identifies a range of concerns, over high rise, rising crime and community decline, for which *Defensible space* "supplied an easily intelligible rationale for linking them together" (1986: 76).

Like Jacobs, Newman started with the contention that modern physical designs often hampered the community's potential for surveillance and social control, and thus made the potential for crime much greater. The physical designs that he implicated specifically included high rise buildings; buildings that looked inwards rather than on to the street; buildings with many corridors and exits; and large estates with anonymous open spaces and large populations, all of which had become more common features of Britain's urban landscape.

Whereas Jacobs' attention was directed to safety and crime prevention on the streets, Newman's proposals had broader appeal, taking in both buildings and streets under the attractively marketable banner of defensible space:

> Defensible space is a model for residential environments which inhibits crime by creating the physical expression of a social fabric which defends itself . . . an environment in which latent territoriality and sense of community in the inhabitants can be translated into responsibility for ensuring a safe, productive and well-maintained living space. (1973: 3)

Newman identified four specific dimensions or aspects to ideal defensible space: first, the territorial definition of space; secondly, the maximization of natural surveillance; thirdly, the design of non-stigmatizing housing; and fourthly, the location of housing projects or estates in "safe" urban milieux. Maximizing these four aspects in planning and design would, Newman argued, lead to a most effective model of crime prevention, utilising mechanical means of target hardening, and corrective means of mobilizing natural social processes of territoriality and surveillance.

Newman's work relied upon evidence from two main sources. First, he compared the crime rates of 100 estates in New York with their design characteristics, arguing that crime rates declined in line with defensible space characteristics: the fewer storeys, for example, the lower the rate. He also provided a more detailed comparison of two "similar" estates, one with defensible space features, and one without. However, this methodology came under sustained attack from his critics: the reliance on a single case study was widely regarded as scientifically inadequate (Reppetto 1976), particularly when there appeared to be other comparative examples Newman could have used, but did not, leading some to wonder (e.g. Bottoms 1974) whether the reason for their omission had anything to do with their possibly not fitting the hypothesis. Furthermore, both the comparison and the larger statistical analysis uncritically accepted the official police data, and did not consider other data that might have been relevant, such as the social class composition of residents, their respective offender rates (Mawby 1977), other relevant social data, and data from the early years of the estates studied, which might have accounted for differences in their reputations. Overall, Hope (1986) characterizes Newman's research as both simplistic and mechanistic.

Despite the strength of these methodological criticisms, they do not necessarily imply that the theory is wrong, and clearly the theory did (and does) resonate with common sense assumptions about the criminogenic nature of certain geographical areas. Consequently, Newman, who was more a planner and architect than a criminologist (Merry 1981), at least set criminological minds thinking, and encouraged a number of studies that sought to test his hypothesis elsewhere. This testing, however, brought to light a number of other weaknesses.

Mawby (1977) found in his Sheffield study that while high rise areas with business premises below did have higher rates of crime this was actually attributable to higher reporting rates, rather than any design feature as such. He noted moreover that Newman's four design aspects carried contradictions, as, for example, stigmatizing housing can actually protect from outsiders, while territoriality may protect from outsiders, but leave delinquent insiders relatively unguarded. Also, while low rise housing may maximize private defensible space, features like gardens can make them difficult to watch over from outside, a point echoed by Power (1989), who found that crime rates can be very high in such low rise areas, despite the apparent defensibility of their space in Newman's terms.

Mayhew (1979) draws attention, among other things, to Newman's rather crass notion of territoriality as a seemingly natural form of social control, which relies upon a particular view of human nature which is by no means beyond contention, and certainly fails to consider its social origins (Hope 1986). As many writers have noted (e.g. LeBeau 1987, Hope 1986, Merry 1981), there is also a tremendous lack of clarity in the link Newman makes between design and territoriality, leading one to suspect a degree of architectural determinism, an issue that is not convincingly dealt with in this refutation of such a conclusion:

> We are concerned that some might read into our work the implication that architectural design can have a direct causal effect on social interactions. Architecture operates more in the area of "influence" than control. It can create a setting conducive to realising the *potential* of mutual concern. It does not and cannot manipulate people toward these feelings, but rather allows mutually benefiting attitudes to surface. (1973: 207)

There is, however, contradictory evidence, gleaned from at least one study into the situational determinants of territorial interventions, which undermines such an assertion, or at least suggests that the influence of design is very weak. Merry's ethnographic research points out that good designs do not necessarily prevent crimes, for "spaces may be defensible but not defended if the social apparatus for effective defense is lacking" (1981: 419). She found that the anonymity produced by ethnic heterogeneity had a significant influence upon people's willingness to intervene, as did the mistrust of criminal justice agencies. Overall (1981: 420) she notes that "The relationship between environment and social behaviour is complex and reciprocal since the environment itself is defined by the ways its users interpret and impose cultural meanings on it." She suggests, then, that defensible space may be a necessary but not sufficient condition for crime prevention, but even this is debatable, for Mayhew (1979) draws attention to the existence of estates that have low defensible space and also low crime rates.

This neglect of social factors is a theme repeated in other research – notably that conducted by the Home Office, which sought to test Newman's theory as it applied to vandalism (Wilson 1980). The results showed that design variables correlated far less closely with crime rates than did a particularly important social variable, namely child density: the more children, the more likely vandalism became. These apparent weaknesses in defensible space led Newman himself to consider the social aspect in more detail, and in his later research (Newman & Franck 1980) he had to concede that social variables had a greater impact that design variables, notably the percentage of families on welfare benefits, the percentage of such families headed by single women, average per capita disposable income, and the ratio of teenagers to adults.

Despite these apparent weaknesses in the original defensible space formulation, it has not been entirely written off. The Home Office vandalism research (Wilson 1980), for example, acknowledges that the theory might fit other crimes better, and concedes that its research was limited, and considered only the aspect of territoriality – although the above discussion has raised doubts also about surveillance and stigmatizing housing, and LeBeau (1987) notes that there is no empirical evidence that locating a housing estate in a safe milieu will reduce its crime rate. The difficulties inherent in testing such an assertion would be formidable, which draws attention to another general difficulty with testing defensible space projects, since they invariably mix physical design changes with other social or law enforcement strategies. Hence, while the jury is still out, it would appear that "defensible space has considerable intuitive appeal, but it may have been over-sold" (Mayhew 1979: 157).

Indeed, as Mayhew also notes, it may be fairer to test defensible space in new housing projects, where negative attitudes and reputations have yet to be formed or hardened. Newman himself recognizes this, suggesting that there may be better ways of preventing crime on existing estates than undergoing prohibitively expensive and high risk design modifications, such as employing security guards in high rise buildings (Clarke 1983). New building, however, may be equally expensive, and high risk relative to the perceived low risk of crime, particularly when defensible space design features compete with fire regulations, segregational zoning, and resident preferences for privacy (Mayhew 1979).

Although it has had its problems, defensible space has also had considerable influence. Its highly practical approach to crime prevention has made it an attractive source for federal funding in the USA under the rubric of Crime Prevention Through Environmental Design (CPTED), and it has also formed a part of similar initiatives in Britain. As Hough and his colleagues acknowledge, Oscar Newman has been a "significant factor behind the increasing interest in situational factors [of crime prevention]" (1980: 4), while Alice Coleman maintains that defensible space is "a brilliant concept" (1990: 13). Indeed, she maintains that what would appear to amount to a conspiracy was launched against Newman's work, not least by the Home Office which, according to her, set out to disprove his theory.

Coleman is correct in so far as, like Jacobs, Newman's theory would have held no appeal for agencies within the criminal justice system (since it offered only a limited role for them to play), or for criminology, which held it to be intellectually sterile (Reppetto 1976) and similarly threatening. However, her allegations ultimately reveal a failure on her part to read the tidal changes taking place in criminology and criminal justice policy in the mid-1970s, which, to the contrary, provided a more receptive climate than the theory actually warranted.

Before closing this section it is worth elaborating further upon Coleman's contribution, since she continues to be a standard bearer for defensible space, elaborating further upon it in her own British research, in which she links not only crime, but also other indicators of "social malaise", namely litter, graffiti, vandalism, faeces, and urine, to design characteristics. In so doing, she particularly implicates five design features (namely dwellings per entrance, dwellings per block, number of storeys, overhead walkways, and spatial organization) in a condition she interestingly names "design disadvantagement", the gist of which is that:

> Shared residential space appears to provide an early-learning environment capable of undermining normal child-rearing practices and promoting child crime on a scale formerly found only in the worst tenement slums – the "rookeries" of British experience. (Coleman 1989: 109)

This can be seen as an extension of Newman's work in so far as it addresses the role of the offender, who is seen to be suffering a design-induced pathological condition, which she proposes may be addressed by a number of practical preventive improvements such as the removal of walkways, walling off residential blocks, and turning blocks into more self-contained units without so many entrances and exits. However, the notion of design disadvantagement seems once again to raise the spectre of architectural determinism, although like Newman she refutes such an insinuation:

> None of this is to be construed as a claim that design is the only factor in the prevention or promotion of social breakdown. On the contrary its influence is bound to be differentially offset or reinforced, diverted or distorted, by innumerable other factors. (1990: 5)

She goes on to say that her contribution is probabilistic, rather than deterministic, and is based upon scientifically observed patterns. However, once again the refutation does not fit the evidence. Design disadvantagement does not sound like a probabilistic condition, and as Hope (1986) points out, there is no attempt to correlate any of the social malaise data with other social variables, with the exception of the number of children in care, which is mystifyingly treated as an indicator of social malaise in the same category as faeces and urine! The scientific pretensions of her research are, in fact, very effectively dismissed in an excellent review article by Smith (1986b), which suggests, among other things, that if Coleman really had seen her work as probabilistic then she might have been a good deal more cautious when interpreting the strength of the relationship between design and malaise, based, as it was, on very low correlation coefficients. Coleman stages her book as a trial of planning and architectural orthodoxy – *Utopia on Trial* – but Smith points out that it is a kangaroo court, where the prosecution evidence is inadmissible. Ultimately, however, as with Newman, the scientific quality of the research is less important than the idea that there might be a link between design and crime, and that this might be a promising criminological furrow to plough.

In summary, then, the revival of interest in the spatial characteristics of crime prompted by Jacobs and Newman heralded in a very fertile period of criminological theorizing in the 1970s and into the

1980s, even though the original theories were less than wholly convincing. This theorizing is discussed below.

Environmental criminology

Environmental criminology is a generic label encompassing a number of different approaches that emerged mainly from the 1970s, and that share an interest in the wider environmental determinants of crime. As Brantingham & Brantingham (1991) observe, crime has essentially four determinants, namely the law, an offender, a target, and a place. The "classical perspective" concerns itself primarily with the law, and positivist criminology's interest is primarily with the offender, thus leaving both the target and the place as relatively neglected features of criminological theorizing. Environmental criminology seeks to redress the balance, without placing as much stress upon design as both Jacobs and Newman do – although the approach's general popularity owes much to their pioneering work and the paradigmatic shift it effected. It also traces its historical lineage back through Quetelet, Guerry and Mayhew in the nineteenth century (Brantingham & Brantingham 1991), the pre-war contribution of the Chicago School (Bottoms 1994), and, in Britain, the post-war areal studies of those such as Mays and Morris (Davidson 1993). However, while a general reorientation towards place and target help to distinguish environmental criminology, it is the relative weight and status accorded to these factors, and their conception of the environment as either physical or social entity, which helps to distinguish different approaches within the paradigm.

Jeffery (1971) was an early advocate of an environmental approach who rejected the mentalistic assumptions underpinning many sociological and psychological accounts of crime, which presented offenders with motives which could never be proven to exist, could be only explicated after the event, and were therefore not truly preventive. He preferred a behaviouristic model of action, with individuals responding to environmental stimuli, and thus responding also to environmental techniques that might "engineer out" stimuli to crime, while "engineering in" aversive responses to them – although he was never clear in his early work what form such techniques should take, beyond expressing an interest in Jacobs' work in this area.

In his later work, Jeffery enlightens us further about his conception of human action, offering an implicitly positivist "bioenvironmentalist" model that is "in favour of scientific efforts to control human behaviour before it occurs" (Jeffery & Zahn 1993: 346). In effect, his behaviourism has been augmented by a more detailed, biologically informed view of how the brain may be affected by environmental stimuli, but not so much design as pollution, including heavy metal contamination and nutritional defects. This approach would seem to characterize the environment more as a chemical entity than anything else, and, not surprisingly, it sets Jeffery apart from the crowd, either moving him out of the environmental criminology camp altogether (he acknowledges the inappropriateness of the "crime prevention through environmental design" label, but still uses it), or making him something of a maverick within it.

A more conventional environmental approach may be found in the work of Patricia and Paul Brantingham, both former students of Jeffery who took up his challenge to establish a basis for environmental criminology. Their work demonstrates, as they (1991) acknowledge, a move from the sociological imagination to the geographical imagination, because of their practical interest in crime control rather than crime *per se*. In so doing,

> Locations of crimes, the characteristics of those locations, the movement paths that bring offenders and victims together at these locations, and people's perception of crime locations all become substantively important objects for research. (1991: 21)

The result is an empirically detailed and highly specific geometry of crime, a "pattern theory" as they call it (1993), which in the course of demonstrating patterns also fulfils the practical end of suggesting preventive interventions that might alter these patterns. Urban environmental planning has a particularly important part to play here. However, while Jeffery might be accused of switching the focus too far away from the environment as conventionally conceived, the Brantinghams arguably produce an approach that, while good enough for the purposes of practical preventive interventions, is lacking as a complete theory of crime. As Hope observes:

> ... a fully "environmental" explanation needs to find a way of

reconciling the opportunities and const
presented by the environment with the deci
taken by individuals in the light of these "
(1986: 70)

Routine activity theory

The same sort of criticism could be levelled at a similar variant of
environmental theory that may be found in Marcus Felson's contributions to a "routine activity" theory of crime, which starts from the
following premise:

> Unlike many criminological enquiries, we do not examine why
> individuals or groups are inclined to criminality, but rather we
> take criminal inclinations as given and examine the manner in
> which spatio-temporal organisation of social activities helps
> people to translate their criminal inclinations into action.
> (Cohen & Felson 1979: 589)

The rationale underlying such a premise may be found in the recognition that post-war improvements in social conditions have been
accompanied by rising crime, which simultaneously weakens the case
for many sociological explanations of criminality (notably the structural ones), and strengthens the case for alternatives such as routine
activity theory. This argues that increases in crime rates have accompanied changing patterns of routine activities, which have affected
the convergence in time and space of the three necessary conditions
for crime, namely a motivated offender, a suitable target, and the
absence of a capable guardian.

The original 1979 formulation of routine activity theory was cast at
the macro-level, analysing changes in national crime rates, and societal
changes, in post-war USA. These changes have reduced the home-
centredness of much American life by increasing the number of working women, of single person households and of students, while also
providing more activities outside the home in the form of holidays and
other leisure activities. Notwithstanding family violence, this has
made homes more vulnerable to predatory crimes by removing large
numbers of capable guardians. At the same time, the consumer revolu-

...as brought into these homes an increasing number of more ...table targets, particularly in the form of automobiles and electronic goods, the latter having become progressively smaller, lighter and more portable – a computer that could be fitted into a small briefcase today might have required something approaching a removal van in the 1960s.

The overall effect, then, is that crime has increased not because of any social decline, but rather because of growing prosperity and freedom. Put simply, the supply of criminal opportunities now far outstrips the capacity of criminal justice agencies to control them.

In a later publication, Felson (1994) extends the routine activity model from predatory crimes to the consumption and sale of illegal products (which require only the convergence of a motivated offender and the absence of a capable guardian), and crimes of violence (which emanate from the differential convergence of combatants, troublemakers, peacemakers, and a wider audience). He also adds to his list of criminogenic societal changes the tendency towards increasingly large schools, which accommodate higher levels of crime by virtue of having less teacher supervision of more anonymous students, more undefended spaces in school designs, and lower participation rates in supervised extracurricular activities. Overall, he builds a macro-level theory of the more criminogenic nature of what he calls the "divergent metropolis" – the contemporary ecological successor to the "convergent city', which is more resonant with Jane Jacobs' (1965) idealized vision of urban life.

However, while Felson's earlier work shares with the Brantinghams a general lack of interest in the offender's motivational circumstances, his more recent work departs from this position and accords much greater consideration to the role of the offender, while maintaining, nevertheless, that crime rate increases do not necessitate any concomitant motivational changes. Felson (1994) considers and rejects a number of criminological perspectives for perpetuating numerous fallacies about crime, but selects Hirschi's control theory as being most in sympathy with his routine activity approach. Incorporating this theory into his model of necessary conditions (1986), Felson is thus able to talk of "intimate handlers" watching over "handled offenders" ("handle" in this instance relating to a capacity for control) in much the same way as capable guardians watch over suitable targets. Intimate handlers are most likely to be family members, but just as capable guardians' absence makes the target more suitable, so the absence of an intimate handler, which can be engineered by the offender, makes the offender more free to exploit any target. Felson adapts control theory, however, in so far as he denies the pervasiveness of the controls Hirschi identifies, stressing instead their situational nature, which also makes them manipulable. In so doing, his position has more in common with Matza's (1964) notion of drift.

Control theory, then, offers Felson an opportunity to identify the sources of self-control that prevent most of us, for most of the time, from taking advantage of the criminal temptations that might fall our way. In an elaboration of this, he seeks to argue that certain macro-level societal changes have served to remove a number of natural (although this is debatable) controls from adolescents. In a previous age, they might have been expected to channel their ample energies into marriage, procreation, building families, and home-based hard manual labour, in the absence of today's time and labour saving devices. Today, however, young people possess the same energies, but lack the same economic function: endurance in education has replaced the need for physical endurance; less meaningful employment has replaced meaningful family supporting work; and family raising has been postponed from the teens to the twenties. The result of all this change has been a significantly increased scope for offending behaviour.

The practical preventive implications of routine activity theory can be found in measures that might be anticipated to change the distribution of routine activities. These include the same sort of strategic planning changes envisaged in the Brantinghams' pattern theory, the aim being to create an "everyday life" in which the necessary conditions of crime are kept apart. In this regard, Felson's (1994) vision of the future is an optimistic one, where the shift towards smaller firms and workplaces, and the opportunities for home-working and home-based education engendered by new technology, offer the potential of greater localism, and the presence of more intimate handlers and capable guardians. Beyond the macro-level, however, Felson also sees a role for the highly crime- and locality-specific interventions characteristic of situational measures of prevention, which find their theoretical home in rational choice theory.

Rational choice theory

Rational choice theory is associated closely with Ron Clarke, the former Head of the British Home Office Research and Planning Unit, which did so much in the 1970s to establish and develop the situational approach to crime prevention, such that it "became the main form of government intervention during the 1980s" (Davidson 1993: 8). Situational crime prevention, which is considered further in the following chapter, represents the practical germination of the seed initially sown by Newman and others that, despite various shortcomings, at least served to engender a spirit of hope among policy-makers that something policy-relevant could be found from criminological research to tackle a crime problem that had become increasingly resilient to the interventions of the criminal justice system. Rational choice, which its authors (Clarke & Felson 1993) prefer to see as a perspective rather than a fully evolved theory, then followed on the heels of the situational practice: it is deduced from it, and has evolved in response to the problems and issues raised by it. As such, it accords strongly with the model of practical theorizing associated with Home Office research (Clarke & Cornish 1983).

While the Brantinghams' work continues to show limited interest in offending motivations (theirs is truly a theory of crime rather than criminality), and Felson has only latterly turned his gaze on the offender in his criminological equation, Clarke's work was more ambitious from the outset. To employ the correct terminology (Cornish 1993), the intention has been to provide an explanation relevant both to the event, and to involvement. These roughly translate, respectively, as crime and criminality, but they are also more complete since they do not imply the mutual exclusivity of the latter two. In other words, in rational choice theory the intention has always been to build a bridge between situation (crime) and disposition (criminality), thereby bringing together what criminological politics has done much to keep apart – something that has increasingly come to be regarded as unhelpful in the name of theoretical integrity (Coleman 1989, Trasler 1993).

With regard to the criminal event, the main influence on rational choice theory has to be the very practical notion of opportunity. Opportunity is implicit in the work of the other theorists considered in this chapter, as well as in macro-level analyses of changes in crime rates such as those proffered by Wilkins or Burt (cited in Mayhew et al. 1976). But in rational choice theory opportunity takes on the central role in explaining a specific criminal event, conceived of in terms of the presence or absence of surveillance and physical security measures, and a constellation of factors weighing as either costs or benefits. However, as Mayhew et al. (1976) point out, at one level opportunities may be seen as occasions whose objective conditions appear conducive to crime (an open window and an unguarded purse, for example), but at another level the occasion has to be subjectively perceived as a tempting opportunity, and it is this that takes us inevitably into the mind of the potential offender – an area that other theories discussed in this chapter either took for granted, or chose not to venture into. Situation and disposition become entwined in so far as one cannot explain the event without reference to the offender's instrumental role therein. In a sense, then, it is the difference, or similarity, between the environment as objectively or subjectively defined.

The decision to engage with this level of analysis evidently runs the risk of revisiting the mistakes of many of the dispositional theories considered in the previous chapter. However, Clarke avoids the dangers inherent in what he terms the "medico-psychological" model of criminological explanations (Clarke & Cornish 1983) by drawing upon a range of theoretical and practical sources that together serve to emphasize the voluntary side of offenders' decision-making. He draws, for example, upon the same empirical reality informing 1960s versions of the sociology of deviance, which shows crime to be generally an essentially mundane activity of relatively "normal" people, in which Matza's (1964) notion of drift via "techniques of neutralization" is perhaps particularly influential. At the same time, however, he seeks to avoid the labelling perspective's failure to deal with other everyday realities, namely that most offenders are law-abiding most of the time, and that most offenders grow out of crime in their twenties. From the more radical sociology of deviance of the 1970s (see Taylor et al. 1973) he similarly draws upon the presentation of crime as a purposive act (Clarke 1980), without subscribing to the view of those authors that its purpose is essentially proto-revolutionary. Rather, he grounds these purposes not in political fantasy, but in the everyday accounts of offenders relayed in interviews with environmental criminologists (Clarke & Felson 1993). It is the empirical grounding of this theory that gives it its apparent strengths:

criminal choice theory is capable of providing answers to many questions lying outside the scope of conventional criminology concerning such matters as temporal and geographical patterns of crime, the isolated offending of otherwise law-abiding people, and changes of course in criminal careers. (Clarke & Cornish 1983: 15)

What this draws attention to above all else is the element of choice: if opportunity is central to the event, it is choice that is central to involvement. Choice in turn naturally draws attention to cognitive processes that have often been underplayed in sociological accounts, but came more to the fore with symbolic interactionism in the 1960s. In psychology, the cognitive equivalent is social learning theory, which stresses mentalism over behaviourism, and employs utilitarian-inspired notions of punishment and reward as prompts to criminal involvement decisions. In this way, then, far from being the break with tradition that accompanied Newman's work, for example, Clarke's rational choice theory merely picks up on the changes occurring within social scientific paradigms, and seeks to incorporate them within criminology.

The emphasis upon choice being rational in Clarke's formulation rests in part upon the utilitarian rationality implicit in social learning theory, and the rationality associated with crime as relatively normal action. Rationality is also a normative construct, and is used as such particularly in another major theoretical influence on Clarke (Clarke & Felson 1993), namely economic models of crime, such as that proposed by Becker (1968). The preventive solution that Becker recommends, namely punitive deterrence, is not one to which Clarke would subscribe, although he would agree over the preventive methodology of seeking to influence the costs and benefits.

It would not be inaccurate to identify an association between the rise of rational choice theory and a growing interest in a sort of "back to basics" return to classicism in both criminology and penal policy. However, it would also be easy to misrepresent the nature of this association, and the emphasis that both might place upon the implications of individual responsibility. Classicism takes free will for granted, whereas rational choice theory unpacks it to expose the essential superficiality of the free will/determinism dichotomy. Hence, for example, Clarke & Felson (1993) note that the theory basically treats the notion of choice as a heuristic device, and refuses to be drawn on the free will debate – another reason why it is a perspective rather than a theory. This is where, however, the label does the theory a disservice, because it implies a model of action that is purely rational. It must be said that the earlier formulations of the theory did display elements of such a model, demonstrating the enhanced initial influence of economic theory, as well as a desire to distinguish the theory from its determinist alternatives. However, latter formulations have taken it from "an environmental/learning perspective to . . . a more complex choice formulation of criminal behaviour" (Clarke & Cornish 1983: 50).

Choices are complex, in fact, precisely because they are not fully rational. Hence, as Cornish & Clarke (1986c) point out, rationality is of a bounded type, constrained by such factors as time, ability, and the availability of information, and beyond the implied materialism of economic rationality we must also make allowance for other more complex motives and preferences, which on the outside might appear as "senseless". As Cornish (1993: 363) points out, "It is neither necessary nor always helpful to use the concept of rational choice as an optimum standard of cognitive efficiency against which the actual decisions of offenders are to be measured."

Indeed, Clarke (1983) suggests that a useful explanatory device might be that of the "standing decision', which has considerable overlap with the notion of disposition. Without such a device, as Mayhew et al. (1976: 17) observe, "it would be difficult to account for the behaviour of the small minority of people who persistently engage in offending".

Overall, then, we are left with the following characterisation of the rational choice perspective:

It is assumed . . . that crime is purposive behaviour designed to meet the offender's commonplace needs for such things as money, status, sex and excitement, and that meeting those needs involves the making of (sometimes quite rudimentary) decisions and choices, constrained as these are by limits of time and ability and the availability of relevant information. (Clarke & Felson 1993: 6)

Given its explanatory ambition to unite crime and criminality, event and involvement, or situation and disposition, it is not surprising that rational choice theory has come under attack from a number of sources, and the sense of much of the criticism is that the focus on both areas means that neither is covered entirely adequately. Hence, for example, Bottoms (1994) makes the point that what he calls "opportunity theory" is not as spatially or temporally precise as routine activity theory with regard to the criminal event.

A more important criticism of this type concerns the theory's use of the term rationality. It is common to find the observation that rational choice theory might fit the materialist rationality underpinning instrumental crimes, but it falls short when it comes to crimes of violence, and expressive crimes in general. Trasler (1986, 1993) is strongly associated with such a criticism, but in many ways it is unfair, since it is clear from the above that the rationality employed in the theory is of a very loose, dilute kind, which does not prohibit links with the notion of a criminal disposition, at least in the form of "standing decisions". Trasler, therefore, overestimates the rationality in rational choice theory. He is, however, on firmer ground in his later work, where he suggests the theory would benefit from a more sophisticated psychological model of action. Like Bottoms' point, the implication is that if Clarke is to go down this avenue, he must explore it in its entirety.

Another type of criticism, based on the same misunderstanding, is that rational choice theory cannot deal with the issue of displacement: displacement is seen as the theory's Achilles heel, its existence taken to be proof of the enduring nature of criminal dispositions. However, as Cornish (1993) points out, the theory was devised specifically to tackle the issue of displacement, and the theory allows for it in its flexible notion of rationality. As Clarke (1980, 1983) has observed in his typology of offenders, displacement is unlikely with the opportunist, most likely with the professional criminal, and most problematic for those that fall between these two extremes. In fact, as Chapter 8 considers, displacement is more a criticism of the practice of situational crime prevention than of the theory of rational choice, yet even there the strength of the criticism is limited.

This distinction between theory and practice is an important one, for right from the very beginnings of rational choice Clarke has made it clear that the primary purpose of the theory is the practical end of crime control (Clarke & Felson 1993), rather than the scientific end of providing sound criminological theorizing. This, however, presents certain difficulties. First, it means that the theory's investment in a practical purpose actually allows it a "get out clause": major theoretical issues about, for example, the integration of disposition and situation (structure and agency?) or the nature and extent of disposition can be side-stepped as not falling within the theory's primary concern. In this regard, then, although the bio-environmental model is no better, Jeffery & Zahn are right to point out that "Choice is neither empirical nor observable, and the investigator can only know when an individual has made a choice when he behaves in a given way" (1993: 339). If the hallmark of science is prediction, this makes rational choice theory scientifically weak, but then so too are other theories employing mentalistic concepts like motives, and indeed the problems of criminological theorizing at large have always been those of either over- or under-prediction, and a lack of scientific exactitude. Nevertheless, rational choice theory is obviously a start, although its practical ends mean that unfortunately (for criminology) it does not have much of an interest in getting that far out of the blocks.

Secondly, the practical manifestation of rational choice theory in situational crime prevention is actually a poor reflection of it – there is a poor fit between the theory, which allows for some element of disposition, and the practice, which rarely does. The consequence is that it is very easy to misinterpret the theory from the practice, which is more conservative than the theory might necessarily imply. The conservatism ultimately comes from the preparedness to satisfice rather than to maximize; to find an approach that is "good enough" to demonstrate success at reducing crime, at least to a certain level, without necessarily looking to reduce it any further. Seeking to control crime is not the same as seeking to eliminate it, and this is therefore a criminology for the real world, and one that understandably finds favour therein.

Summary

In this chapter we have reviewed a number of important theoretical contributions to the development of contemporary crime prevention practice. Initially, in the 1960s, these emanated from outside of criminology, but in the 1990s they are now an integral part of it, or at least one of its key competing paradigms – there is probably no such thing as a criminological mainstream.

This tradition of theorizing about crime picked up on the lead given by control theory and the labelling perspective, which helped to divert attention away from the offender as the key explanatory variable. However, whereas the rationale for the latter two was mainly theoretical, for the approaches considered in this chapter it was mainly practical. Importantly, it was also of a practicality that was not confined to the repertoire of traditional criminal justice system responses to crime, and this gave it the necessary freedom to be innovative. Unusually, and in stark contrast to the late 1950s, for example, this applied even to the research conducted by the British Home Office, which formed the basis of the situational approach and rational choice theory.

These, then, are not so much theories of crime as theories of crime control, where, initially at least, pragmatic ends took precedence over scientific ones. This can be seen in the limitations of the theories that have been developed: Jacobs, Newman and Coleman all acknowledge, not always convincingly, that their ideas were never intended to be taken as the whole story; whereas Felson, for example, had the liberty in his early work of taking the presence of a motivated offender as given. Ultimately, these limitations were glossed over, being presented as less important than any potential contribution the theories might make to effective crime control. In addition, this pragmatism brought in explanatory variables, such as time and space, which mattered a great deal in the real world, but from which academic criminological theorizing had, very much to its detriment, become detached.

The practical impact of these theories has been considerable. They have contributed to the development of a range of preventive approaches that have focused not upon the offender, but upon the environment of the victim and potential victim – the community. To employ a well-used phrase, the onus has shifted to design against crime. They have thus increased the repertoire of official and indeed unofficial responses to crime, taking in a range of criminal justice and non-criminal justice agencies, and in so doing sharpening the politics of crime control, especially at the mezzo- or organizational level.

These theories have also contributed to further theoretical developments in the discipline of criminology. As Bottoms (1993) observes, it has become increasingly incumbent upon theorists of crime to move towards the integration of individual and community explanations of crime and criminality, of subjective and objective data, and of agency and structure. This can be seen in a number of recent developments, such as in the work of Braithwaite (1989), Gottfredson & Hirschi (1990), and in the contribution of the left realists and their notion of the square of crime (Young 1994). However, as Bottoms' criticisms demonstrate, the task of theoretical integration is far from easy, even though its reward, of greater theoretical integrity and holism, makes it a worthwhile venture.

The goals of integration and holism have also permeated the practical sphere, as crime prevention policy has moved increasingly towards the more general approach of community safety, although the theoretical contribution to this development is not necessarily as significant as the political contribution. This will become clearer as we now turn our attention towards crime prevention policy.

CHAPTER 4

The emergence of crime prevention as a major strategy of crime control

Introduction

In this chapter we turn our attention towards accounting for the rise to prominence of crime prevention in the 1980s and 1990s, from a position of relative obscurity and unpopularity in the 1950s. Of course, in so doing we are operating with a particular notion of crime prevention, for clearly if we were to consider all policies and practices that have been justified, at one time or another, in such terms then this book would have to be considerably more weighty than it is, taking in the combined efforts of at least the entire contribution from social policy and criminal justice policy domains. However, any attempt to provide a clear distinction between the kinds of crime prevention included in this chapter, and those excluded, would be doomed to failure, for ultimately the distinction is arbitrary, with such arbitrariness being facilitated by the flexibility of the concept, its political usage, and a collective amnesia that seemingly allows us to forget that existing practices were once considered crime preventive, thus allowing us, from time to time, to re-invent the wheel. Such issues have already been touched upon in Chapter 1.

Consequently, this chapter is interested in practices and policies currently regarded as earning the title of crime prevention, and in tracing their roots, recognizing, with Tuck (1987), the lack of any clear analytic scientific distinctions between past- and future-oriented actions, for example. Tuck does, perhaps, come closest to capturing the essential ingredient that binds contemporary crime preventive approaches together when she talks of contemporary crime prevention in terms of a paradigmatic shift from the state, and from institutional crime control, to crime control within the community, although as with community care there is an essential ambiguity about whether this control is supposed to be by or in the community. Tuck notes, then, that

> there is some ideal not in the past but in the future towards which we are groping; which is a world in which authority and law and the prevention of crime are not solely the responsibility of the state, but emerge from living associations of citizens who control themselves, because it is in their joint interest to do so. (1987: 7)

Now Tuck is certainly not naïve enough to believe that such a position has yet been reached, but she may be premature in dismissing all but the recent past of modernity, for in many ways the community thrust of crime prevention, or community safety, which others might call simply privatization, represents an endeavour to turn the clock back two hundred years to before the emergence of the modern state, although the implicit social contract underpinning her statement suggests something similar, if less monolithic, in its place. There is an idealism inherent in such a view, and in the case of crime prevention it is one that neglects the necessities of state agencies' continued involvement in order maintenance, and the realities of social control, which are considered in more depth later in the book. For now, we turn ourselves to an evolutionary account of what shall be termed unfocused crime prevention. It is unfocused in the sense that it is mainly primary (see Ch. 1), and oriented towards a general crime problem rather than focused upon specific and often localized problems: it is more general crime prevention than crime reduction.

Historical antecedents of unfocused crime prevention

Unfocused crime prevention, which is of a primary sort, targeted at the general population, has been traced back into the mists of time. Laycock & Heal (1989), for example, note that palaeolithic man used property-marking, albeit not with a UV pen, while the constructors of the Egyptian pyramids clearly pursued something akin to a strategy of design against crime. Clearly, whenever individuals or groups sought to protect themselves or their property from the depredations of outsiders their activities were preventive in one way or another, although the attribution of crime prevention to such activities presupposes a legal category of crime, which, in the case of England, and especially in the case of judicial interpretation, was far from unambiguous until the codification of the criminal law in the course of the nineteenth century.

To this extent, then, crime prevention might be more properly associated with the period marking the emergence of the modern state, although the paradox of this is that this is exactly the same time at which the responsibility for crime prevention came to be taken over by state agencies and located in an institutional form – exactly the situation from which the contemporary crime prevention paradigm is retreating. Hence, virtually the entire nineteenth century was taken up with the use of crime prevention to justify institutional forms of crime control, first with policing, for which the preventive principle was paramount, and then with penal policy, in the form of prisons, alternative arrangements for managing juvenile offenders, and noncustodial alternatives, culminating at the beginning of the twentieth century with the statutory establishment of the probation service. Many of these changes entailed an extension of crime prevention from criminal justice to social policy (Garland 1985), but few if any entailed any consideration of the part of the wider community of civil society: indeed, a failure to consider this may often have exacerbated the problems these institutions encountered, notably the police (P. Cohen 1979, Clarke 1987).

Now throughout this period it must have been the case that the community continued to take its own crime preventive precautions – indeed, the growth of private associations for the prosecution of felons in the first half of the nineteenth century demonstrates the extent of interest in direct participation in crime control, albeit among the propertied classes. However, the essential point is that very little was made of this, and there was not much official interest in harnessing the community's potential contribution to crime prevention. Rather, there was a pervasive belief that the new criminal justice institutions would prevent crime alone, and propaganda to the effect of their capacity to do this was an important element in their legitimation.

Nevertheless, even in these optimistic days, there was one lone voice, from a very unexpected and in retrospect unlikely source, which identified the potentially important part the community had to play in all this, in a mode of crime prevention that is very resonant with the dominant situational model of the 1980s. That lone voice belonged to Edwin Chadwick, the utilitarian reformer and erstwhile secretary to Jeremy Bentham, who did so much to rationalize the incremental expansionism and interventionism of the mid-Victorian state. Chadwick had been appointed as a member of the Constabulary Force Commission, established in the 1830s to consider the state of policing outside of London, and to make recommendations about possible reforms. This Commission collected evidence from across the country on the nature of the crime problem and crime control (although it has been suggested that the collection and presentation of the evidence was less than scientific), and reached the following conclusion:

It is the honest portion of the community only who are in ignorance, who require to be put on their guard and convinced of the necessity of taking effective measures for the abatement of the evil. More effectual measures than have yet been taken can only be founded in more close enquiries than have yet been made, and a better knowledge of the habits and practices of the classes to be guarded against than has yet been obtained. (Lefevre et al. 1839: 55)

In effect, this is a plea for situational crime prevention, complete with problem-oriented methodology, and, of course, the academic convention of calling for more research. This, evidently, did not fall on deaf ears, and a decade later Reith (1956: 260) reports the then Home Secretary Palmerston making the following commission to Chadwick in the following undated and unsigned letter:

Viscount Palmerston is especially desirous that you should investigate and distinguish in your report as closely as the evidence will permit:
1. what offences admit of prevention by the action of a police alone
2. what by a police in concert with the public

3. what offences must be prevented, if at all, by the care taken by the public themselves.

Such a question was clearly pertinent at this time, only a few years before the 1856 Obligatory Act, which established permanent policing across England and Wales, when central government must have been considering the nature and extent of police responsibilities. It is a great pity, then, that the research was either never done, or at least never reported, for it might have pre-empted developments over a century later. But the question did not appear to get raised again, and the preventive mantle was left to the police, although not to everyone's satisfaction.

Tallack, for example, the first Secretary of the Howard Association, which had been established with the intention of discovering the best methods of crime prevention, berated the police for focusing too much upon detection (tertiary prevention) to the detriment of (primary) prevention, accusing them of abstaining from "exertions which might, by destroying or obviating criminality, at the same time deprive themselves of the opportunities of earning reward and promotion" (1889: 327). In this regard, he suggested, they were like rat catchers who needed rats to justify their existence! Tallack's alternative preventive vision for the police, however, was not the situational form intimated by Chadwick, but rather the social rejoinder, based upon moral education, religion and training. Situational and social crime prevention, then, clearly have their antecedents, even if in the nineteenth century they existed more at the level of ideas than action.

The twentieth century: the decline of confidence in traditional crime controls

In terms of criminal justice policy, the first half of the century was characterized by a period of considerable stability, in which the major criminal justice institutions appeared to contain crime. Up until the Second World War crime rates in Europe remained relatively stable (notwithstanding a number of new automobile offences; Morris 1983), prison populations fell from their high nineteenth-century levels to hover around a modest 10,000 mark (Windlesham 1993), the probation service professionalized (May 1991), and policing experienced something of a "golden age" (Reiner 1992). There was certainly the odd crisis, and concern that there was room for improvement, but in general the system appeared to be coping relatively well with the demands placed upon it, and there was therefore little need or incentive to consider extending the responsibility for crime prevention into the community, beyond perhaps a softening of attitudes towards juvenile offenders that prompted the beginnings of a more welfarist, social work-oriented approach, necessitating increased interventions from agencies in this field.

After this tranquil period, crime rates suddenly rose during the Second World War, but this was attributed at the time to the unique pressures and conditions of wartime experience, and it was widely expected that things would return to normal after the war (Bottoms & Stevenson 1992). Even when this did not happen, however, and the prison population nearly doubled from its pre-war level to some 20,000 by 1948 (Windlesham 1993), there was nevertheless still no sense of crisis, of the system being unable to cope. Consequently, with in the main cross-party consensus on the issue, law and order was hardly a political issue in the two decades after the end of the war (Downes & Morgan 1994).

The widespread belief was that the criminal justice system was fit for its intended purpose, and that while they might need an element of fine-tuning in response to the changing times, institutional responses were generally up to the task of crime control. The fine-tuning was prompted by a renewed increase in levels of crime from the mid-1950s, and by the accompanying greater use of custodial sentences that led in turn to greater pressure on the prisons, culminating, inevitably, in overcrowding.

This fine-tuning took three main forms. First, by the late 1950s there was a recognition that penal methods had to be grounded in sounder research into the causes of crime (the Home Office Research Unit and the Cambridge Institute of Criminology had been established partly for this purpose in 1957 and 1960 respectively), the underlying assumption being that these causes often lay in individual pathology. The hope was that research would point the way to better diagnostic methods for identifying and ultimately treating such pathology, and that these might be allied, for example through observation centres, with a more effective and appropriate allocation of offenders to a range of disposals, many of which, such as detention and attendance centres, served the dual purpose of taking pressure off the over-crowded prisons. Secondly, fine-tuning was also applied to a chronically understaffed police service, where the hope was that policing in the 1960s might be made more effective by the injection of a number of technological innovations, which might strengthen the police's hand against an increasingly sophisticated criminal fraternity. Thirdly, and finally, attempts were made to reform the structure of juvenile justice, by focusing more preventive intervention on families in need, and by a stronger dose of welfarism – essentially an acceleration of the trend first evidenced before the war.

Unfortunately, however, traditionalist opposition from a number of quarters blunted the force of these intended reforms and rationalizations (Bottoms & Stevenson 1992). More significant for our purposes, and with a heavy dose of irony, the research that had originally been intended to underpin the so-called "treatment paradigm" (Bottoms & McWilliams 1979) of penal methods ultimately proved to be their Trojan Horse. By the end of the 1960s, and certainly by the 1970s, the most significant finding to emerge was that penal policies and methods were largely ineffective in crime reductionist terms (Brody 1976). In this light, the optimism of the late-1950s, that the system could be adapted to control crime, initially gave way to crisis management, as measures such as the suspended sentence, parole and community service were designed to take some pressure off our bulging prisons, and latterly melted into a pessimism that "nothing works".

It is against this change that we must measure the contribution of unfocused crime prevention, and the role of the wider community in controlling crime. The beginnings of this, for our purposes, can be traced back to the mid-1950s and the combined effort of the Home Office and the insurance industry to launch a publicity campaign that urged the public to take greater care over the security and protection of their property (Greater London Council 1986). The publicity campaign has since formed an integral part of unfocused crime prevention policy, despite evidence (Weatheritt 1987) that casts doubt on its capacity to deliver the desired effect among its target audience. Nevertheless, this early initiative is significant in so far as it draws attention to an alternative, largely non-institutional means of preventing crime, and a concern from outside of the criminal justice system that the system lacks the capacity successfully to control crime by itself. In this regard, one might draw a parallel between the concerns of the insurance industry in the middle of the twentieth century, and the concerns of private businesses in the nineteenth century that, mindful of the limitations of the criminal justice system then, formed themselves into private associations for the prosecution of felons.

These humble beginnings of unfocused crime prevention were barely significant in the overall context of a criminal justice policy that in the 1950s saw the control of crime almost exclusively in institutional terms. Moreover, the opportunistic view of crime on which they rested was not even articulated by criminologists until the 1960s (see Wilkins 1964, Radzinowicz 1966), and only obtained official support in the 1970s (Mayhew et al. 1976). Indeed, in retrospect, Bottoms & Stevenson (1992) may attribute rising crime rates to increased opportunities, increased individualism following the relaxation of social controls, and declining informal social controls as a result of changes in families and communities, but of these only the latter two held any currency at the time. In the 1950s, when the treatment paradigm was in ascendance, the opportunistic view of crime must have seemed very simplistic and unscientific. Nevertheless, the seed had been sown, and the same forces that conspired to bring down the treatment paradigm served to increase the stock of unfocused crime prevention.

The rise of unfocused crime prevention in the 1960s

Perhaps the key moment for unfocused crime prevention was the decision of the then Home Secretary to establish, in 1960, the Cornish Committee on crime prevention and detection – although the Committee did not report officially until 1965. Despite its focus upon prevention *and* detection, the significance of the Committee lies in its preparedness, despite the general mood and direction of criminal justice policy in the mid-1960s, to recognize the potential of unfocused crime prevention, and the vital roles to be played therein by both the police and the wider community. With regard to the police, the Committee recommended that the practice of appointing specialist crime prevention officers and departments, which had been pursued by some forces from the late-1950s (GLC 1986), and which had received further support with the establishment in 1963 of the Home Office's National Crime Prevention Centre at Stafford for training purposes, should be adopted by every police force on a divisional or sub-divisional basis.

The essential point, recognized by the Committee, was that the police were needed to deliver locally the sort of message that could be generated through publicity at the national level, and that trained officers could be used to pinpoint areas of particular vulnerability, especially amongst private businesses. However, the Home Office was also alive to the possibility that the creation of specialist departments might encourage an abrogation of responsibility for this kind of crime prevention elsewhere within the police organization. Hence, it took the opportunity, through a 1968 circular, to suggest that the new area constables established under the unit beat policing plan might be in a good position to provide crime prevention advice direct to the community, or to put them in touch with the more specialist services offered by the crime prevention departments.

The same national–local framework applied to the community. Thus at the national level the Committee recommended the formation of the Standing Committee on Crime Prevention to be based at the Home Office. This corporatist body was duly formed in 1966, comprising representatives from the Confederation of British Industry, the Trades Union Congress, chambers of commerce, the insurance industry, and the Association of Chief Police Officers. The focus of this body was clearly upon property crimes, and in practice it was functionally split into two subcommittees, one on buildings and property, and the other on vehicles and goods in transit. In its early years this Standing Committee was responsible for engendering industry-wide agreements on, for example, the standard fitting of steering locks to all new cars, and the institution of a minimum standard security code for all newly built houses.

At the local level, the Cornish Committee recommended the establishment of crime prevention panels, under the aegis of the Standing Committee. The purpose of the panels was envisaged as being to establish a local corporate body, consisting of representatives from local businesses and industries, voluntary organizations and statutory services, which might be capable of maintaining a two-way dialogue with the police: to enable the police to channel crime prevention advice and publicity through the panel, and to enable the panel to identify local crime problems that might either be brought to the attention of the police, or form the focus of a community-based preventive initiative (Partridge 1984, Symes 1984). Another Home Office circular in 1968 urged local police forces to set about establishing such panels, and by the end of 1969 some 58 of these were in existence (Her Majesty's Chief Inspector of Constabulary (HMCIC) 1970). By the mid-1970s the number had risen to 134, and by the mid-1980s this had risen still further to more than 200 (Windlesham 1987), reaching 450 by the 1990s (Home Office 1991).

Also as a consequence of Cornish Committee recommendations, as a means of establishing a practical channel of, and vehicle for, communication between the centre and localities, the Home Office launched, in 1969, a journal entitled *Crime Prevention News*, a free publication that reported news of national policy developments and local schemes and initiatives, and a short while later it produced a *crime prevention index* as a repository of information about the best preventive methods and security products (HMCIC 1972). Overall, then, as Laycock & Heal (1989: 315) observe, the Cornish Committee "laid the foundations of a structure for crime prevention still visible today".

The Cornish Committee had grasped the central importance of unfocused crime prevention and the notion of collaboration. Ultimately, as Chadwick and his colleagues had recognized well over a century before, the prevention of crime in terms of the blocking of opportunities depended upon ordinary people taking sensible measures that made themselves, or at least their property, less vulnerable to the depredations of potential offenders. To do this, they needed to be reminded that it was their responsibility (and not solely the police's), that the means were available for such an end, and that expert advice existed about how such means could be put to best use. The crime prevention infrastructure put in place after the Cornish Committee Report had these points very much in mind, although the mere existence of such an infrastructure is, of course, no guarantee of the desired outcome.

Indeed, one can identify a number of difficulties standing in the way of a successful outcome to these reforms. Heal (1987: 9), for example, argues that "the climate was against it. It was the period of fast developing technology and information systems and, for many people, these wonders seemed to be the answer to rising crime." Heal suggests that the police made more effort than most to comply with the Cornish reforms, but even this is debatable, since these changes resonated strongly with the mores of the rank-and-file occupational culture, while traditionalists within the police (HMCIC 1965: 44) displayed some resistance to this unfamiliar conceptualization of crime prevention in arguing that "there is still widespread support for the view that the constable patrolling in uniform is still the best means of preventing crime and that his presence on the streets acts as a deterrent". Police support, then, was pivotal, yet problematic as crime prevention stood, in effect, between a rock and a hard place. The police role in crime prevention is considered in greater detail in Chapter 5.

Another set of related problems emanate from the structural position of the Home Office, and the nature of its policy-making in a context in which many of the interested parties lie outside its direct sphere of influence (see Tilley (1993a) for an informed discussion of this). This means that while the Home Office can have some influence on the creation of certain infrastructures or forms of crime prevention, it cannot predict contents or outcomes with any degree of certainty. The police, for example, may have been encouraged to act as catalysts for the creation of crime prevention panels, and to set up their own crime prevention departments, but thereafter the nature of business conducted within these panels or departments was beyond Home Office control. To the author's knowledge there has been no research of any note conducted into crime prevention panels, but it is apparent that in the 1970s and beyond many may have lost their way in regard to their original intended purpose, as police support was not as forthcoming as had been hoped, and as interest groups establishing themselves on the panels strove to pursue alternative agendas, including moving more towards social approaches to crime prevention. These may be classified as implementation difficulties, although underpinning them one finds the political and criminological discursive differences that have consistently lain at the heart of the concept of crime prevention.

The situational paradigm:
from the margins to the mainstream

By the beginning of the 1970s, then, crime prevention had an institutional framework, even if it did not amount to very much. In the course of that decade, however, it was to undergo what Laycock & Heal describe as a renaissance, so that "[by] the end of the 1970s several influences were coming together which were to result in prevention being given greater weight" (1989: 316). In the context of the previous couple of decades, many of the influences that Heal & Laycock draw attention to are relatively unexceptional, including such factors as rising crime, bulging prisons, growing costs, falling detection rates, and a generally increasing strain on the system. However, there were other more significant influences, prompted particularly by the dissemination of those ironic research findings, noted earlier in this chapter, which showed both sentencing (Brody 1976) and, later, policing (Clarke & Hough 1980) to be of limited effectiveness. In addition, although it was not until 1982 that the Home Office undertook its first British Crime Survey, experience elsewhere pointed to the immutable fact that the vast majority of crimes went either unreported or unrecorded, and thus their prevention lay beyond the reaches and best efforts of the criminal justice system anyway. Moreover, it became equally apparent that in the process of attrition through the criminal justice system only something like three per cent of offences resulted in a conviction, so that the vast armoury of penal policy only ever touched the tip of the iceberg. So, in contrast to the 1950s and 1960s, the implication in the 1970s was that no amount of fine-tuning was going to solve the problems of the criminal justice system and make it work more effectively.

Recognizing this fairly early on, researchers within the Home Office, as opposed to their political masters, drew inspiration for an alternative vision of crime control, not from the emerging paradigm of unfocused crime prevention, which remained relatively marginal, but from the theoretical influences considered in Chapter 3, and the organizing concept of crime as opportunity (Mayhew et al. 1976) in particular. While this concept was greeted by the criminological community with as much scepticism as that with which criminal justice agencies greeted unfocused crime prevention, it did nevertheless feed into a policy review process within the Home Office (1977: 9–10):

> In view of the limitations in the capacity of the agencies of the criminal justice system to reduce the incidence of crime, the scope for reducing crime through policies which go beyond the boundaries of the criminal justice system merit particular attention. In recognition of this, work is already in hand exploring how the Home Office could more readily involve other Government Departments, local authorities, and agencies outside

government in the crime prevention field ... Work on the broader aspects of crime prevention should be pressed forward as speedily as possible.

This work took a number of forms, from circulars exhorting other welfare-oriented agencies to participate in intermediate treatment and cautioning schemes for youths, to research projects intended to explore other avenues of crime prevention, particularly with regard to vandalism and theft (Clarke & Mayhew 1980). At roughly the same time as the unfocused crime prevention infrastructure created in the 1960s entered a period of relative stasis (although there was at least room for inventiveness in publicity slogans, such as "watch out, there's a thief about" or "lock it or lose it"), experience derived from these projects was distilled into a distinctive, specific approach to crime prevention. Gladstone (1980) reports on how this approach was arrived at by a Home Office Working Group on Crime Prevention, on which Home Office researchers were represented, and which came up with the proposal that crime prevention should follow a methodology that was problem- rather than practice-oriented.

This new approach or model obtained the label of situational crime prevention, derived from the starting point of the methodology, namely the background situation of, or facts known about, a particular offence category, although the label has subsequently been used as much to refer to techniques of crime prevention as the methodology that informed their selection (see Ch. 1). From the situation of the offence, the idea was that a number of potential preventive approaches might be identified, of which the most promising could be selected, implemented, monitored and evaluated (Laycock & Pease 1985). The model was the epitome of the rational approach to policy-making, and it offered a great deal of promise, for in contrast to the policy that preceded it, which effectively established an infrastructure before the problem, it sought to establish an infrastructure in response to the problem, thus making it considerably more focused and purposive. More importantly, it dovetailed neatly with the collaborative message of unfocused crime prevention policy, for as Gladstone observes

This [the situational approach] implies a need for increased liaison and co-ordination of effort because knowledge, skills and responsibility for decision making with respect to each approach [to crime prevention] are frequently divided between several agencies. (1980: 139-40)

Laycock & Heal imply that the force of this logic effectively "opened the door to prevention" (1989: 317), but this in turn implies an open-mindedness among the criminal justice community that does not sit comfortably with past experience. If situational crime prevention was to avoid befalling the same fate of marginality as the policy of the 1960s, it faced two formidable barriers.

First, there was the problem of implementation, which took a number of forms. For example, where the situational approach had been tried, such as in a schools vandalism demonstration project in Manchester (see Hope & Murphy 1983), it had proved difficult to get all the relevant agencies "on board", hence Croft's (1980: v) observation that "The problem of preventing crime is not so much knowing what to do but of persuading people to undertake the necessary action."

Secondly, there was the related problem of politics, for while the research community had become accustomed to the pessimistic conclusion that "nothing works" in the way of traditional criminal justice responses to crime control, this was not necessarily accepted elsewhere. In particular, at the party political level, the Conservatives had been elected to government in 1979 on a law and order ticket (Brake & Hale 1992), and in pursuit of policies, notably in terms of industrial relations and welfare retrenchment, which were likely to have significant law and order implications and thus be subject to heavy political investment. Moreover, established criminal justice institutional interests, of either liberal or punitive persuasions, were hardly likely to accept a need for finding alternative approaches to crime control that might simultaneously undermine their own positions. Indeed, they were not under any substantial pressure to do so as, for example, the increased investment in policing immediately after 1979 heralded in another golden age of a kind, and there was a certain element of hay-making while the sun shone, especially as storm clouds gathered over other more vulnerable areas of public policy.

Although implementational difficulties have remained a thorn in the side of the situational approach to crime prevention, as events transpired the political barrier was eventually overcome, and the momentum continued to build. Laycock & Heal point to the key influence of a speech made in the House of Lords by the Lord Chief Justice in March 1982, which emphasized the importance of looking beyond, and before, the criminal justice system in the search for a solution to continually rising crime rates. The speech prompted the Home Secretary to make a similar speech in the House of Commons the following day, and from this a number of more specific initiatives followed, beginning with the announcement of the establishment of an interdepartmental working group on crime reduction, and a conference at Bramshill Police Staff College. However, while these speeches undoubtedly helped to move things forward, it remains pertinent to ask what prompted them, for research rarely has such direct influence at the political level.

Since the police were at the time the sole agency with a statutory responsibility for crime prevention their role in this is understandably vital. In this regard, Reiner (1992) identifies a number of factors that effectively softened them up, and made them, and by implication the Home Office too, more accommodating of crime prevention cast in its situational mould. First is the impact of the research on the effectiveness of policing, which made it increasingly difficult to cling to the sacred cows of patrolling and detective work as the main forms of crime prevention. Secondly, the aftermath of the 1981 urban riots left the police in a more politicised position, experiencing a crisis in public confidence that Weatheritt (1986) suggests made them more ready to turn to the government for advice and assistance over operational priorities. Thirdly, the government's stringent Financial Management Initiative from 1982 finally eclipsed the sun that had been shining over the criminal justice system, and gave the police the incentive to find more efficient and effective ways of tackling the crime problems they faced.

The police arrived at a position of support for collaborative crime prevention, somewhat surprisingly, via the efforts of those from within the service who had been responsible for developing the philosophy and practice of community policing, notably John Alderson, the former Chief Constable of Devon and Cornwall. The essential point here is that community policing and collaborative crime prevention dovetail in much the same way as unfocused crime prevention and the situational approach do. Alderson's definition of community policing makes this abundantly clear:

The prevention of crime can be achieved by proactive measures including education, social welfare, environmental planning and socializing influences of a multifarious kind. It can in part be achieved by police guarding, patrolling and scaring off; or by use of alarms and security technology; or by detection, conviction and penal measures and supervision. They are all important as a whole crime prevention and fear prevention strategy. Community policing is concerned mainly with the proactive. (1983: 3)

The problem for community policing is how to decide which in this inventory is proactive, and which is not, although the principle of shared responsibility underpinning it is apparent enough, even if in practice this "translates into a fairly disparate set of proposals ranging from the highly idealistic to the prosaic and down to earth" (Weatheritt 1983: 130).

The Bramshill conference in 1982 represents the coming together of community policing and crime prevention, and the crystallisation of the pressures on the police to change their approach. Hence, the conference was addressed by Sir Brian Cubbon, who also chaired the interdepartmental working group on crime reduction; and it was held at Bramshill, which then fell under the leadership of Kenneth Newman, who was soon to become Commissioner of the Metropolitan Police, and whose views were not that dissimilar to Alderson's, having been informed by a problem-oriented approach to management acquired in part from American industrial experience (GLC 1986). Moreover, as Gordon (1984) points out, many of the conference papers were of presentations by police students who had visited inner city "ethnic flashpoints" with the purpose of finding multi-agency solutions: hence community policing was a way of responding both to the crisis in public confidence and to the Home Office's pressure to become more effective by becoming more preventive.

Indeed, this was given greater urgency through the influence brought to bear on the conference (Heal & Burrows 1983) of a contemporaneous contribution to criminology – Wilson & Kelling's (1982) "broken windows" thesis – which suggested that a failure to attend to relatively minor disorders risked setting off "cycles of decay" that would plunge areas into unmanageably high levels of crime and disorder. The implication underlying such a position was that minor disorders, rather than deep-seated socio-economic problems, were causes of these cycles about which something realistically could be done. The question remained as to what, however. Wilson & Kelling favoured an emphasis on the police's "order maintenance" role: an emphasis that Kinsey et al. (1986) claim had much influence on the Home Office's promotion of beat policing. But clearly crime prevention, with the right collaborative structure, had as much potential here, even if its application had not yet lent itself to the kinds of disorders envisaged by Wilson & Kelling in their thesis.

This is a very interesting point in the development of crime prevention policy, because it marks the recognition of the variety of ways in which crime can be prevented. The Wilson & Kelling line opens up a potential distinction between the police order maintenance role and crime prevention, but it also distinguishes between different modes of crime prevention – crudely, situational and social – by de-emphasizing the role of the latter in breaking the cycles of decay to which high crime rates may in part be attributed. This was a relatively new way of thinking that was prioritized in the Bramshill conference, and that received further, more explicit backing in the report of the interdepartmental working group on crime reduction, which clearly associated situational crime prevention with opportunity reduction and went on to make the point that "this "situational" approach affords the best immediate prospect for significant crime reduction" (Home Office 1983: 1). Such a position corresponded well with the government's political position with regard to social policy-type interventions in terms of crime control, as well as with the research evidence that pointed to its apparent lack of effectiveness in such terms.

This preferred direction of crime prevention policy was threatened somewhat when Kenneth Newman took over as Commissioner of the Metropolitan Police, for he immediately set about instituting a new vision of policing – very similar to Alderson's community approach – which he termed "multi-agency" policing. By this he meant

> police collaboration with other agencies, "social, economic, cultural and educational', to develop solutions which address the root cause rather than the symptoms of crime. The assumption is that through better understanding of all the facets of any type of anti-social behaviour, the community, including the police,

should be able to produce constructive, co-operative ventures to prevent or reduce the phenomenon, so avoiding costly reactive policing. (Newman 1983: 8)

The emphasis upon cost demonstrates the immediacy of the priorities instilled by the Financial Management Initiative, and following Weatheritt's judgement of community policing (1983: 130), the emphasis upon collaboration succeeds in making a virtue out of necessity. However, the worrying thing about this definition of multiagency policing from the Home Office's point of view was that it eschewed the Wilson & Kelling and situational approaches, and seemed rather to promote a welfarist view of the causes of crime, a deep irony given that this came from an organization not renowned for its liberalism. Evidently a politics of crime prevention was emerging, although in fact when Newman's vision was distilled into an action plan, it was also transformed into something altogether more acceptable and consistent with the situational approach (Weatheritt 1986).

In the context of the early 1980s, the vision of social crime prevention implicit in much of the community policing rhetoric served less as a block on progress than as an indicator of a contest that lay ahead, and in effect the Bramshill conference served to provide situational crime prevention with "the seal of legitimacy as a major new element in British crime policy" (Stern 1987: 209). This in turn ensured, as Heal (1987: 10) correctly observes, that "Unlike members of the Cornish Committee, those seeking to establish prevention in the early 1980s were swimming with, rather than against the tide."

The major task confronting the Home Office after the Bramshill conference and the deliberation of the interdepartmental working group on crime reduction was how to encourage agencies beyond the boundaries of the criminal justice system to play a role in crime prevention: essentially, this was the same task confronting those in the 1960s, but the main difference was that the focus had been broadened from the general public and private sector to also take in public sector agencies. The working group had recognized, however, that this was no easy task, drawing attention once more to potential implementational difficulties:

While it may be obvious what should be done to reduce opportunities, it is frequently difficult to persuade the people or organisations concerned to take the necessary action. The costs of action may be high in relation to the benefits; the necessary measures may be construed as inconvenient or intrusive (though in practice these problems are usually surmountable); and where a number of agencies (public or private) are involved it can be difficult to achieve the necessary co-ordination. (Home Office 1983: v, *Annex B*)

Attempts were made to overcome these possible pitfalls on a number of fronts. First, the Home Office established a separate Crime Prevention Unit (CPU), which included a small group of research staff, with the purpose not only of consolidating knowledge of what works, but also of seeking to promote crime prevention within public agencies, and within the community at large. Secondly, the Standing Committee on Crime Prevention was transformed into a Standing Conference, and given a higher profile with the appointment of a Home Office Minister to the chair. Thirdly, a draft interdepartmental circular drawn up by the working group in 1983 was issued in its final version as Home Office Circular 8/84, addressed to an unusually wide audience of police, probation, education and social services, and especially the chief executives of local authorities. Its message was plain from its opening paragraph:

A primary objective of the police has always been the prevention of crime. However, since some of the factors affecting crime lie outside the control or direct influence of the police, crime prevention cannot be left to them alone. Every individual citizen and all those agencies whose policies and practices can influence the extent of crime should make their contribution. Preventing crime is a task for the whole community. (Home Office 1984: 1)

The issuing of the circular just after the wider dissemination of findings from the first British Crime Survey, which made it clear that most crime was either not reported or not cleared up, made the case for crime prevention that much stronger. The circular argued, after the 1983 working group, that situational crime prevention offered the greatest prospect for success, and stressed the importance both of following a problem-oriented methodology in respect of established crime problems, and of making crime prevention a standard consideration in all policies with a bearing on crime. However, it did not make any additional resources available for this, and while the incorporation of crime prevention considerations into mainstream policy planning might not have had major resource considerations, the tackling of established crime problems potentially did. Resource limitations thus limited the impact of the circular, as did the Home Office's reluctance to identify an agency with a lead responsibility (Bright 1991), which facilitated a certain amount of buck-passing.

It was probably with an awareness of these difficulties that other initiatives were set in motion. An attempt was made, for example, to raise the profile of crime prevention panels so that they might act in effect as local pressure groups (Smith & Laycock 1985), ensuring that local agencies took crime prevention seriously and did something about it. To this end a national conference for crime prevention panels was organized in 1984, and subsequent attempts were made to raise their profile, and to give them a national focus, so that models of good practice might be identified and disseminated. However, while the numbers of such panels has grown quite considerably and rapidly since the mid-1980s, the nature and quality of their work has been very variable, and in places they have been seen as little more than marginal bodies that drain the police resources generally required to sustain them.

The CPU also sought to determine the level of response to Circular 8/84 by implementing a hurried nationwide survey of chief constables and local authority chief executives in 1985, requesting information on crime prevention projects and activities at the local level. To an extent this survey was doomed from the beginning because of inherent problems in knowing who to ask and what counted as an individual project, and thus it seemed reasonable to conclude that the survey had uncovered only the tip of the iceberg of local activity (CPU 1985). Nevertheless, one significant and rather worrying finding was that the vast majority of the projects that were uncovered were not evaluated in any rigorous way. It was impossible to say, with any degree of confidence, whether crime prevention was a success, and given the Home Office's prior understanding of implementational difficulties, there must have been concern that much of this local "activity" might actually be leading nowhere. This was dangerous, because crime prevention was being cast as a high profile new initiative, and given that it issued a political challenge to the main institutions of the criminal justice system, there were likely to be several interested parties standing by not that unhappy to see it fail.

The CPU must have been anxious, therefore, to see local crime prevention succeed, and to identify models of good practice that might illuminate the way for others to follow. This anxiety probably lay behind the decision to launch a series of demonstration projects in late 1985 under the title of the Five Towns Initiative, taking in the areas of Bolton, Croydon, North Tyneside, Swansea and Wellingborough. The Initiative itself began in January 1986, to run for 18 months. The CPU kept a tight rein on the initiative by providing research and technical support, and the funding for a co-ordinator post in each of the five towns, the object being that the co-ordinator should service an inter-agency committee in each area. As Bright (1991) observes, the model owed a lot to the pioneering work of NACRO in the 1970s (see Ch. 6), although the focus of the committee was adjusted from area-based to authority-wide, albeit with subcommittees or individual projects working at an area level beneath this.

The status of demonstration project meant that publicity was afforded a high priority, and each of the five towns paid attention to involving the local media, as well as producing glossy brochures of their 18 months' experience. Publicity was also a motive in the establishment of a ministerial group on crime prevention within central government in 1986, initially chaired by the then Prime Minister Margaret Thatcher – although Laycock & Heal (1989) point out that this group was also responsible for effecting a much greater concern for crime prevention within a number of departments, notably Transport, Energy, Health, Education and Environment.

The effectiveness of the Five Towns Initiative was variable, and the CPU's figures suggested only small reductions of crime in some of the areas (CPU 1988). A more conspicuous success was that each of the areas had worked with situational methods of crime prevention, although given the limited time scale involved, there was little other realistic alternative. Also, each of the local authority areas had been sold on the benefits of crime prevention, and had agreed to take over financial responsibility once the Home Office funding period came to an end, thereby lending support to the aspiration that the widespread adoption of crime prevention might be achieved at minimal cost to the Home Office, barring investment in a few demonstration projects that might serve the purpose of pump-priming.

This aspiration was further assisted when the Department of Employment agreed to collaborate with the Home Office in the 1985 launch of the "Crime Prevention and the Community Programme" initiative, whereby a significant part of the government's job creation scheme for the long-term unemployed was to be focused upon areas of relevance to crime prevention, thereby providing a significant staffing resource both for the Five Towns Initiative and other contemporary schemes across the country. By the end of 1986 some 5,000 people were employed under the scheme on 200 local projects (CPU 1986), and in 1987 this figure reached 8,000 (Laycock & Heal 1989). Wages were relatively low, and the initiative was therefore a low cost, productive alternative to supplementary benefit (now income support), although the quality of the work produced under these schemes, and the commitment of the managing agencies to their crime preventive effectiveness, remains open to question, for crime prevention was not necessarily the primary object of the exercise. Indeed, the crime preventive need was still there when the scheme came to an end in 1989.

By 1986 crime prevention had moved to centre stage in crime control policy, and yet, despite the Five Towns Initiative, and the availability of funds under the Community Programme, there was still no ground swell of support where it mattered most at the local level, leading Laycock & Heal (1989: 322) to observe that "The notion that crime and its prevention is the responsibility of the police and the criminal justice system is entrenched; it is hardly going to be turned round overnight." Restricted finances did not help the situation, and the argument that crime prevention can save money in the future with a little investment in the present carried little weight in the climate of short-termism generated by restrictive forms of financial management.

Consequently, the Home Office was faced with little alternative but to pursue more of the same, especially as there appears to have been strong political resistance to the path taken in other countries in Europe, where a strong local-national infrastructure of crime prevention councils had been put in place (see, for example, King 1991) – rather like the infrastructure envisaged in the 1960s in England, but with significantly enhanced powers and responsibilities, notably for local authorities. This "more of the same" took the form of the announcement of the launch of the Safer Cities Programme in March 1988. It was modelled on the Five Towns Initiative, but was conceived as something much bigger, initially scheduled to run in 20 "cities" (some of them were actually towns, or London boroughs, and all were selected from the 57 Urban Programme areas); for three years (this was later extended to five); and with an annual budget of £250,000 for each city to spend on crime prevention projects, albeit with the proviso that all bids of over £1000 should be referred to the CPU for prior approval. The idea was that a Co-ordinator would act as a catalyst to bring local agencies together, to encourage them to think about crime prevention, and to motivate them to make individual project bids for Safer Cities funding.

While there is continuity between the Five Towns Initiative and the Safer Cities Programme, there are also elements of discontinuity. One of the most important of these stemmed from the signs that crime prevention was now being tied to the coat-tails of urban economic policy. Hence, the Safer Cities Programme formed an element of the "Action for Cities" initiative launched by central government as the crystallization of the pledge made by the Prime Minister on the eve of her third general election victory in 1987, largely as a response to the Conservatives' failure to make many inroads into inner city Labour strongholds. As a consequence of this, according to the press release that launched the scheme, Safer Cities was as much about "creating a safer environment in which enterprise, community activity and personal responsibility can flourish', as it was about preventing crime. Crime prevention was once again becoming infused with politics, albeit of a different sort, as it became enmeshed within the ideological project of the third Thatcher government.

The rise of community safety

Another source of discontinuity, of an equally profound importance, arose from a paradigmatic shift in the nature of crime prevention being pursued within the boundaries of the Programme, for while a problem-oriented methodology remained paramount, much greater space was given to the development of social approaches to crime prevention alongside the more established situational ones. Together they formed the core of a hybrid approach that attracted the label community safety. There appear to be two main reasons for this shift.

First, one can discern within the research community a dampening of enthusiasm for a purely situational approach to crime prevention that is probably not entirely unconnected to personnel changes within the Home Office, and notably the departure of one of its most ardent enthusiasts. This dampening can be interpreted either as a reflection of the political sympathies of the new dominant research personnel who were more accommodating of social policy-type interventions, or as a rational response to the perceived inadequacies of situational crime prevention. With regard to the latter, Heal draws attention to the theoretical inadequacy of the situational approach's rational choice underpinnings in explaining criminal behaviour where, as he puts it (1992: 260) "There is clearly a difference between those who see an open window as a passport to crime, and those who view the same window as an aid to ventilation." At the very least, it was apparent that the situational approach was less than ideally suited to dealing with some crimes, in some contexts. Overall, dampened enthusiasm for situational crime prevention was probably a consequence of a number of different factors, including perceived theoretical weaknesses, the apparent Achilles heel of displacement, and the general discomfort many people experience with the surveillance and target-hardening technologies that underpin it.

Whichever the exact cause, it can be seen in the more cautious welcome extended to situational crime prevention in a major Home Office text that appeared on the subject (Heal & Laycock 1986), and it can be seen in the blueprint established for the famous and highly successful Kirkholt Project (Gilling 1992), which envisaged a model of collaborative crime prevention combining social and situational approaches, whereby police-led initiatives focused upon target hardening, while probation-led initiatives followed up in order to counter the criminal motivations of those frustrated by the target hardening. In other words, the blueprint assumed displacement, which was deeply ironic, because the evidence for it proved to be scanty indeed (Forrester et al. 1990). The research community, then, was slowly moving towards a position more accommodating of community safety, rather than just situational prevention. Indeed, this position became clearer still a couple of years later, following the publication of "Communities and Crime Reduction', which showed a much less ambiguous orientation to this approach (Hope & Shaw 1988), and which assembled a collection of papers from a conference of a similar title organized by the Home Office Research and Planning Unit in 1986, suggesting that the change in policy and emphasis had been under consideration a few years earlier.

The second reason for the "reconciliation" between social and situational crime prevention can be found closer to the action on the ground, among the agencies pulled into the collaborative net by Circular 8/84 and the subsequent initiatives. Situational crime prevention required a very specific form of inter-agency collaboration, between agencies who in the course of their normal functioning could reduce the opportunities for crime by environmental manipulations, or by the use of security and surveillance technologies. However, it is apparent that many of the wrong sorts of agencies were brought to the collaborative table to fulfil this requirement, for the agencies that showed the greatest readiness to collaborate, such as the probation and social services and a number of voluntary agencies, did not necessarily belong, whereas a number of other agencies, such as education and housing departments, had other interests beside situational crime prevention that were just as likely to take priority.

Indeed, even the police were not necessarily certain of the rules of the game that they had been invited to play, and they too had a mixed agenda as can be seen from the definition of community policing considered above. The inter-agency context of crime prevention is considered in more detail in Chapter 7 and here is not the place to dwell on it, but clearly it had a vital role to play, because it ensured that while the Home Office initially emphasized the preferability of situational crime prevention for quick results, local agendas were often quite different. Heal's account (1992) broadly concurs with this when he implies that the shift from a purely situational approach was less the result of a theoretical breakthrough than an unintended consequence of the development of a multi-agency structure, which brought together agencies with very different views and crime prevention agendas. While, however, he paints a picture of a resultant "composite" strategy for crime, it is equally plausible that the outcome is conflict, as the supporters of social and situational approaches take up their entrenched positions, regardless of the occasional artificiality and arbitrariness of the distinction between them.

Ultimately the question of whether the policy shift from a purely situational approach to one that was more accommodating of social crime prevention was intentional or unintentional is less important than the fact that it happened, and that it eventually received backing at the political level. This can be seen in the comments of the then Home Office Minister, who noted in *The Guardian* that "The language of five years ago about crime prevention, of "target hardening" or the "external enemy" now has an archaic ring to it" (Patten 1989). The acceptance of the legitimacy of social approaches to crime prevention should not necessarily be regarded as a softening of attitude, for as King (1989) has so ably demonstrated, social approaches are quite amenable to an illiberal ideological bent, particularly when practised in the wrong hands. However, the evidence of a right wing conspiracy to deliberately capture the social agenda at this particular moment is weak, not least because it would appear, as Jones et al. (1994) discovered, that the main influence behind crime prevention policy emanates from departmental officials, rather than politicians. Thus while Patten's comments are remarkable as a demonstration of the political change of attitude, and have a "road to Damascus" feel to them, it must not be forgotten that the itinerary had been provided by Home Office officials, quite literally in so far as they had "nudged" Patten to visit and draw lessons from the much more socially informed preventive policies found in France and Germany (Jones et al. 1994).

The Conservatives' conversion to its version of community safety has to be seen within a wider context of that party's political position in the law and order debate. In the first half of the 1980s the emphasis upon crime prevention had been a good deal quieter than that upon punitive law and order; something that Brake & Hale (1992) have portrayed as a necessary element of a political project intended to break the power of organized labour, and to keep a lid upon the social consequences of stringent economic policies, especially in the inner cities. This position was relaxed in the latter part of the 1980s, or what Nash & Savage (1994) characterize as the age of reason (although in truth it was more reason tinged with ideology), not least because the lid was in danger of blowing off, with the mid-1980s round of riots and spiralling rates of crime that appeared resistant to law and order strategies for reasons already cited above. More pragmatic solutions such as crime prevention had to be found, with the form of crime prevention itself being more subject to pragmatic choice than just ideological predilection.

Nevertheless, one of the hallmarks of Conservative success in the 1980s and 1990s has been the tactic of making virtue out of necessity. Hence, in much the same way as alternatives to custody came to be cast as punishments in the community, so the softer form of crime prevention being pursued towards the end of the 1980s acquired "the ideological clothes of right-wing rhetoric" (Nash & Savage 1994: 145). If the seeds of criminality lay within the community, it was the community's task to do something about it, either by preventing its manifestation as crime, or (and this is the new departure in policy) by tackling its origins in broken down communities. In this way, the spatial concentration of crime in urban neighbourhoods made so apparent by successive British Crime Surveys served a similar purpose to the rediscovery of pockets of urban poverty in the 1960s, since both were used to reinforce the notion of social pathology. According to Hale (1992), the government had to tread a thin line here, for in citing risk factors associated with criminality, such as low school achievement and poor parenting, it risked arming those who could use such information to push for broader-based social policy interventions, which the previous decade had done so much to sideline from criminal justice policy.

Consequently, from the end of the 1980s, the community safety phase of crime prevention policy tended to rely upon a dual strategy, which mixed reason and ideology. First there was a concerted effort to pass the responsibility down through the community to the individual citizen, and secondly there was an attempt to locate it within multi-agency structures. The concept of partnership linked the two.

Brake & Hale (1992) trace the first strategy back to the 1987 election, after which time Prime Minister Thatcher and Home Secretary Hurd worked tirelessly to stress the theme of the active citizen, particularly through the vehicle of Neighbourhood Watch, which had first appeared in England in 1982. Moreover, in January 1988 a publicity campaign was launched under the slogan "crime, together we'll crack it', which was accompanied by a booklet demonstrating "practical ways to crack crime". Neighbourhood Watch is considered in more detail in Chapter 6, and the limited effectiveness of publicity campaigns has been commented upon previously, although they have the obvious political benefit of publicizing policies if not actually effecting behavioural changes. Here it should perhaps be noted that the promotion of Neighbourhood Watch was a resounding success in terms of numbers recruited: in the years 1988 and 1989 its schemes increased from approximately 50,000 to 80,000 (McConville & Shepherd 1992). Indeed, John Patten felt confident enough to declare that the five per cent fall in recorded notifiable offences in 1988 – the first fall for five years, and the biggest fall for considerably longer – was largely attributable to the massive increase in Neighbourhood Watch membership. Ironically, as Johnston (1993) wryly observes, the increase in recorded crime in the following year was attributed by the same Minister to not enough households being covered!

The Safer Cities Programme was the main plank of the second strategy, but in addition the government sought to make good its 1987 manifesto commitment to establish a national body for crime prevention. All the main political parties had made a similar commitment in 1987, but as events transpired the Conservative solution rested less upon a statutory infrastructure (notwithstanding the previously formed ministerial group), and more upon an independent sector solution. Thus in 1988 it set up Crime Concern, which is considered in more detail in Chapter 6. Here it is worth noting that it provided a bridge between multi-agency and community efforts, for it was given the brief of developing Neighbourhood Watch, but also crime prevention panels, and encouraging a more meaningful contribution from the private sector, as well as engaging in its own consultancy work with local authorities and local partnerships.

Crime Concern secured relatively few consultancies with local authorities, which, together with its limited success with the private sector delayed its objective of becoming financially self-supporting. More tellingly, perhaps, the small number of local authority consultancies drew attention to a familiar problem from the early 1980s, namely the general lack of local commitment to take crime prevention forward. Underlining this, at the end of 1989 NACRO's Safe Neighbourhoods Unit produced a survey of all English and Welsh upper and lower tier local authorities that was only completed by 105 of them. Only 19 had corporate crime prevention strategies., while only 21 had specially nominated crime prevention units or posts (Association of Metropolitan Authorities 1990). Outside of the Safer Cities Programme and other small demonstration projects it was evident that developments were patchy indeed, and multi-agency crime prevention was still developing more by short-term projects than by programmes. With Safer Cities funding only initially available for a three year period its claim to programme status was somewhat weak.

Home Office ministers had tried to engage local authorities and the police in crime prevention through a series of regional conferences in 1987 and 1988, but the lack of a sustained decline in crime after 1988 brought a renewed sense of urgency to the task, even though each of these agencies had begun to respond to the idea by establishing various subcommittees and working parties on their representative bodies. Nevertheless, while crime prevention was undoubtedly seen as a good thing and a worthy pursuit, there was still some kind of blockage preventing the flow of ideas and good will into action. Judging by its subsequent response, the Home Office interpreted this blockage as a lack of inspiration, prompting it to bring forward another of its commitments from 1988, namely the issuing of a follow up circular to 8/84.

Home Office Circular 44/90 differed from 8/84 in three key respects. First, it was accompanied by a booklet entitled "Partnership in Crime Prevention', which provided concrete examples and models of good practice that localities were invited to emulate. Secondly, it required a response from local authorities and the police about their own strategies, thus providing a sharper focus than the regional conferences of two years earlier. Thirdly, it was not so prescriptive in terms of the form of crime prevention to be pursued, not showing the leaning towards the situational approach that had been in evidence in 1984. Rather, it stressed the importance of establishing durable local structures at both strategic and operational levels, of basing initiatives upon sound information, and of ensuring that crime prevention did not become submerged beneath competing objectives. Like Circular 8/84, however, it made clear that resources had to be drawn from a redirection of priorities, and it was noncommittal on the matter of local leadership.

Leadership was a matter of some controversy. Rationally, because of a desire to promote a fully multi-agency composite strategy against crime, the Home Office was reluctant to identify a single lead, through concern that this might encourage others to off-load their responsibilities in much the same way as, historically, the criminal justice system has come to be regarded as solely responsible for crime rates, despite the obvious absurdity of such a view. Moreover, it has been suggested that the identification of a lead agency might discourage a holistic view of the crime problem. Furthermore, at this time there was no obvious agency with the skills or expertise to deliver crime prevention locally. Thus, as Heal (1992) observes, it does not matter which agency leads so long as all agencies work together.

In addition to the Home Office's practical or rational reasons for not wanting to identify a lead agency, however, government ideology ensured that there was no prospect of passing on a statutory leadership responsibility to the most obvious local agency, the local authority (Loveday 1994a). Not only are most local authorities not Conservative-controlled, but they have also been perceived by central government as generally profligate and incompetent, and on the basis of this view policy has been geared towards taking responsibilities away, and certainly not adding to them.

This combination of practical and ideological reasons for not identifying a lead agency was nevertheless alleged to be responsible for holding up the local development of crime prevention. Local authority associations lobbied hard for such a responsibility, the Labour Party supported this lobbying in its own policy documents, and it was also the main conclusion reached by the Morgan Committee, which had been set up under the auspices of the Standing Conference on Crime Prevention indirectly to review this very issue, for one of its terms of reference was "to consider and monitor the progress made in the local delivery of crime prevention by the multi-agency or partnership approach in the light of the guidance in the booklet, 'Partnership in Crime Prevention'" (Home Office 1991: 10).

The Morgan Committee had been established in early 1991 because of the difficulties encountered in the local co-ordination of crime prevention, but if the official expectation was for a report consisting solely of a range of practical and technical recommendations, that hope was most definitely dashed. While, certainly, the Morgan Report did make practical recommendations concerning such topics as training and resourcing, the Committee refused to neglect the wider context, and thus produced a critical report, noting crucially that "crime prevention is a peripheral concern for all the agencies and a truly core activity for none of them" (Home Office 1991: 15). It continued that because of this fact local initiatives relied too heavily upon committed individuals, whereas centrally driven projects such as the various urban initiatives were viewed locally with confusion and mistrust, because of their short-termism, potential duplication, and use of "outsiders". As a consequence, the Committee recommended that local authorities, in conjunction with the police service, should be given a statutory responsibility for crime prevention, with direct grants from the Home Office, and that central government's own crime preventive activities, ordered around the ministerial group and the Standing Conference, should be given a stronger focus.

The Morgan Report also went further, to address the issue of the nature of crime prevention. It suggested that much more attention than hitherto should be addressed to youth, and that the term crime prevention was both inaccurate and misleading – community safety was eminently preferable because it "is open to wider interpretation and could encourage greater participation from all sections of the community in the fight against crime" (Home Office 1991: 13). So, although this phase of policy has been characterized as community safety, until this point in time the word had been rarely used, restricted in the main to developments in the local authority sector and in left realist literature. The Morgan Committee, however, clearly felt that the wider use of the term could help to clear the blockage in local developments. Indeed, there was some precedent in central government, since safety had become an explicit objective of urban policy back in 1988 as part of the Action For Cities package (Deakin & Edwards 1993).

While Heal (1992), a key figure within the Home Office in this period, acknowledges that the lack of a local structure for crime prevention stands as an obstacle to progress, the Morgan Committee proposals were not warmly received as a solution by the government, and many have been conspicuously ignored, although others have been addressed. Hence, while Crime Concern has since 1988 sought to raise the profile of youth crime prevention by such measures as establishing youth crime prevention panels, and the Standing Conference has produced a number of reports on the matter in the late 1980s, in early 1992 the then Home Secretary Kenneth Baker conceded to an Association of Chief Officers of Probation conference that social approaches were an integral part of tackling youth crime.

Plans to launch a package of measures were unveiled in 1992, but were subsequently vetoed in the run up to the 1992 election, partly on grounds of cost, and partly through concern about the potential political fall-out from publicly linking crime with social conditions that might have been exacerbated by government economic policies. Nevertheless, after the election in 1993 a £4 million youth action scheme was announced, and youth was identified as a priority group for the new National Crime Prevention Board (see below). In the end, however, the commitment to a more liberal conception of youth crime prevention proved short-lived, and by the end of 1993 the preventive emphasis had switched to more punitive forms of crime control, including the doubling of the maximum custodial sentence for young offenders, and the establishment of the new secure training order, both included in the regressive 1993 Criminal Justice Act. Also, taking an adaptation of Neighbourhood Watch with him as he moved ministerial office from the Home Office to the Department of Education, John Patten launched a heavily surveillance-oriented truancy watch scheme between 1993 and 1994.

At the national level, the Morgan Committee's criticisms were responded to by revamping the ministerial group on crime prevention in 1993, and by creating a wholly new body, the National Board for Crime Prevention. As with the establishment of Crime Concern back in 1988, this was another occasion in which the government elected to shun the continental model of statutory infrastructures (see Graham 1987), this time in favour of a preferred inter-sectoral corporatist equivalent, drawing representatives from a wide range of statutory, voluntary and private agencies, and with a Home Office minister as chairman. Its stated purpose was to find new ways of involving all sections of the community in measures to reduce crime and the fear of crime which could be put into effect at the local level (National Board for Crime Prevention 1994). The acceptance of fear of crime as an explicit object of preventive effort demonstrates a continued adherence to a model of community safety. The Board met only occasionally, and developed strategies with regard to repeat victimization and retail crime (although it prioritized youth, it never developed a strategy), but its large membership and uncertain status made it rather cumbersome in operation.

As the Morgan Committee had identified, however, the major problem concerned the local level. In so far as there was a response to Morgan, it took the form of a continuation of the crime prevention by exhortation approach. Hence in 1993 Crime Concern was enlisted to produce a guide entitled "A Practical Guide To Crime Prevention For Local Partnerships', disseminated to "local agencies" (Home Office 1993a), on each occasion therefore avoiding explicit mention of local authorities. This brought an acerbic comment from the outgoing president of the Association of Chief Police Officers' Crime Prevention Committee (Owen 1994: 7) to the effect that "Crime prevention activity needs core funding, not more glossy brochures endorsing the partnership approach."

As is so often the case, however, local authorities were indirectly assisted by a further new measure, namely the planned expansion of the Safer Cities Programme. Most of the original 20 Safer Cities had wound down, in terms of central funding, by early 1994, and so a second phase was announced with an intended 40 new schemes. The period of funding for these second phase schemes was, however, reduced from five to three years, with the amount of funding also being pegged back to a modest £100,000 for each of those years. As with the first phase, an explicit objective was that this Programme would establish a local infrastructure that could be left in place at the end of the funding period. However, with local authorities clearly expected to be a key element within such a structure it was deeply ironic that the local management of each Safer City was located with either NACRO or Crime Concern, although the Society of Voluntary Associates (SOVA) was also used in a few cases. While such agencies have some virtue as independent and impartial outsiders, and "honest brokers", it is also true that their use is consistent with the general tenor of central government policy and ideology towards local government.

The Safer Cities Programme was initially managed from within the Home Office, but from April 1994 its management was transferred to the Department of the Environment as it became a part of the new unified Single Regeneration Budget (SRB), which aimed to rationalize urban policy by bringing together 20 disparate government programmes into a more coherent whole. In the longer term, the purpose of the SRB is to change the nature of funding urban initiatives from a predetermined bureaucratic allocation according to some measure of need, to a competitive bidding process in the mould of one of its predecessors, City Challenge. There are several bidding criteria, one of which is crime prevention/community safety, and any bids have to be accompanied by evidence of partnerships between public, private and voluntary sectors, and the community. In theory, then, this means that local partnerships outside of Safer City areas should be able to bid for funds for crime prevention to a number of regional SRB offices. However, at present the majority of the funds available through the

SRB is committed on existing projects: the amount of available money in the first spending round is a very modest £100 million, although more will become available as existing commitments such as the Safer Cities Programme are fulfilled.

In theory, then, the SRB potentially makes more resources available for crime prevention to local authorities, so long as they can demonstrate a commitment to partnership, which is very much a theme of crime prevention anyway. In practice, however, the advent of the SRB may be a mixed blessing, since it takes some responsibility away from the Home Office, where a certain expertise had been developed in problem-oriented work. Even if there is still some Home Office representation in the administration of the SRB, the important point is that by tying in crime prevention to the wider needs and goals of urban policy, the centrality of specificity and relevance to the former is potentially lost. Moreover, as both Loveday (1994a) and Burton (1995) note, the SRB comes with a number of strings attached, which serves to undermine both its localism and its relevance for crime prevention, as its main aim remains urban regeneration for purposes of private sector investment.

Beyond Safer Cities and the SRB, local authorities have been the recipients of other exhortations and minor inducements to crime prevention. In the run up to the 1994 local government elections, for example, John Major made an infamous speech about the importance of planting heavy duty shrubbery around vulnerable premises – "back to berberis", as one commentator wittily observed (Loveday 1994b). Major also urged local authorities to consider the widespread adoption of closed-circuit television (CCTV), following its high profile usage in the James Bulger abduction and murder case, and its reported success in cutting crime rates in city centres such as in Newcastle and Wolverhampton. To facilitate this, in late 1994, the Home Secretary Michael Howard announced a CCTV competition, with local agencies invited to submit bids for local schemes. The competition was heavily oversubscribed, attracting nearly 500 bids, of which the government eventually accepted 113, in the process having to increase the funds available from £2 million to £5 million. Even this, however, did not pass without controversy, as concerns were raised that the selection process might have favoured bids from Conservative-held electoral constituencies, although this did not halt the announcement of a second phase of the competition in late 1995.

In the middle of the 1990s, it has been suggested by some that there has been some withdrawal from the "age of reason", to a more explicitly ideological stance with law and order, which has tied in with the arrival of Michael Howard as Home Secretary, and the beginnings of a political campaign seeking to put "clear blue water" between the Conservative and Labour parties on an issue that is likely to feature prominently in the 1997 general election. One element of this change, noted by Taylor (1993), has been a loss of patience with the corporatist approach. In crime prevention, this can be seen in a few areas. For example, since the passing of the 1994 Police and Magistrates' Courts Act, central influence has been increased, with the Home Secretary having a new power to set national objectives, thereby forcing the police's hand somewhat.

Also, following on from a commitment made at the 1995 Conservative Party Conference, the National Board for Crime Prevention was transformed into the National Crime Prevention Agency Board, which among other things entailed trimming down its membership to a smaller core, and discarding representatives from agencies such as the probation service and national youth agency, which were less likely to fit in with government priorities for crime prevention for the 1990s. This does not, however, necessarily mean that the social perspective has been lost. The Agency Board, as a result of the shifting of crime prevention from the Home Office Police Department to the Criminal Policy Directorate, has also taken on a responsibility for criminality prevention. Thus, the social focus remains, but in the hands of agencies other than the excluded ones noted above. Moreover, the Agency Board has been given a sharper remit, with a directive role over the work of a new Crime Prevention Agency, which now incorporates the Home Office Crime Prevention Unit, and the Crime Prevention Centre, which has been relocated from Stafford to Easingwold.

Finally, returning to the other element of the dual strategy that the Home Office has promoted, it has been noticeable that the impatience with the corporatist approach has been accompanied by a renewed call-to-arms of the active citizen, whereby the Home Secretary has set very ambitious targets for the future growth of Neighbourhood Watch, as well as employing more special constables and encouraging citizen patrols. These developments are considered in more detail in Chapter 6.

103

Summary

This chapter has covered a considerable amount of ground in accounting for the rise to prominence of crime prevention, and considering some of the issues that have arisen in this process. It has identified a number of distinct phases, from the unfocused and theoretically uninformed form that predominated from the 1950s to the mid-1970s; to the situational model that came to the fore from the mid-1970s to the mid-1980s; to the more holistic but ideologically manipulable community safety, which held sway from the late 1980s onwards.

In practice, the phases have not been as neat and as discrete as this distinction implies, and one form has increasingly come to be superimposed upon the other: hence, in the mid-1990s, while community safety is very powerful, there is still some importance attached to unfocused crime prevention as resources continue to be devoted to publicity campaigns, and such industry-wide initiatives as, for example, "secured by design".

The key moment for crime prevention's entry into the mainstream of crime control policy was its political acceptance in the early 1980s as a route out of a number of blind alleys and potential crises into which the criminal justice system had been led. However, while this moment transformed crime prevention's fortunes it also had the effect of politicising it. Before this time, crime prevention was largely regarded as a technical and technocratic affair, with its politics confined to the small scale implementational difficulties it encountered at the local level. After its acceptance into the mainstream, however, the politics was projected on to the big screen, and crime prevention found itself as a site of conflict between left and right wing crime control agendas, in regard to theory, form, and institutional structure in particular – often manifested in the competition between situational and social prevention (see Ch. 8). Consequently, this politicization has meant that in addition to its projected role as a form of crime control, crime prevention policy has often had as much to say about such matters as the respective roles and responsibilities of state and citizen, the balance of powers between central and local government, and the proper limits of the state's welfare responsibilities.

The great irony of this, of course, is that as its political star has risen, its particular strength, lying in its problem orientation and close attention to detail, has come under increasing threat of eclipse, as other interests come more and more to the fore. With the benefit of hindsight, this appears to have had some inevitability to it, as the story of crime prevention has been increasingly hard to tell without incursions into the wider world of politics. Indeed, even if we shift the focus from the macro to the micro or mezzo, the same inevitability manifests itself in the fundamental difficulties that crime prevention has encountered as its pure scientific ambitions have been diluted by occupational and organizational agendas. We turn our attention to these in the next chapter, with regard to the police and probation services, before considering other aspects of the mixed economy of crime prevention in Chapter 6.

CHAPTER 5

Crime prevention within the criminal justice system: the police and probation services

Introduction

The last chapter emphasized the promotional role performed by the Home Office in seeking to bring crime prevention more to the fore as a serious and credible strategy of crime control. Ultimately, however, the success of this endeavour rests upon the roles performed by others closer to the ground, although as the last chapter also pointed out, there are various political and implementational difficulties that can render these problematic. In this chapter we focus our attention upon the roles performed by criminal justice agencies in crime prevention, and specifically the police and probation services. Both of these are central elements of traditional criminal justice responses to crime, and both have a long and established history in this regard. Finally, both also possess their own distinctive discourses of crime prevention that are not necessarily in harmony with that – or those – currently being promoted at the national level, and for each the story revolves mainly around the accommodations that have had to be made, or that have been resisted, in response to contemporary crime prevention policy.

The police

The historical background

Permanent professional public policing in England can be traced back to 1829, when the Metropolitan Police Act was taken through Parliament by Sir Robert Peel; and right from the very beginning, crime prevention was uppermost in the minds of those who issued the force instructions to the new police:

> It should be understood, at the outset, that the principal object to be obtained is the prevention of crime. To this great end every effort of the police is to be directed. The security of person and property, the preservation of public tranquillity, and all the other objects of a police establishment, will thus be better effected, than by the detection and punishment of the offender, after he has succeeded in committing the crime. This should constantly be kept in mind by every member of the police force, as the guide for his own conduct. (quoted in Reith 1956: 135–6)

There are two related questions emanating from this: the first is what is meant, in this context, by prevention, and the second is why prevention is prioritized over detection and punishment, which in Brantingham & Faust's (1976) typology are alternatively identified as tertiary prevention. Answering the questions takes us into an appreciation of the political and pragmatic appeal of crime prevention to police reformers at the beginning of the nineteenth century.

Without going into a lengthy and detailed historical account, which would be inappropriate here, it is important nevertheless to acknowledge that the introduction of permanent, professional public policing was a matter of deep controversy, and that the passing of the 1829 Act represented the triumph of a lobby that had been campaigning for the best part of a half-century for such a reform. As ever, political and pragmatic concerns lay behind the reform: the urban bourgeoisie supported it for the protection it afforded to their propertied interests, while the aristocratic state, which benefited from the existing arrangements, held out for as long as possible for the status quo.

In this political contest, it would appear that the idea of prevention played an important part in helping to win the argument. As noted in Chapter 1, prevention is an idea close to utilitarian hearts, because it seeks the avoidance of the painful side of the utilitarian calculus, both in terms of avoiding a nasty problem such as criminal victimization, and in terms of avoiding the costs of seeking to right the wrongs incurred by the problem through detection and sentencing. Consequently, it will come as no great surprise that the main players in the police reform movement – characters such as Bentham, Colquhoun, Peel and Chadwick – were all committed utilitarians, drawing their inspiration in part from the classical perspective of Cesare Beccaria. For these people, policing formed a central part of a classical criminal justice system, because it was part of the matrix of deterrence, in which a uniformed, visible presence ideally reminded any potential miscreant of the certainty of apprehension. In this regard, the model of prevention was primary, based principally upon police patrolling, or what Reiner (1992) has prosaically termed the "scarecrow function".

Before the passing of the Metropolitan Police Act, there were a number of small-scale patrolling experiments in London that apparently proved the worth of the idea. Many of these emanated from the Bow Street magistrates' office: the Runners were the detective agency (Palmer 1988), but they were supplemented by day patrols, night patrols, mounted patrols (which apparently put paid to the highwayman), and the curiously named dismounted patrols, where presumably horses, like pistols, were at the ready. Colquhoun was responsible for establishing the Thames Marine Police, where teams of uniformed officers patrolled the river in a bid to deter pilfering from docked cargo ships. All these experiments secured elements of public funding, which suggests that the pragmatic logic of this kind of prevention was hard to resist.

Prevention cast at the level of police patrolling also had considerable political appeal. It is now widely recognized that the establishment of the Metropolitan Police, despite Peel's eloquent parliamentary speeches, had rather less to do with the problem of rising crime than with the threat of political disorder from the capital's "dangerous classes". Uniformed policing provided a safer means of dealing with this than did a reliance on the army or local militia, not least because preventive patrolling afforded the police the opportunity to penetrate working-class communities on a regular basis, and in so doing to extend the supervisory arm of the state that could potentially preempt manifestations of disorder. In this regard, Colquhoun's (1969) plans for the police have particular relevance, for his vision of the police's preventive role included, in addition to patrolling, what he termed "internal regulation". This, as briefly mentioned in Chapter 2, meant morality enforcement alongside law enforcement, using the police to clamp down on "private offences" of immorality that he saw as the causes of "public crimes". This takes policing into the domain of secondary prevention, and draws an historical parallel with some critics' perceptions of community policing in the twentieth century (e.g. Gordon 1984).

At the same time, preventive patrolling provided a means of overcoming the traditionalist civil libertarian opposition that had blocked many previous efforts at reform, and that contrasted English freedoms with the menacing continental alternatives, especially in France, where policing was portrayed as a corrupt network of spying and informants. Of course, the Parliamentary Rewards system in England, where those who apprehended and successfully prosecuted suspected felons received financial rewards, was scarcely any better in this regard, contributing to a thriving but corrupt private sector of policing. Nevertheless, the clear distinction between prevention and detection helped to allay these concerns, and it was not initially envisaged that the Metropolitan Police would have to become involved in the latter.

Although the Metropolitan Police were given this preventive mandate, it did not sit well with the reality of the position in which they found themselves. It took them a number of years to gain public acceptance, but whether they were liked or disliked, their main problem was that they were not that great a deterrent to potential offenders, who recognized that the thin blue line was spread very thinly. As early as the 1830s controversy was caused when it was discovered that, contrary to their force instructions, police officers were engaging in plainclothes detective work, which was supposed to be the preserve of the Bow Street Runners, with whom there appeared to be a territorial dispute (Tobias 1979). Consequently, by the end of the 1830s the police role in detection had been acknowledged, not least on grounds of effectiveness as the first Metropolitan Police Commissioners had pointed out that 75 per cent of all arrests were accounted for by officers working in plainclothes.

Thus there was pressure from the top of the police organization to move away from the preventive principle. This pressure was intensified after 1856 when the Metropolitan Police model (with variations for local control), was imposed across the country, with the "sweetener" that central government would pay for 25 per cent of the costs of uniforms and equipment. This is because in return for the grant each local constabulary had to prove its efficiency to the Home Office's Inspectorate, and it was quickly recognized that efficiency was easier to prove with regard to detection than to prevention:

> If the extent of crime prevention is difficult to prove, and while burglaries and robberies continued in spite of the new preventive measures, the larger nineteenth century police forces could prove efficiency with arrests for public order offences and petty misdemeanours. (Emsley 1983: 130)

In this way, then, prevention as deterrent patrolling was undermined and made even more difficult as working-class communities objected to and indeed resisted the methods by which the police sought to prove their efficiency by enforcing a law that criminalized many of their every day activities (P. Cohen 1979). However, while this is certainly attributable to pressure from the top of the organization, it is unlikely that it went without support at the bottom. Hence, foot patrol was probably as unpopular and as uncomfortable then as it is now, whereas "collar-feeling', particularly without the paperwork that it entails in the 1990s, must have looked like a glamorous and more productive alternative to an occupational culture geared primarily to the removal of sources of trouble from the streets (Holdaway 1983). Whatever, after 1856, the professionalization of policing became inextricably linked with detection over prevention, with patrolling increasingly coming to be seen as an initiation stage to be passed through before entry into an array of more exciting specialisms that have emerged over the course of the twentieth century.

The crime prevention specialism

As with other aspects of the criminal justice system, policing entered a period of relative calm from the late nineteenth century to the middle of the twentieth century, and in this period there was little if any questioning of their preventive role, and the tertiary prevention of detection came to be seen as legitimate as the primary or secondary prevention of patrolling. However, as the Home Office set about developing a specific functional crime prevention policy, so the police organization experienced once again the need to accommodate a different discourse of prevention.

Unfocused crime prevention policy, which required the police to establish specialist crime prevention departments from the late 1950s onwards, issued a challenge to policing on a number of grounds. First, it was an implicit criticism that existing policing methods could not be expected to stem the tide of rising crime. Secondly, it required the police to re-think their preventive role: did the establishment of crime prevention departments mean that existing policing methods were not crime preventive? Thirdly, it required the police, or at least a specialist part of them, to find a new way of working, to move from a position of traditional independence and isolation to one that entailed the development of much closer working relationships with outside agencies, and a certain dependence upon these agencies to contribute towards the uncertain end of crime prevention.

For various reasons, this challenge has resulted in the marginalization of crime prevention departments within the police organization. To begin with, as mentioned in Chapter 4, crime prevention departments were introduced into policing at much the same time as unit beat policing, which, with its heavy reliance on new technology, resonated much more strongly with the preferred occupational view of prevention than did the work of crime prevention officers, which could be cruelly caricatured as little more than glorified leaflet distribution and generalized crime prevention publicity. As Weatheritt (1986) points out, the departments also began to appear in the 1960s at the same time as the community relations departments that were the forerunners of community policing in the 1970s and beyond, which emphasized a more social approach to crime prevention, and which have attracted a strong level of support from certain sections of the police. Consequently, crime prevention departments often find themselves between at least two stools, and the police organization has consistently tended to look elsewhere for crime prevention, with the result that these departments remain marginal in terms of establishment strength. In 1989 the National Audit Office counted no more than 500 full time crime prevention officers, less than half of one per cent of the total police establishment (Loveday 1995).

Crime prevention officers perform a number of specific tasks, although in 1979 the Association of Chief Police Officers (ACPO) had quite unrealistically identified as many as 68 different ones that they might perform. As the activity analysis of Johnston et al. (1993) shows, their main tasks include conducting domestic or commercial premises surveys, dealing with an increasing number of alarm problems and firearms enquiries, and arranging talks and displays. It is no surprise that not long after the Cornish Committee had recommended the general adoption of crime prevention departments, to formalize and professionalize previously patchy and *ad hoc* approaches, that a Home Office circular of 1968 expressed a concern that the establishment of specialist departments might encourage an abrogation of responsibility for these practical tasks elsewhere within the police organization. Such a concern expressed the view that this form of crime prevention would encounter both ideological and practical problems in seeking to gain acceptance within the police organization.

This circular proposed that ordinary permanent beat constables should also have a responsibility for these practical crime prevention tasks, although it is not apparent that this has been a spectacular success. On the face of it, no matter how important they might appear to be, they are deeply unattractive. A knowledge of the technology of physical crime prevention, and a responsibility to transmit this to the community does not do much to advance the professional credentials of policing to the outside world. These tasks, in the main, present the crime prevention officer as an intermediary, passing on relevant information on which consumers are expected to act. As well as not being occupationally glamorous, both of these things weaken the police's professional standing, by implying acceptance of the idea that the key to crime control is not actually held by the police, and that the police's role is reduced to that of a mere technician. In more recent times, this has made the crime prevention specialism vulnerable to privatization, as the threat is made that core professional tasks may be separated from ancillary tasks that can be done more efficiently by outside agencies (Home Office 1995). This has created a paradoxical situation where such crime prevention is professionally undefended, yet it is strongly defended at the political level, not least because it represents the thin end of the wedge, where core tasks might shrink and ancillary ones might grow. Consequently, it becomes easy to see why Weatheritt (1986) has identified two histories of this kind of crime prevention within the police: generally poor achievements, set against strong rhetorical support, which is hardly less than could be expected given the police's statutory responsibility in this field.

Up until the mid-1980s, crime prevention officers were trained as technical experts in physical crime prevention methods, but as Harvey et al. (1989) point out, these methods have tended to be very unfocused, mirroring the unfocused nature of this sort of crime prevention in general, which was initially oriented towards generalized publicity and advice, indeed, they go on to complain that much of this is not really crime prevention at all, and has as much to do with such ends as public relations. The unfortunate result is that crime prevention department resources are often deployed in areas where they are least needed, according to an assessment of the risk of criminal victimization. This means that such resources have not been effectively deployed, although it is telling that until comparatively recently effectiveness has not been a major consideration, as demonstrated by the absence of any endeavour to find ways of measuring the impact of crime prevention departments (Weatheritt 1986). In a results-oriented organization such as the police, the absence of an uncomplicated measure of effectiveness means the odds are stacked even higher against this kind of crime prevention.

Chapter 4 told the story of the paradigmatic shift in crime prevention policy in the late 1970s, where unfocused crime prevention came to be replaced by the situational methodology. This eventually brought crime prevention from the margins to the mainstream, from the general to the specific, and from the reactive or demand-led to the proactive. However, since crime prevention departments were certainly none of these things at this time, it did not necessarily bring them along too, and in many ways it marginalized them further. Writing in 1986, Weatheritt shrewdly observed that crime prevention departments were philosophically at odds with the new crime prevention of the 1980s, which their training did not equip them to deal with, because it was generalized and unfocused, it lacked a strong research base, and it did not prepare them for working closely with other agencies.

Following a review in the mid-1980s, however, it is apparent that the curriculum of the Home Office National Training Centre changed, as it broadened out from physical security to include such other aspects as community participation, inter-agency working, and crime pattern analysis (Laycock & Heal 1989). It might have been expected, then, that crime prevention departments would have steadily grown more accustomed to situational crime prevention, and come to play a more instrumental role therein. However, such an expectation neglects problems beyond the purely philosophical. In particular, the structural difficulties remain, and the high political profile attached to crime prevention in the 1980s and into the 1990s make it very unlikely that a responsibility for it would be entrusted to a marginalized part of the police organization. This is especially the case as crime prevention has taken on a strategic role as much as an operational one, with high-level managerial commitment across a number of local agencies. Since there are no crime prevention officers of a sufficiently senior rank, and according to the Sheehy Report's (Home Office 1993b) ranking none likely to attain such a rank in the future, then crime prevention departments are unlikely to have a place at the collaborative table at this level.

The Home Office continues to churn out generalized crime prevention publicity and advice, and so a role will remain for crime prevention departments in this area, but the main thrust of contemporary policy threatens to leave them more and more out of the picture. A parallel can be drawn here with the fate of the crime prevention panels. They were established in the late 1960s as the main vehicles to take forward the crime prevention message at the local level, although they have always been heavily dependent upon the support and enthusiasm of local police forces. However, in the 1980s their role came to be usurped by a number of other local bodies, which have served to muddy the crime prevention waters considerably: first there was Neighbourhood Watch, then the community liaison panels established following the 1984 Police and Criminal Evidence Act, then the various inter-agency committees, with community representatives, established following the exhortation of the 8/84 Circular. Depending upon the locality, these may or may not be overlaid by the structures put in place by the Safer Cities Programme, the Priority Estates Project, and various other central or local initiatives. An attempt was made to resurrect crime prevention panels in the 1980s, but by then the writing appeared to be on the wall, although that is not to say that there are not any successful panels in existence: nevertheless, they are the exception rather than the norm.

The question for the police is whether a similar fate awaits the crime prevention department. The research of Johnston et al. (1993) momentarily suggests optimism, where the crime prevention department was brought up to date and more into the mainstream of police crime management. However, this was only achieved by doubling resources, securing unusually strong support from senior management, and acquiring a special project status that lifted the experiment out of the ordinary. Such conditions are unlikely to be found elsewhere, and even where they are, it is not inevitable that crime prevention departments should be the principal beneficiaries of them. Hence it is deeply revealing that the new discourse of crime prevention foisted upon the police has been accompanied by the establishment of some new occupational positions: at least one force, for example, now has a "crime reduction officer', while several have begun to appoint "community safety officers". In terms of its crime prevention role, policing is very much in the process of change.

Without radical reform, then, it is unlikely that the police crime prevention role will be taken forward into the twenty-first century by its crime prevention departments. However, while this much may be clear, it is not so easy to see how the role will be taken forward. The Home Office's vocal support and promotion of crime prevention has not fallen on deaf ears, as witnessed by the establishment in 1989 of a crime prevention subcommittee by the Association of Chief Police Officers (ACPO). Moreover, the more detailed Home Office Circular 44/90 has pushed the police to review their crime prevention arrangements in more depth. But it is not yet clear where they are going, and Jones et al.'s recent research into a few local forces came up with the pessimistic conclusion that there is "little evidence of concrete policy initiatives embodying a major transformation away from narrow target-hardening initiatives and towards the multi-agency approach" (1994: 88).

The authors attribute this state of affairs to "the wider confusion of government policy" (1994: 95). By this they mean that for various reasons the Home Office has been reluctant to specify exactly what the police role should be, and what the relative role of the numerous other agencies exhorted to collaborate in crime prevention should be. As Chapter 4 demonstrated, the Home Office has pursued crime prevention simultaneously across a number of fronts, drawing in the private and independent sectors, as well as local government and various central initiatives, leaving the police in a position where they and others are unsure who should take the initiative, and who should be the leader. The problem is further compounded by the nature of contemporary crime prevention, which requires local flexibility: initiatives are to be informed by local problems rather than central strategies, which to some extent necessitates an inversion of the traditional organizational hierarchy. Increasingly, under the rubric of managerialism, this change is being required across a range of public services, where leaner and meaner agencies must orientate themselves more towards the problem and the customer, rather than letting the practice become an end in itself. But in the traditional militaristic bureaucratic command structure that characterizes the police service, this change is probably harder to make than for most.

This last point draws attention to the possibility that the problem lies at least as much with the police organization as it does with external Home Office policy. In essence, it is a problem that requires that sense be made of crime prevention as a distinctive and unfamiliar practice. One element of this is the problem-oriented methodology, but much more important is the inter-agency context in which this methodology is supposed to be pursued. The contemporary buzzword is partnership, and in many ways it is the concept of partnership that now lies at the heart of the police organization's difficulties with crime prevention. This point will be returned to in Chapter 7.

The probation service

Unlike the police, the probation service has never been charged with a statutory responsibility for crime prevention. Nevertheless, the statutory establishment of the probation service at the beginning of the twentieth century, along with that of its voluntary predecessors, the police court missionaries of the late nineteenth century, was largely predicated upon the assumption – sometimes explicit but more often implicitly – that these bodies had a substantial role to play in the prevention of crime.

If policing took its cue from classical theory, the probation service's theoretical origins and justification can be found in positivist criminology that, as Chapter 2 discussed, came to prominence towards the end of the nineteenth century for a number of reasons. Initially, as May's (1991) historical account makes clear, the theoretical and scientific basis of probation work was weak, based upon a philanthropically inspired moral correctionalism (Bottoms & McWilliams 1979) that sought to reform the character of the wicked and often inebriate individual in much the same way as envisaged by Colquhoun (1969) in his science of policing, although by the late eighteenth century the direction of police professionalization had made them an inappropriate vehicle for such a task. However, as the probation service came to be placed upon a statutory footing, and as the institution of training courses underpinned their growing professionalization from the 1920s onwards, so the theoretical basis of the probation service's crime preventive role became more solid, manifested in rehabilitation and the well-named treatment paradigm.

As Hall-Williams (1981) notes, psychoanalysis was very influential upon the emergent probation profession, and helped to secure one-to-one casework as the mainstay of probation work, whereby offenders "who had more often than not been thought of as emotionally or mentally disturbed, even ill and in need of a cure" (Ryan 1983: 50), could be helped over their problems by the skilled therapeutic intervention of the probation officer. The theoretical ascendance of positivism in the middle decades of the twentieth century, especially within the Home Office, provided a fertile bed in which the service could thrive, as did the practical problems identified in Chapter 4, when growing crime rates steadily increased the pressure on the prisons, and made the search for non-custodial alternatives more and more pressing. With a virtual professional monopoly in this area in the case of adults and young adults, the probation service was well placed to take advantage, and the organization expanded rapidly in size and function in the 1960s and into the 1970s.

In the 1970s, however, the bubble burst in so far as the probation service's crime prevention rationale was called into question, and no longer taken for granted. The catalyst for this was the research that cast doubt upon the effectiveness of probation interventions in crime control terms, but this was joined by the force of a paradigmatic shift in criminology away from a determinist conception of the offender cast in terms of individual and social pathology, and towards a conception of the voluntary nature of offending (Sumner 1994). This rendered any notion of treatment as fundamentally misguided, and worse, as potentially abusive: the probation officer was transformed from offender's friend to controlling arm of a coercive state. There was still an important role for the probation service in the criminal justice system, but with its crime preventive credentials undermined the role was beginning to lack professional credibility, and to look more like an administrative one of offender-processing.

It was against this background that Bottoms & McWilliams (1979) noticed the writing on the wall, and set about rebuilding a credible basis for professional probation work. Underpinning this was a recognition that it could no longer be assumed that traditional probation work would contribute towards crime reduction, and that this should be cast now more at the level of help than treatment. In addition, however, they argued that it was important that the probation service should contribute in a meaningful way to crime reduction, and that their best prospect of so-doing was to participate in community-based crime prevention initiatives of the kind undertaken by NACRO in the late 1970s, and in which the probation service had been involved. They made the point that "crime is predominantly social, so . . . any serious crime reduction strategy must be of a socially (rather than an individually) based character" (1979: 189). This meant working in high crime communities, and advancing approaches that would enable communities to develop the strong informal social controls that tended to characterize most low crime areas. In other words, this implied a measure of community work.

In essence, this implied a very different notion of crime prevention that, as with policing, undermined the existing professional basis of probation, and recast the role of the professional as a catalyst – helping others to help themselves. This, however, was not entirely unfamiliar terrain to the probation service, because under the strong tradition of main grade autonomy (Fielding 1984) a number of officers had become involved in community-based social interventions, in such areas as housing and employment. These, however, had been regarded largely as sidelines to the main business of casework, and they had not been explicitly rationalized in terms of crime prevention, which was now required under the non-treatment paradigm.

Survey research by Henderson (1986a,b, 1988) into what he calls community probation work has demonstrated how widespread this sideline is, with only 10 per cent of probation teams not having been involved in something that could be so described, and 40 per cent of probation officers having undertaken training in the area, although the timing of the survey in the 1980s does not enable us to see whether this kind of work has increased following the publication of Bottoms & McWilliams' influential article. Henderson does, however, make the point that there have been a number of other influences affecting such developments, including the general drift to a community orientation that has characterized the response to crises of both confidence and competence in other public services, including the police and social services.

It is also true that this kind of work has a strong elective affinity with the problem-oriented methodology of situational crime prevention being developed by the Home Office around the same time: it is problem-oriented in so far as it is generally focused on high crime areas, or high criminal propensity groups, although not as specifically problem-oriented as the Home Office ideal. However, the similarity ends there, and the crime prevention methods themselves have more in common with the social crime prevention part of NACRO initiatives, than with situational crime prevention. Nevertheless, it is likely that points of potential similarity and overlap were noted within the Home Office, because Circular 8/84 was issued to local probation areas as well as the police and local authorities.

Alongside Circular 8/84, in the same year, and as if to ensure that the probation service got the message, two other central pronouncements urged the service to orientate itself more towards crime prevention. Hence Objective D of the Statement of National Objectives and Priorities (SNOP) stressed

> encouraging the community in the widest practicable approach to offending and offenders, taking account of the influences of family, schools, and other social factors and of the other potential contributions of other agencies; developing the service to the wider public by contributing to initiatives concerned with the prevention of crime and the support of victims, and playing a part in the activities of local statutory and voluntary organizations.

Similarly, Rule 37 of the revamped 1984 Probation Rules (quoted in Harding 1987: 10) required the service "to take part in crime prevention projects, reparation schemes, victim support and other work in the wider community".

There was, however, a certain contradiction between these instructions from on high, for while Circular 8/84 was explicitly supportive of situational methods of crime prevention, SNOP appears to look favourably upon social crime prevention and community approaches of the kind envisaged by Bottoms & McWilliams. Thus, while the probation service was left in no doubt that it was expected to become more involved in crime prevention, and the wider politics surrounding the application of SNOP to the probation service meant this could not safely be avoided (May 1991), the detail of such involvement was a source of confusion; a confusion that Lloyd's (1986) survey of local responses to SNOP clearly picks up. Lloyd's findings suggest that local probation areas were uncertain as to whether they were to commit resources to the practical implementation of crime prevention projects, or whether they were supposed simply to be represented on inter-agency groups.

In this climate of uncertainty, a number of things emerged. Initially, in 1984 the Central Council of Probation Committees (CCPC) established a working party to consider the implications of crime prevention to the service, noting in its report three years later that it was "sensitive to the implications for the service in not participating in crime prevention initiatives at a time when the subject was featuring significantly on the political and criminal justice agendas" (1987: 5). In 1985, the Home Office sponsored a conference for the service on the subject of crime prevention, with the outcome following the tone of an Association of Chief Officers of Probation (ACOP) report of 1985, which cautiously welcomed crime prevention, while clearly conceiving of it in broader social terms – a wider perspective that flowed from the service's knowledge and experience of offenders' motivations.

Laycock & Pease tried a different tack, writing an important article in 1985 that suggested that there was scope for the service to become more involved in situational crime prevention, for example by eliciting information from offenders about their offending techniques, and passing this information on to agencies better placed to put into place appropriate forms of physical security. But they also acknowledged that this would be controversial, and they were right, for in 1984 the National Association of Probation Officers (NAPO) had issued a policy document that was prepared to support situational crime prevention, while seeing "few direct opportunities for probation officers to become directly involved" (1984: 3). The support it offered situational crime prevention, moreover, was limited by its conviction that it was only a partial solution, neglecting the broader social causes of crime with which the service more usually dealt.

NAPO was more supportive of social crime prevention, but this did not amount to an endorsement of the ACOP position, because it simultaneously stressed that

> It is important in this context to make links with other groups who may be in a better position to develop particular initiatives and that involves probation officers knowing the limits of working within a statutory agency. (NAPO 1984: 3)

This introduced a clear distinction between offender-centred crime prevention, which was the traditional mainstay of probation work, and had NAPO's full backing, and community crime prevention, which was better left to other agencies that had the necessary expertise and responsibility. NAPO, however, was isolated when in 1987 the CCPC finally produced the results of its deliberations, in which it effectively endorsed the ACOP position, while also being prepared to consider the more situational role envisaged by Laycock & Pease (1985). Its concerns were more practical than political, and in this regard the question of resourcing was identified as a potential sticking point.

Its solution, rather like that found in Circular 8/84 to the same problem, was to suggest that crime prevention considerations could be incorporated into mainstream activities such as community service and day centres. However, it was possibly shrewd in anticipating that this might result in no visible change from the outside (for these activities were already crime preventive in the probation ideological sense), and so it also suggested that each local service should nominate a member of headquarters management to have special responsibility for crime prevention, while the CCPC itself would explore closer links in this regard with police authorities with which they were coterminous. This shrewdness might have fed off an ACOP survey into local crime prevention activity in 1986, which came back with the not surprising result that there was plenty of crime prevention activity, albeit buried within traditional areas of probation expertise or involvement, including the various sidelines. This was confirmed later in a 1988 ACOP survey that showed that crime prevention was often incorporated into community service order work schemes.

Although, as the above discussion makes clear, there was an obvious internal politics of crime prevention within the service in the 1980s, in some ways it did not matter, because the momentum building up behind crime prevention made it virtually unstoppable, particularly when the Home Office had a financial carrot to dangle over local agency heads in the shape of such things as the Five Towns Initiative, Crime Prevention and the Community Programme, and the Safer Cities Programme.

Developments in the latter half of the 1980s and beyond, when a narrow version of crime prevention has gradually given way to a more integrated notion of community safety, have generally benefited the service, by bringing national policy more into line with the preferences and values of those within the service who have supported the social side of crime prevention. In so far as community safety seeks to tackle the causes as well as block opportunities, and in so far as those causes are seen as residing within the community rather than the individual, then clearly it fits in very well with the community probation/ crime prevention discourse that had been generated particularly within ACOP, while simultaneously allaying some of the concerns that involvement in crime prevention might compromise the service's softer side of social control.

Nevertheless, while crime prevention policy has become more accommodating of the probation perspective, the Home Office has failed to be explicit about exactly what it expects from the service in this field, and in this regard there are obvious parallels between the police and the probation service. As Raynor et al. (1994: 118) have commented, "The Home Office has been clear in broad policy statements that crime prevention should be a part of the work of the probation service, while being less clear about what this should entail in practice." Hence in the 1990 White and Green Papers that preceded the 1991 Criminal Justice Act the Home Office urged the service to develop its inter-agency crime prevention role further, and gear its operation more towards crime prevention. But these have to be made sense of, if there is to be any substance to the exhortations.

The decision by ACOP to establish its own crime prevention subcommittee in 1987 clearly reflects a desire to find a clear plan of action. But an audit survey of four probation areas conducted by Geraghty, a member of this subcommittee who was under temporary secondment to the Home Office Crime Prevention Unit, demonstrated that this was going to be no easy feat:

In summary, there is clearly much variation in the nature and
extent of probation representation in local crime prevention
initiatives. There are differences in commitment and understanding of the service's role and potential that suggest the need
for an identified policy, strategy and system in order to promote
consistent and high quality practice that is closely linked to
service objectives. What is also revealed, however, is the need
for guidance on, for example, level of representation, time commitment, use of information and training. (1991: 13)

Geraghty limited her quest for examples of crime prevention to
primary and secondary forms, thereby excluding tertiary prevention,
since this covered traditional offender-centred work that all areas
would have been doing as a matter of course. Even so, the decision to
exclude this from the survey's purview is not without consequence,
and has important political implications within the service for how
crime prevention is conceived. Indeed, Geraghty acknowledges the
difficulty of establishing categories of crime prevention for her survey: her choice to look for three categories, where crime prevention is
either a central, additional or incidental concern of the activity arguably covers all angles, and is inconsistent with her exclusion of tertiary prevention. Nevertheless, this exclusion is consistent with the
Home Office's statement of purpose for the probation service, which
clearly distinguishes two goals, namely reducing and preventing
crime, and the supervision of offenders.

Similarly, the typology that orders Geraghty's findings into issue-
focused, crime-focused, area-focused and representational forms of
crime prevention activity is not without its problems. Nevertheless,
the problems with the survey are largely the problems with the service's role in crime prevention, and she draws attention to the need for
greater clarity about the specific purpose of crime preventive activities. Moreover, she identifies a related lack of interest in implementation and impact evaluation, the marginalization of crime prevention
as a specialism within the service, and a cleavage between headquarters and front line staff wherein the former appear a good deal more
committed to crime prevention than the latter.

In one way this is similar to Weatheritt's (1986) identification of two
histories of police crime prevention: the rhetorical support from
management, but the problems "at the coalface", although the prob-

lems here are less about resistance than about the chaotic organization of the probation response to crime prevention. Understandably, management show a greater sensitivity to the political importance of being seen to respond to Home Office proposals, as evidenced by the CCPC response in 1987, noted above. At the same time, however, they also show a sensitivity to probation values, and in this regard Bryant, the then chair of the crime prevention subcommittee, accepts the legitimacy of situational crime prevention, but cleverly interprets the service's role not as criminal opportunity reduction, but legitimate opportunity creation, incorporating components of traditional probation work and social policy. Crime prevention thus becomes "a major opportunity to present some traditional probation service objectives in a way which commands widespread public support" (Bryant 1989: 15).

The awareness of the importance of public relations is instructive, and Bryant goes on to make the point that the other side to crime prevention, which entails working with communities and victims, may equally benefit the service's and ultimately its traditional clients' profile, for if the service is seen to support the community then the community is more likely, in turn, to support the service in its work with offenders. A similar argument is advanced by Raynor et al. (1994), who fear the service otherwise becoming trapped within the punitive confines of the criminal justice system, and by Nellis (1995) in his proposal that community safety should be a core value of probation work, for without it the service would lack the political base from which to advance the other core values he proposes, namely anti-custodialism and restorative justice. Above and beyond this reason, however, Nellis makes the point that crime disproportionately affects and oppresses poor communities, and that involvement in community safety therefore becomes an essential element of anti-oppressive probation practice.

This may be so, but using crime prevention or community safety as a means to other ends is dangerous if the need for specificity over the crime prevention role is not first met, and it is apparent that as the service moved into the 1990s, there was still a good deal of confusion about this, notably about whether the service should be working in the community, with offenders in the community, or both. Moreover, the climate of the early 1990s was not conducive to this issue being resolved, because the service found itself being forced into the more punitive discourse of punishment in the community, which did not sit easily alongside community safety. Given that punishment in the community affected the mainstay of probation work, the impression was conveyed that the service's crime prevention role had only been tacked on as something of an afterthought.

Sampson & Smith (1992) identify some of the difficulties in this area, with one of the main ones being that while crime prevention or community safety implies working in the community, probation officers are far from clear about what communities are, and what they should be doing should they find them. With regard to the first question, probation officers' traditional individualized work makes them sceptical of communities, for their clients rarely belong to any: rather, they tend to exist on the margins, by virtue of their criminality and associated difficulties such as homelessness or drug misuse. While Sampson & Smith are right to criticize those situational approaches to crime prevention that artificially distinguish offenders from the wider community, they could be more explicit about the constraints that some offenders' frequent marginality brings, even when they are themselves victims of crime.

With regard to the second question, a problem similar to that first identified by Lloyd (1986) in the response to SNOP still remains: namely, that it is unclear whether the probation role should be representational, or based upon direct work, and Geraghty's (1991) survey shows examples of both. The list of skills for community-based work identified by Raynor et al. (1994) tends to emphasize the representational, including such things as inter-agency working, articulating the probation view, and managing meetings. Bryant (1989) and Wilson-Croome (1990) also stress the importance of the representational role, where the probation service may be able to inform other agencies about the motivational causes that they may be able to alter, and to ensure that issues of equal opportunities are addressed. In these cases, however, representation is not simply about public relations. Rather, it is based upon an acknowledgement that other agencies are more experienced and better placed to take action in certain fields of social intervention. There is some wisdom in this, for if the probation service were to become too heavily involved in direct work with the community then there would be a danger of criminalizing the discourse of social policies (Sampson et al. 1988), justifying measures aimed at social justice purely in crime control terms. More pragmatically, the probation service lacks expertise beyond its work with offenders. Nevertheless, while a representational role seems the most prudent, a general vagueness still remains.

Summary

This chapter has explored the difficulties that both the police and probation services have encountered in interpreting their crime preventive roles in the light of the different emphasis that has been placed upon crime prevention in Home Office policy. This different emphasis has clashed with these agencies' traditional discourses of crime prevention, and has prompted a degree of soul-searching and internal disagreement. Traditional discourses retain a strong influence over practice despite being increasingly politically marginalized as realists within each service recognize the necessity of moving with the times.

In this regard, however, they have not been assisted by the lack of specificity or clear guidance in Home Office policy. The police remain uncertain about the extent to which they should take the lead, and how far this should be through the seemingly inappropriate vehicle of the specialist crime prevention department. The probation service, meanwhile, are clearer about values than about exactly what they should be doing, unaided by the Home Office's three year plan for 1996 to 1999 that includes a responsibility for the service to help communities to prevent crime, but in contrast to other identified responsibilities says nothing about how this should be done or measured. ACOP (1993) has recognized that if the service is going to make its distinctive mark it is vitally important that it bases its proposals on sound socio-economic data, but it is not clear whether the Home Office shares such a view, and the exclusion of service representation from the Crime Prevention Agency Board does not bode well.

The problems these two agencies have encountered demonstrate the political nature of crime prevention at the intra-organizational level. When, however, this becomes the inter-organizational level, as agencies are increasingly pushed together into crime prevention partnerships, it will come as no surprise that these politics become further enhanced. We turn to this issue in Chapter 7, following our exploration of the role of other agencies and sectors in Chapter 6.

Crime prevention beyond the criminal justice system: the mixed economy

Introduction

Contemporary crime prevention policy relies increasingly upon a partnership or multi-agency approach that takes in contributions from a range of agencies other than the two considered in the previous chapter. This includes those within the statutory sector, such as local authorities, but also those outside of it, in the voluntary, private and informal sectors. It is these agencies that form the focus of this chapter, and each shall be looked at in turn in the context of government policy, and in terms of the potential contribution they can make to crime prevention strategies.

Local authorities

The discussion in Chapter 4 made it apparent that local authorities were identified as key players in crime prevention in the 1980s and 1990s. The government has identified very good reasons why local authorities should be involved in crime prevention in Circulars 8/84 and 44/90, and elsewhere, and yet it has consistently shied away from providing them with a statutory responsibility for this task. Among other things, this section seeks to explore the rationale behind this, and subject it to critical scrutiny.

In the context of changing views of crime causation and theories of prevention, the potential contribution of local authorities is obvious. A considerable array of services for which local authorities are responsible have a bearing on crime patterns. Planning and environmental design, for example, can seek to secure defensible space, and to secure routine activities that reduce the coincidence of those necessary minimum conditions for crime to occur. Environmental maintenance has an important bearing on criminal opportunities, whether it be the provision of street lighting, the planting and maintenance of shrubbery, or the installation of CCTV, which since the mid-1980s has become an increasingly common aspect of the local authority landscape, particularly in city centres. Schools are not only major sites of criminal attacks that require some protection, but they also provide an important environment in which children learn to be law-abiding, and acquire the qualifications that give them the opportunity to have a stake in society. Social services have a particular responsibility for delinquent youth, but also for preventive family services that seek to make families safe and supportive environments for their members, and important sources of informal social control.

In some parts of the country, local authorities are major landlords, and as such they have a responsibility and an incentive to prevent criminal attacks against municipal property, and to provide a safe environment in which tenants are not fearful or inclined towards a fortress mentality. Moreover, as local authorities provide the elected members of police authorities, they have an interest in the nature and direction of policing in their areas, and in many ways share a concern with the police's statutory responsibility for crime prevention, although the revised constitution of those authorities since the passing of the 1994 Police and Magistrates' Courts Act means their influence is now less. Nevertheless, in so far as elected members and local authority officers are also represented on the community liaison panels established after the 1984 Police and Criminal Evidence Act, and which are supposed to consider crime prevention matters within their brief, there is an alternative channel of communications for local authority views on policing matters, even if it is only "consultation".

There are, then, good reasons for local authority involvement in crime prevention. Many of the above points are echoed by Michaelson (1991), who adds the financial incentive: investment in crime prevention, he says, can save policing costs, although it can also save local authority costs in other areas. He also makes the point that local authorities have a general interest in the quality of life of citizens resident in their areas, and since crime threatens this, it should be a natural concern. However, as the above also makes clear, this concern has many aspects to it, reflecting a very catholic approach. It is not surprising, therefore, that those local authorities developing an interest in crime prevention have generally been quick to substitute the similarly catholic term community safety.

The main problem, nevertheless, has been the relatively small number of local authorities that have shown a corporate interest in crime prevention or community safety, and neither Circulars 8/84 nor 44/90 have effected a major ground swell of opinion in favour of action, although there has certainly been some. The NACRO Safe Neighbourhoods Unit survey at the end of the 1980s, cited in Chapter 4, showed that only a limited number of local authorities had established any special crime prevention initiatives or machinery, while an Association of Metropolitan Authorities survey (AMA 1990) showed much the same thing, with local authorities generally failing to identify a nominated officer, or a dedicated budget, or to disseminate any information, or to monitor any initiatives that were implemented, or to attempt to assess the costs of crime to the authority.

One must be careful in interpreting these surveys. First, they were done at the end of the 1980s, and things have changed since then, although not necessarily a great deal. Secondly, while the surveys point to a general lack of action in the way of corporate strategy, it does not mean that most local authorities were not doing anything crime preventive. Rather, they have been, but without necessarily recognizing it as part of a strategic responsibility or concern. There tends, for example, to be good liaison between police crime prevention officers, or architectural liaison officers, and local authority planners and architects, whereas much of the local authority routine can be connected to one or other discourse of crime prevention. However, the important point about crime prevention policy in the 1980s and 1990s is that it has increasingly required agencies such as local authorities to explicitly acknowledge their contribution towards crime prevention, to incorporate this into their corporate policy-making machinery (and often within multi-agency structures), and to direct it in a problem-oriented way towards specific crime problems in order to reduce their incidence. Crime reduction is in many ways a better term for such a thing than crime prevention.

Many local authorities have had trouble accommodating this requirement, for a number of reasons. First and most obvious is the question of resources: outside of specific government initiatives, none have been made specially available for the purpose, and given the squeeze on local finance few authorities have been in a position to countenance taking on what is perceived to be an added responsibility for a new area of concern, even though the perception is not strictly accurate. There is a strong argument that crime costs local authorities a great deal, particularly in terms of property repairs and replacement, but when crisis management is the norm such strategic arguments do not always cut much ice. This is a reason why the Morgan Committee (Home Office 1991) recommended that the Home Office should provide a direct crime prevention grant to local authorities, while the AMA (1990) suggested that such a grant might be based upon the submission of specific local plans, submitted to the Home Office so that it was clear exactly where the money would be spent.

The Morgan Committee also recommended that local authorities should have a statutory responsibility for community safety, noting that they provided "a natural focus for co-ordinating, in collaboration with the police, . . . community safety" (Home Office 1991: 19). The deeper reasoning behind this argument, however, reflects a certain dissatisfaction with the direction of crime prevention policy when local authorities lack a lead role. There are a number of dimensions to this. As Loveday (1994b) notes, one problem relates to the profusion of central government initiatives that have some bearing upon crime prevention, such as the Safer Cities Programme, Task Force, City Challenge, the Priority Estates Project, and the SRB. These tend either to by-pass local authorities, or to involve them in ways that limit local autonomy. The consequence of this is a general lack of co-ordination or strategy. Indeed, the irony that central government expects greater co-ordination from local authorities, while itself lacking co-ordination, is not lost on the AMA (1990).

In addition, bearing in mind the financial difficulty cited above, this profusion of central initiatives affords some local authorities the opportunity to escape one difficulty, but to find another, as these initiatives come with strings attached, such as the requirement to involve the private sector, and to work with unelected bodies. McLaughlin (1994: 108) puts the problem well:

These initiatives posed a dilemma for radical local authorities. At a time when their powers and resources were being severely curtailed, the crime prevention proposals held out the promise of both an enhanced role for local authorities and extra central government funding.

A further element of this dilemma is the sense that where local authorities lack a leadership role, the resultant nature of crime prevention is more situational than anything else. As far as many local authorities are concerned, this is generally not enough, because situational approaches tend to be highly localized, rather than authority-wide (AMA 1990). If these approaches encourage displacement, then from the local authority perspective problems are merely shuffled around, and never eradicated, especially if the crime reduction is only short term. Loveday (1994b) points out that the authorities with the most intractable problems tend to be those with the sharpest levels of economic decline and social dislocation, and here local authorities would be more concerned with social approaches that might address, among other things, work opportunities. The Association of District Councils (ADC) (1990) makes a similar point, arguing that the local authority role entails a combination of practical strategies and social policies, a form of community safety that is more liberal than that countenanced by the government.

Herein lies a major difficulty for central government in its approach towards local authorities. The emphasis has been upon soliciting greater responsibility for, and interest in, crime prevention, while simultaneously seeking to control the terms of this. This is because while local authorities are accepted as necessary, as the Home Office's various promotional activities demonstrate, they are not well trusted. There are a number of well rehearsed reasons for this, ranging from their alleged profligacy, to their political opposition, especially in some urban areas, to their status as part of a local administrative state that is being restructured away from direct service provision and towards an enabling role within a mixed economy. An example of what concerns central government can be found in McLaughlin's (1994) account of the transformation of Manchester's police monitoring group into a community safety group. While McLaughlin might bemoan this as the desertion of a previously radical position, government concerns might centre rather on the unlikelihood of leopards changing their spots, and the unwelcome nature of an explicitly left wing discourse on crime prevention, which related it more to social structural interventions, rather than situational ones.

In general, then, central government finds itself in the position of having to tread a fine line between encouraging local authorities, and keeping them under control. But other than relying on central initiatives that dictate the terms of local authority involvement, and that are self-defeating in so far as they undermine the objective of redirecting local resources and priorities, this is no easy feat. In the late 1980s, for example, both the ADC and the AMA have established crime prevention working parties, and these have lobbied for a much broader-based notion of community safety than that envisaged by central government, and they have been joined by the Labour Party in so doing. The result is that the local authority role in crime prevention has become a delicate issue that central government has preferred to side-step rather than confront, and under Michael Howard's tutelage crime prevention policy has come to place a much stronger emphasis upon the local potential of private citizens and the private sector (Loveday 1994a).

Officials within the Home Office have had to sit uncomfortably between these two parties. Their more practical concerns have enabled them to rationalize the government's failure to identify local lead agencies as the preservation of the essential prerequisite of flexibility in the local delivery of crime prevention, where structures are less important than appropriate problem-oriented action. However, as the AMA (1990) convincingly argues, while flexibility might be important at the operational level, it is not at the strategic level, and indeed in many ways this is already implicitly recognized in the administrative arrangements for the Safer Cities Programme, where there tends to be a standard formula for the constitution of steering committees. Of course, the Safer Cities Programme is only temporary, and its objective to leave behind a permanent structure is less likely to be realized if the statutory responsibility is left entirely to the police. The practical perspective of the Home Office, then, inevitably flounders on the rocks of crime prevention politics.

It may be argued, however, that in the event government policy has proved to be quite shrewd. For while it has held out and refused to concede either extra resources or a statutory responsibility, the number of local authorities developing a corporate crime prevention or community safety strategy has slowly increased, if only because of a recognition that in the long run it is cost effective. Moreover, the criterion of cost effectiveness naturally tends to favour situational strategies of a sort with which the government would find favour, while simultaneously limiting the potential of social policy-type interventions, which find it hard to demonstrate such a thing. This, however, remains to be seen: the corporate move to crime prevention has been slow, and the rhetoric thus far has emphasized a more liberal notion of community safety. Meanwhile, developments elsewhere have been more noticeable.

The voluntary sector

Crime prevention within the voluntary sector has been dominated in England and Wales by two bodies, the National Association for the Care and Resettlement of Offenders (NACRO), and Crime Concern. Each is considered in turn.

NACRO

NACRO was originally formed as a voluntary organization to assist, as its name indicates, in the care and resettlement of offenders, notably those released from custodial institutions. However, like other criminal justice-related agencies operating in the 1970s, NACRO was influenced by the wider criminological context in which it operated. This was not only critical of the rehabilitative ethos and its practical expression in the treatment paradigm, but it also began to place greater faith in alternative approaches such as Oscar Newman's concept of defensible space, which was discussed in Chapter 3.

As befits a voluntary organization, NACRO possessed a pioneering spirit and a freedom from statutory responsibilities and controls that enabled it to respond flexibly to these changing times. Whiskin (1989) and Poyner (1986) mention that in the mid-1970s a number of members sought to effect a change of direction in the agency's work, from concentrating solely on offenders to looking more closely at the areas of high crime and criminality from whence they came. In 1975 a number of multi-agency conferences were organized by NACRO to explore the possibility of crime prevention in such areas (Rock 1988), and the eventual upshot was NACRO's first estate-based project, in Cunningham Road, Widnes. This ran from 1976 to 1979, and from it NACRO derived its familiar problem-oriented and consultative methodology.

Whiskin (1989) describes this methodology as a four stage process in which, first, a steering group of agencies working on an estate is convened; secondly, residents are consulted and urged to participate in the process; thirdly, public meetings are arranged on the estate, for small and large groups; and fourthly, an action plan is devised between residents and agencies, and it is implemented and monitored. This methodology became institutionalized as the NACRO *modus operandi* in its Crime Prevention Unit, which was established in 1979, and in its Safe Neighbourhoods Unit, which was established in 1980 to engage in action specifically within the London area.

The NACRO methodology was developed at broadly the same time as the ostensibly similar situational crime prevention methodology was devised within the Home Office Research and Planning Unit, and it may well be that there was some cross-fertilization of ideas. There is, however, no direct evidence of this, and it is important to stress the difference between the two approaches, as well as their similarities. In this regard, they have quite different ways of identifying both problem and solution, despite both being problem-oriented. The situational approach relies mainly on agencies with hard data, and assumes that agencies will be well placed to identify both problem and solution from within a range of essentially opportunity reducing technologies. The NACRO approach is, however, less controlled, eliciting the views of the community as well, and being more open in its choice of potential solutions. Indeed, these may be either situational or social, and are also quite likely to address the fear of crime. Consequently, in so far as all approaches are usually employed, it is within NACRO's work that one finds the earliest references to community safety, although the term applies increasingly to local authorities now, as noted above.

NACRO's consultation with residents did much to "discover the victim', which proved to be very influential on criminal justice policy from the mid-1980s onwards. However, in so doing, it demonstrated that the problem-oriented methodology depends very much upon whose problem one is addressing. The assumption underpinning situational crime prevention is that problems reveal themselves statistically, and are thus amenable to reduction, but NACRO's methodology challenges this by asking residents, whose problems may have no statistical foundation and may therefore not be amenable to reduction. However, NACRO's approach also complicates matters by involving official agencies that act more in ways envisaged within the situational approach. Consequently, the issue of competing priorities may be more apparent in NACRO strategies.

As a voluntary organization, NACRO's funding base is insecure, but in crime prevention it has been able to rely upon an array of urban policy initiatives linked to depressed and high crime areas: what is confusion and poor co-ordination from a local authority perspective is an opportunity from NACRO's. Whiskin points out that since its first scheme in the 1970s NACRO has extended its crime prevention work into 40 local authority areas, working on more than 70 individual housing estates, and obtaining considerable benefit from manpower resources made available under the Community Programme, which ran until the late 1980s. The further spread of NACRO's work was, however, probably limited by the somewhat similar central government initiative, the Priority Estates Project.

In 1988 NACRO lost a number of key experienced personnel to its new rival Crime Concern, but its influence has remained such that it was still one of the agencies consulted before the final issuing of Circular 44/90 (Jones et al. 1994). In the 1990s, NACRO's fortunes in its crime prevention work have become tied to those of the SRB, which is no longer a specifically urban policy, and therefore loosens the convenient ties that used to exist between urban initiatives, depressed areas, and high crime. Nevertheless, NACRO presents itself as a consultant and potential partner in the preparation of SRB bids, which must show consultation with the community and a partnership approach. Moreover, its role in crime prevention has been made more secure by the announcement in 1994 of its new role as managing agency of a number of the Safer Cities announced in the programme's second phase.

Essentially, NACRO's role has been that of a catalyst in estate-based schemes, while at the national level its independence has been presented as a virtue as it has acted as a pressure group, seeking broader changes in the approaches of the police (NACRO 1988) and local authorities (Bright 1987, NACRO 1989) towards crime prevention.

Indeed, the pressure group activity has broad similarities with the promotional work of the Home Office Crime Prevention Unit, and this may explain some of its apparent success in achieving at least limited change. With regard to the success of its estate-based schemes, however, the evidence is rather less positive.

Stern (1987) notes that the independent evaluation of the Cunningham Road project showed that the crime and disorder problems had not disappeared, although in many other ways the project was a success. However, this shows how problematic the nature of success is: rather like Neighbourhood Watch (see below), NACRO's estate-based work has a multiplicity of objectives, some of which are not geared unambiguously towards crime prevention. As Poyner (1986) observes, some of the activities, such as establishing tenant associations, or improving housing management, may in fact be legitimate ends in themselves.

Following an approach from NACRO to the Home Office, Poyner (1986) was specifically asked to evaluate the effectiveness of NACRO's estate-based schemes in crime preventive terms. Poyner noted the problem of what information to use in such an evaluation, but sided with the use of official police statistics, if only because ultimately "it is the officially reported crime that is in the end the most influential on political debate about crime" (1986: 14). He then raked through the 60 NACRO projects then up and running, rejecting random sampling in favour of the selection of the 15 projects that were the most established and the most likely to be successful. On closer scrutiny, these 15 were eventually whittled down to just five, since only this number had police data for purposes of comparison, and only this number had parts of their action plans implemented.

Poyner's team noted that NACRO's methodology tended to produce a fairly standard approach to crime prevention, employing such measures as building modernization and external improvements, environmental management, security measures, community organization, and housing management. However, when these were scrutinized for their combined impact on crime, the overall conclusion was that "the evidence does not suggest that the programme is a particularly effective means of reducing crime" (1986: 61), although some of the elements did appear to show some signs of success, notably the opportunity reducing security measures, and targeted intensive policing where these coincided with and were incidental to project areas.

In essence, then, while it is always possible to take issue with Poyner's evaluative methodology, NACRO's estate-based work appears to suffer from two basic difficulties. The first is that despite the profusion of projects, relatively few appear to make much progress towards their objective, and Poyner notes, for example, that some projects failed to obtain data from the local police, while others had difficulty turning their plans into action. Evidently, in such cases NACRO representatives lacked the authority to make things happen, which demonstrates how an alleged advantage, namely independence, can also be a disadvantage. Secondly, it is apparent that action plans can lack a strong problem-orientation, addressing concerns that are only tangentially related to the crime problem identified in police statistics.

As Rock (1988) observes, NACRO's main claim to success lies in the belief that by involving the community informal social control will be increased, and relations with service providers will be improved, with these changes having a long-term impact on crime. However, between NACRO's essential idealism and Poyner's (1986) evaluation, which employs official statistics for practically sound rather than methodologically sound reasons, Rock adds that the reality is that we still understand relatively little about how estate-based initiatives work, especially with regard to their differential impact on a street by street basis. Moreover, it is difficult to untangle the effects of a package of measures (Rock 1988: 109), so that too often "The result has been a succession of reports that offer simple, condensed glosses on what must have occurred, each gloss passing as an explanation for practical purposes." Rock's preference is for qualitative work that seeks such an understanding, such as that undertaken by Foster (1990), although inevitably such research rarely meets the needs of policy-makers.

Crime Concern

Crime Concern is a difficult body to classify: Jones et al. refer to it both as a voluntary organization and a quango, and also as a "curious hybrid" (1994: 101). As described in Chapter 4, it was brought into existence by central government following a manifesto commitment it had made in 1987, and Home Office officials attribute the idea very much to the politicians rather than to themselves. As such, it understandably displays elements of the ideological antipathy to statutory solutions to crime prevention that have become a characteristic of policy, at least on the surface, thus setting developments in England and Wales firmly apart from those of its continental neighbours (Graham 1987, NACRO 1992).

Crime Concern was established by central government in 1988 as a voluntary organization, if such a thing is possible. Of course, there are very close links between many voluntary organizations and government, although it is more usual for the former to have been established independently before forming links with government agencies, generally as a consequence of financial dependence. This is not, however, what happened with Crime Concern, which was set up with an advisory board consisting of representatives drawn from the Home Office, the police, the business community, and other voluntary organizations (Whiskin 1991), and a chairman who was a former Conservative MP. It initially received three years' funding from the Home Office, under the condition that it should become financially independent after this period, although in the event it was not, and so the funding was continued for a further period. Finally, as if none of this is enough to question its independence, it was given a series of specific objectives to work towards by the Home Office, including a responsibility to develop and maintain the momentum behind both Neighbourhood Watch and crime prevention panels; a brief to enhance the profile of crime prevention with regard to youth; and an opportunity to develop consultancy work of a kind carried out by NACRO among local authorities.

Crime Concern recruited wisely, bringing in crime prevention experts from academic institutions, from NACRO, and from Safer Cities Programmes, and it quickly set about its tasks, adding another, namely the promotion of crime prevention within the business community, including sponsorship of its own operations. In so far as this was promoted on the basis that crime prevention stimulated enterprise, it repeated the Safer Cities theme established in the same year as Crime Concern's creation.

Turning to Crime Concern's work with regard to Neighbourhood Watch and crime prevention panels, the common theme has been an attempt to make these institutions as free-standing and independent as possible, so that they do not place an excessive burden for their maintenance upon the police. This has been achieved in the case of Neighbourhood Watch by engineering sponsorship and support for a series of national Neighbourhood Watch conferences and special

Neighbourhood Watch weeks, and disseminating publicity and practical guides about the purpose and operation of schemes. In theory, the establishment in 1995 of a national Neighbourhood Watch organization should provide a focal point for individual schemes, further reducing reliance on the police, while giving Neighbourhood Watch a potentially powerful national voice, speaking as it does on behalf of more than five million households. The approach towards crime prevention panels has been similar, with Crime Concern designing a good practice guide and a national organizational focus, assisted by annual conferences and the publication of a dedicated magazine (Whiskin 1991).

Crime Concern has developed its consultancy work with nearly 50 local authorities, with more in-depth NACRO-style involvement in a further 10 (Crime Concern, undated). Like NACRO, it also received a fillip in winning contracts to manage the majority of Safer Cities announced in the second phase of the programme in 1994, and it has received further work from central government in the form of a commission to produce the 1993 guide on crime prevention for local partnerships. To an extent, this also follows NACRO's lead of pressure group activity towards local authorities, although in Crime Concern's case its role is more officially proscribed: for example, it is noticeable that Crime Concern addresses its good practice guide to local partnerships, using terminology that is more government-friendly than that used by NACRO (1989), which directed its guide explicitly to local authorities.

Finally, Crime Concern has also shadowed NACRO in its focus upon youth crime prevention, developing a number of specific targeted local projects in a more "hands on" approach, as well as focusing upon the development of local structures through which specific projects might be developed. To this end, a strong emphasis has been placed upon the development of youth crime prevention panels or youth action groups, which by 1991 had reached 240 in number (Whiskin 1991), increasing to more than 650 by 1994 (Crime Concern, undated).

Crime Concern has undoubtedly become a major force in crime prevention, and its chief executive has been appointed to the national Agency Board for crime prevention in 1996. However, Crime Concern's status sits uncomfortably between statutory and voluntary sectors, and it mirrors much that its statutory and voluntary "twins", namely NACRO and the Home Office Crime Prevention Unit, do. But in sitting between both sectors it arguably loses the benefits that each in a pure form should hold, namely independence or accountability. Its lack of full independence makes it unwilling to question the brief it has been set, which leads ultimately to the proliferation of piecemeal local schemes and projects, rather than a clear national crime prevention infrastructure and programme. Its quasi-independence, however, also means a lack of traditional lines of accountability, and thus the perpetuation of an illusion of a crime prevention strategy that has been rationally rather than politically and ideologically determined.

The informal sector: the case of Neighbourhood Watch

In the 1990s the preferred direction of crime prevention policy has been to stimulate the private and informal sectors above all else. In the case of the informal sector, it must be stated that the theme of citizen participation and collaboration has been a consistently strong theme running across the development of crime prevention policy from its beginnings in the 1950s, in each of its unfocused, situational and community safety forms. Hence, for example, publicity campaigns seek a greater security consciousness from the private citizen, while situational crime prevention often does likewise, having first pinpointed and analyzed the crime to be reduced by the effort. Community safety seeks to combine security consciousness with more communitarian concerns, about restoring informal social controls and support mechanisms.

However, both publicity campaigns and situational crime prevention have their critics in this regard. Publicity campaigns often fail to inspire their intended targets into action, or if they do, it is determined more by ability to pay for security hardware, rather than by need as measured by victimization risk. The situational approach is similarly dependent upon ability to pay, or the availability of special public funds, which is inevitably limited. Consequently, by the middle of the 1980s, while the salience of the law and order issue demonstrated the public's concern about crime at a general level, private citizens were not necessarily any more inclined than before to see themselves as responsible for its prevention. Indeed, given the heavy emphasis on law and order policies, and the propaganda that is an inevitable part of the professional aspirations of criminal justice agencies, this "dependency culture' was as not surprising as it was contradictory with crime prevention policy. In this light, the phenomenal growth of Neighbourhood Watch from a single scheme in 1982 to 147,000 by early 1996 was both remarkable and fortuitous. Whatever the shortcomings of existing policies that failed to inspire citizen action, Neighbourhood Watch was the spark that finally succeeded in igniting the flame, or so it appears.

It is inaccurate to conceive of Neighbourhood Watch as a single entity because it has a number of manifestations depending upon the context in which it is applied; from home watch, to school watch, farm watch, pub watch, and even plant watch. In addition, while it has received particularly strong support and promotion from central government and the Home Office since the late 1980s, both before this time, and subsequent to it, it has been implemented by individual police forces, with subtly different variations, as Bennett (1992) describes. Although the origins of the idea are North American, derived from the conspicuously successful Seattle project, it has not been transplanted root, stem and branch into the UK. Thus, not only were there similar predecessors in the UK on to which Neighbourhood Watch was grafted, but also in the process of grafting the element of citizen patrols – an integral part of North American schemes – was discarded as unsuitable and undesirable in the UK. Moreover, while North American schemes typically comprise only 20 to 30 households – literally a block – UK equivalents may be considerably larger, with the size having an important bearing upon the kinds of activities that can be undertaken.

The variation that is a part of Neighbourhood Watch in the UK makes it rather difficult to characterize its purpose, especially as there is then additional variation between the formal characteristics of schemes, and their actual practice. Formal elements tend to include such activities as property-marking, security surveys and upgrading, and surveillance, but in practice many so-called participants engage in none of these activities. There may be good grounds for suspecting that, beyond the erection of signs and placement of stickers in windows, a large proportion of schemes are in fact dormant, if not entirely lifeless. In theory, however, among other objectives, Neighbourhood Watch is intended to prevent crime both by enhancing surveillance and other opportunity reducing measures, and by building or exploiting informal social controls, essentially a combination of situational and social crime prevention. In practice, neither objective may be realized as the implementation of the idea falls short of the ideal that accompanies its enthusiastic promotion.

Initially Neighbourhood Watch was imported into the UK not by central government, but by the police, although their actions in so doing had an obvious elective affinity with emergent crime prevention policy, previously considered in Chapter 4. The first scheme established itself in Cheshire in 1982, but the real seal of legitimacy, depending upon one's perspective, was obtained when Kenneth Newman made it an integral part of his strategic plan of multi-agency policing for the Metropolitan Police in 1983, emphasizing a crime control partnership between police and public (Donnison et al. 1986).

This means that Neighbourhood Watch has to be seen in the context of the enforced recognition that the police's effectiveness depends upon the active co-operation of others, particularly in respect of opportunistic crime: Neighbourhood Watch is presented as a solution to a police problem. Investigating opportunistic crime brings the least reward in terms of clear-up rates, and thus there is pressure to limit the deployment of scarce police resources in this area. Neighbourhood Watch offers a way out of this difficulty, with the added bonus that it routinizes and formalizes the collection of low-level intelligence from the public, acting as the "eyes and ears" of the police. In theory, then, Neighbourhood Watch is of great potential benefit to the police, and by the mid-1980s this point was quickly accepted by other police forces, which hurriedly sought to follow the Metropolitan example.

Police support for Neighbourhood Watch, allied to the fact that it is they who authorize schemes, helps to explain its almost exponential growth in the second half of the 1980s, from approximately 4,000 schemes at the beginning of 1985, to more than 75,000 towards the end of 1989. During this time, however, central government also started to promote it under the theme of "crime: together we'll crack it", and the Thatcher–Hurd promotion of active citizenship, while from 1988 Crime Concern also took an interest in its development, as noted above. In addition, the domestic insurance industry has increasingly taken membership of Neighbourhood Watch into consideration in its calculation of insurance premiums, allowing a discount of five per cent or more that provides an obvious incentive for public participation. Overall, there has been strong pressure on the public to join Neighbourhood Watch, and indeed the success of this can be seen from the shift from most new schemes being police-initiated in the early 1980s, to most schemes being public-initiated in the late 1980s (Husain 1988, Bennett 1992). Police-initiated schemes continue, however, not least through pressure operating on the police as a result of the inclusion of a performance measure of "neighbourhood watch schemes per 1000 households' by Her Majesty's Inspectorate of Constabulary.

The rapid expansion of Neighbourhood Watch has continued into the 1990s, along with the heavy promotion of it: since the late 1980s a number of national Neighbourhood Watch conferences have been held, at which, more recently, medals have been awarded to model members among the five million or so households that are members. Indeed, in 1992, 20 per cent of all households were members, and given the increase in membership since then, the overall proportion of member households must in early 1996 be in excess of the 25 per cent rate of coverage reported in Canada in 1988 (Bennett 1992). In addition to the national Neighbourhood Watch conferences and special Neighbourhood Watch weeks, in 1994 a national Neighbourhood Watch Association was established under private sector sponsorship to represent the interests of scheme members. Interestingly, the rationale for such a body emanated in part from the need to oppose the Home Secretary's proposals in 1993 to transform Neighbourhood Watch schemes into street watch patrols, although the combined opposition of the national conference and the police ensured that such proposals were hurriedly discarded. Consequently, Michael Howard's aspirations for Neighbourhood Watch have become more conventional, especially in terms of the emphasis on quantity, having set a target of 200,000 schemes by the end of 1996 in his 1994 "partners against crime" campaign initiative.

This emphasis on quantity is, however, somewhat problematic, since it relates to form rather than content, and it gives no necessary indication of minimum standards. It suggests that Neighbourhood Watch has been valued more for its public relations than its crime prevention, for quantity is no guarantee of success, and even Home Office researchers are moved to observe that "It may be that there is more to gain by improving existing schemes – especially in needy areas – than by starting new schemes for the sake of increasing numbers" (Dowds & Mayhew 1994: 4).

One major problem for Neighbourhood Watch has been that with so many agencies promoting it, purposes have often been confused. In addition to situational and social crime prevention, it is variously seen as an aid to detection by improving the flow of information to the police, as a source of recruitment for special constables, and as a means of simply off-loading some of the responsibility for crime control. It is also often conceived less as a means of preventing crime, relying as it does on public "amateurs", and more as a means of addressing the fear of crime. In some quarters, moreover, and particularly among front line police, it might not be seen as having any purpose at all beyond the symbolic one of being seen to respond to Home Office and managerial priorities, as indicated by performance measures. To assume that those police officers developing Neighbourhood Watch know why they are doing it presumes a level of communication of purpose that might not necessarily be the case.

This assemblage of different purposes for Neighbourhood Watch – which are not always in harmony or complementary – provides one means of making sense of some of the more important research findings about it, although Hope (1995) suggests another angle, in so far as its main problems all stem from a reliance on voluntarism, while Bennett (1989) suggests another in raising the related aspects of theory and programme failure, which essentially cut across these other areas. Whichever way it is to be regarded or evaluated, the overwhelming point from the research is that it does not work very well as a crime prevention measure.

Before the question of what Neighbourhood Watch participants do can be answered we need to ask who joins, and the evidence from research conducted both in North America and in the UK, notably that by Bennett (1989, 1990, 1992) and from sweeps of the British Crime Survey, is that participation is predominantly slanted towards households in the more affluent, low crime areas. This means individuals who conform to the general stereotype of the volunteer, namely white, middle class and middle aged. In other words, Neighbourhood Watch schemes are most likely to be found where they are least needed in terms of risk of criminal victimization. In so far as Neighbourhood Watch schemes are most easy to recruit from these areas, some doubt must be expressed about the strength of the commitment to crime prevention in setting them up, if by crime prevention we mean crime reduction in high crime areas, which is the problem-oriented view taken by the situational approach.

The nebulousness of the term crime prevention allows some protection from this sort of criticism, for in neutral terms and contexts crime prevention is as legitimate in one area as it is in another. Crime, however, is not neutral in either its impact or its prospect, for as the proliferation of Neighbourhood Watch schemes in affluent areas shows, it unites citizens against a perceived outside threat, whereas in poorer areas where schemes do not take root it divides and weakens the community.

It is often assumed that Neighbourhood Watch reduces fear of crime, although the mechanism by which this is intended to happen is rarely specified. The research from North America (Rosenbaum 1988), nevertheless, suggests that quite the reverse may be true: bringing concerned people into close proximity with those who have been victimized can increase the concern rather than diminish it. Bennett's (1989) research in London contradicts this somewhat, although the decline in fear that he found in his experimental area was only marginal.

It has already been mentioned above that while Neighbourhood Watch seeks to increase the deployment of opportunity reducing technology, notably property-marking and stronger bolts and bars, the reality is that few scheme members actually do this, rather tending to restrict their activity to "wearing the badge". This is hardly surprising, because Neighbourhood Watch participants are not necessarily exposed to any more crime prevention information than other citizens (although there may be notable exceptions where more enthusiastic co-ordinators reside), and the capacity of the police to provide security surveys cannot possibly keep pace with the growing demands placed upon them by the rapid expansion of the initiative.

The other element to the situational agenda is increased surveillance, but the research here is ambiguous. Bennett's (1989) study showed reporting rates declining in the Neighbourhood Watch areas, not only for the reporting of suspicious persons, but more alarmingly for actual criminal victimization. McConville & Shepherd's (1992) research showed that there was no greater level of vigilance among participants over non-participants. Even were there to be greater vigilance among the former, there is some concern (Bennett 1992) that co-ordinators might actually reduce the information flow to the police by acting as unofficial gatekeepers. Against this, however, Dowds & Mayhew (1994) note that while the British Crime Surveys of 1988 and

1992 showed similar levels of witnessing of suspicious incidents between participants and non-participants, the fact that participants lived in low crime areas suggests that their vigilance must be sharper. More clearly, these surveys both showed an increased willingness to report suspicious incidents to the police among Neighbourhood Watch participants, even when demographic backgrounds are controlled for. And if reporting rates increase, this might help to explain increased crime rates in such areas.

Whatever the true picture with regard to surveillance, Hope (1995) perhaps makes the most telling contribution when he points out that there is a limit to how far natural surveillance can be increased when the trend in routine activities tends to be to leave homes unoccupied for longer periods of the day. This fact suggests that Neighbourhood Watch might attract a lot of what he calls "free riders", who may seek to benefit from any enhanced surveillance that membership might bring, without any necessary concern for reciprocity.

It is not apparent that the social crime prevention ambitions of Neighbourhood Watch stand any greater chance of success. Some schemes have demonstrated a very high level of community activity, but it has tended to be restricted to those middle-class areas where voluntary activity and community social controls are already well established, rather than in those areas where communities are suspected of being in terminal decline. Moreover, the potential contribution of Neighbourhood Watch to any improved sense of community is somewhat undermined by the limited activities undertaken by the majority of participants, and by the 1988 British Crime Survey's finding that a mere 13 per cent of respondents felt that it had improved neighbourliness in any way (Hope 1995).

Indeed, since social crime prevention is generally perceived of as a developmental long-term objective, it seems particularly ill suited to the general pattern of experience with Neighbourhood Watch, which demonstrates a marked tail off in levels of enthusiasm over time. This is mainly seen as being a consequence of a single issue focus, where the single issue is a comparatively rare event that may, in the initial flurry of publicity surrounding the launching of a scheme, significantly recede, only to return later, as the follow-up evaluation of the original Seattle scheme showed (Bennett 1992). This means that Neighbourhood Watch may, if marginally successful in the short term (although this might simply be the vagaries of crime rate fluctuations), contain the seeds of its own demise. This could affect not only the prospects for social crime prevention, but also those for the situational approach, for as Shapland & Vagg (1988) speculate, in so far as Neighbourhood Watch is often simply imposed upon pre-existing informal networks of surveillance, its own potential demise may well weaken these, with a resultant net loss rather than simply no gain.

The short shelf life of Neighbourhood Watch has become an issue of increasing concern in recent years, and it is apparent that it requires more support than the police are either willing or able to give. Indeed, it has proved very problematic for the police organization. It was intended initially as a means of off-loading responsibility, and potentially freeing up resources to be deployed elsewhere. However, its growth has fuelled an increasing demand for police support, and since it has grown most where it is least needed, this diverts police resources from areas of greater priority. Moreover, if the public demand is not met, then the possible result is declining public confidence, which then affects another objective of Neighbourhood Watch, namely the improvement of the flow of information between public and police, on which police effectiveness so demonstrably depends.

But if we take a closer look at the nature of a good deal of this information flow, we find that it is taken up with matters that are generally regarded as being of secondary importance to policing. They relate often to quality of life issues, regarding such matters as environmental services and decline. The public link these to crime, but the police normally do not: thus to them Neighbourhood Watch is something of a Pandora's Box, although ironically it is these sorts of concerns that enhance the longevity of schemes. Indeed, both Whiskin (1989) and Bennett (1992) suggest that Neighbourhood Watch should not be confined to crime prevention, which might anyway more profitably be pursued through other channels. Others such as Husain (1994) suggest that other forms of support could be found for Neighbourhood Watch, such as the local authority, where the more mundane concerns of participants would be considered more relevant. However, local authorities are not that much better placed to cope with the demands, and if the objective is to improve levels of consultation and participation, they would probably have to be a lot more certain of Neighbourhood Watch's representativeness.

In summary, then, Neighbourhood Watch continues to be heavily promoted, but without convincing evidence of its crime preventive effectiveness, and arguably without full regard to the excessive burden, including that of expectation, which it imposes upon the police, although in so far as it was initially a police idea they are to some extent the architects of their own misfortune. However, if its crime preventive effectiveness is not convincing, its ideological value is, and in the emphasis upon quantity rather than quality it at least does much to promote the active citizen. In the mid-1990s the objective appears to have become to make the citizen so active that Neighbourhood Watch becomes self-supporting, and the new national organization has an important contribution here. However, this organization and the annual conferences and prizes that provide a focal point for the movement are heavily dependent upon private sector sponsorship, which is by no means certain or secure. It is to the role of the private sector that we finally turn in this chapter.

The private sector

The private sector has a number of different roles in crime prevention, for which the following is not a comprehensive list, although it covers the major areas. First, the private sector is itself a victim of crime, and as Tilley (1993b) points out, far more crime is committed against businesses than against individuals or households. A large proportion of this is fraud, and Andrews & Burrows (1988) cite the estimate of the Home Office Standing Conference's working party on the costs of crime, that the cost of fraud is nearly double that of all other property crime. It is not all property crime, however, as crimes of violence against staff also indirectly victimize companies, depending upon the effect such victimization has upon such a valuable resource.

Secondly, the private sector produces a range of goods and services that are used or purchased by private individuals or organizations, but that may be made more or less vulnerable to criminal attack depending upon the amount of diligence and crime-related concern that has gone into their production. The issue here is whether private businesses should be concerned about the vulnerability of the goods and services they provide, when they themselves either do not bear the costs of crime, or may actually benefit from them. As Burrows (1991: 38) observes, businesses have no responsibility for crime prevention equivalent to that of the police, and "Appeals to companies' social responsibilities invariably cut little ice." Nevertheless, there remain very good reasons why the private sector should take some responsibility for "design against crime".

Thirdly, crime prevention actually provides opportunities for the private sector, and as it grows, so too do these opportunities. This is a key area of the privatization of crime control, and the growth and expansion of the private security industry bears testimony to its importance, mainly in the areas of private policing and patrolling, and the provision of an increasing array of security technology, from alarms to CCTV, with much in between (see Johnston 1992 for an excellent overview of developments). In addition, within this role we must note that crime prevention provides an opportunity for private sponsorship, primarily engaged in for purposes of public relations, although it would be too cynical to completely overlook the philanthropic rationale.

Underpinning these three different areas of involvement, which will be considered in more detail in the following discussion, is, as one might expect with the private sector, the issue of profitability. Unless crime prevention can be seen to enhance profitability, it is unlikely to be taken seriously, especially when private organizations are generally satisficers rather than maximizers, which means that the profits have to be considerable, and obvious. Consequently, it is easy to see why, of the three main roles the private sector possesses in relation to crime prevention, the one that has been most unproblematic in terms of willing involvement has been the last one, where crime prevention provides a business opportunity. However, this area throws up other concerns, about the propriety of crime prevention for profit, and the accountability of organizations operating in this area.

The private sector as victim, or as responsible provider of goods and services

To a large extent, before the advent of a distinct crime prevention policy in the post-war period, these roles were the sole responsibility and concern of the private sector. But central government has come to take a greater interest in them for a number of reasons. Most obviously, the costs of crime fall not only upon private businesses, or the consumers who make use of their goods and services, but also upon the public purse, through the criminal justice process. A collection of small dents in profit margins may be of negligible concern to private businesses, but together they make a much larger impact upon public resources. Credit card fraud provides an excellent example of this: as Levi et al. (1991) report, it is something that absorbs a great deal of police time, and incurs even more police frustration, because of the simplicity of preventive measures that, until comparatively recently, the industry has been reluctant to take.

Another reason for interest in this area has been the growing conviction that crime actually creates conditions in which enterprise suffers, which then has wider economic repercussions in terms of disinvestment, unemployment and so forth. This link between crime and enterprise became a more consistent theme in crime prevention policy from the mid-1980s onwards. In so far as governments are judged on their economic records, this reason also has underlying political motives, but more obviously political is the fact that governments are judged on the crime rates, and while crime might not be perceived by private businesses as a major problem, reported incidents count against the government's record, and are thus a cause for concern. Finally, since 1979 the focus upon the private sector has been an important element in the pursuit of the ideological project to relocate the responsibility for crime prevention away from the statutory sector.

If we look at how central government has sought to stimulate the private sector into action, we can see the pursuit of a number of different approaches. Initially the impetus actually came from the private sector, in the publicity campaign launched by the insurance industry and Home Office back in the 1950s. In the 1960s a corporatist approach was taken in so far as the private sector was represented locally on crime prevention panels, and nationally on the two subcommittees of the Standing Committee. Moreover, as a consequence of the deliberations of one of these subcommittees, legislation was passed in 1969 that required all car manufacturers to fit steering locks as standard on new cars, although since then the legislative approach has not been employed again.

The corporatist approach continued during the 1970s through the infrastructure that has been established in the 1960s, and a significant change in policy was not that apparent until the 1980s, when the Home Office Crime Prevention Unit began to produce a number of small studies on crime within different areas of the private sector. These studies, and a number of others, set about demonstrating the seriousness of the problem of crime to the private sector, and in the process uncovered a number of difficulties in the private sector response.

The costs of fraud have been cited above, while a Home Office Standing Conference report on the prevention of arson also showed the devastatingly high costs of this, which was often enough to drive companies out of business. Moreover, Cubbon (1988) cites figures that suggest that as little as a two per cent loss in turnover can translate as a 20 per cent loss of profits. However, while certain projections like this can be made, a problem is that information is difficult to come by. The police recording of crimes against businesses is inadequate (Tilley 1993b), and businesses themselves are not forthcoming with information (Andrews & Burrows 1988).

This is partly because there is a reluctance among managers to reveal information about something that might be regarded as their fault, or that might show their business in an unflattering light relative to competitors. But, more worryingly, it is also because there is a cultural inclination (Stenning 1988) to view crimes more as economic losses than legal categories of behaviour. These losses can be tolerated if the solution incurs still more loss, or is indeed more costly than the initial loss incurred by the crime, and thus there is a disincentive to prosecute, or to install preventive technologies. Moreover, losses tend to be measured in terms of the proportion of turnover rather than the financial cost (Andrews & Burrows 1988), which given the trend to multinational businesses means that quite significant costs can be written off as minor losses in the global context. As Pease (1994: 680) argues

> There is no doubt a threshold of cost above which simple crime prevention will come into play in commercial judgements, but that threshold is massively above the point at which the crime represents a significant social problem.

The implication of this is that crime prevention is less likely to be taken seriously in businesses where there is a high volume of transactions (Burrows 1991), unless the risks are extremely obvious, undeniable and controllable, such as is the case with money in transit, or warehousing. But Burrows points out that businesses are rarely equipped to think rationally about crime risk management, not only because they lack the information, but also because they lack the expertise. This is a point echoed by Clarke (1992) who points out that until it gains more of an in-house capability, the business sector, which is not well inclined to hear or heed the research findings or promotional activities of the Home Office, is unlikely to be a prominent player in problem-oriented crime prevention. However, as with other areas of crime prevention, resource availability may be inversely related to need here, for it is among small businesses that the costs of crime are least likely to be absorbed, and yet they have fewer resources to devote to any in-house capacity for expert crime risk management.

Without an expert view on how best to prevent crime, businesses which do invest in crime prevention ironically find themselves in the position of the ill-informed consumer. In a study of crime on industrial estates, for example, Johnston et al. (1994) note that many businesses employ unproven methods of crime prevention, or they take action independently of others operating on the same estate. This latter point demonstrates another cultural tendency of some businesses, to operate in competitive isolation, which spills over into areas where it is not necessary, and in the case of crime prevention simply risks displacement (Tilley 1993b). Against this, however, the proliferation of local chambers of commerce, and their representation on crime prevention panels, shows a potential for collective action.

The private sector is by no means completely immune to the crime prevention message from central government. It is most likely that a more successful strategy than relying on publicity was the approach taken by the Prime Minister in 1986, who chaired a seminar on crime prevention with representatives of the private sector, and certainly with regard to the automobile industry a number of new security standards ensued not long afterwards. Indeed, theft of or from motor vehicles was a major focus, because it accounted for approximately a quarter of all recorded crime by the late 1980s.

Also, although it was not originally charged with this responsibility, Crime Concern saw the stimulation of the private sector's role in crime prevention as one of its core tasks. Moreover, the private sector has been well represented on the National Board for Crime Prevention, and one of the more conspicuous examples of achievement by this body relates to the actions of a subcommittee looking at solutions to the problem of retail crime. The National Agency Board set up in 1996 gives an even stronger focus to private sector representation.

One noticeable theme in crime prevention policy from the late 1980s has been the attempt to present crime not so much as a problem for individual businesses as a problem for business, or enterprise, in general. At one level central government has attempted to tackle this problem itself: this was an important part of the Action For Cities initiative and the subsequent Safer Cities Programme. However, at another, particularly through the vehicle of Crime Concern, it has solicited contributions from the business community to general crime prevention initiatives that seek to improve the quality of life within an area, on the basis that happy customers are ultimately good news for sales. However, as the AMA (1990) points out, this has proved difficult, since private funding tends to favour short-term, highly localized initiatives. The difficulty is increased when the crime prevention objectives are social ones, for as Miller & Brown (1994: 439) observe, "The processes of crime prevention aiming to address social causes are often vague and long term and do not always fit easily into a corporate culture centred on firm targets and visible solutions."

Finally, in the 1990s we have also seen the emergence of a different strategy to make the private sector more crime prevention conscious. Rather than relying on gentle persuasion, this has entailed shocking businesses into action. For example, with ministerial backing, in 1991 the Home Office produced the Car Theft Index, which listed in order the makes and models of cars that were most at risk from theft. Also, Webb et al. (1992) report on police efforts to reward safe car parks with a "secured car park" status that might encourage customers to use them in preference to unsafe ones. The problem, of course, is that there may be no alternative car parks, and that such an initiative might end up increasing street parking, and thus displacing the risks. There is thus a limit to how far such a strategy can be taken, especially when it might be perceived as undermining confidence in the private sector, which is quite at odds with government policy elsewhere.

The private security industry

Encouraging the private sector to acknowledge that the costs of crime are sufficiently great to warrant serious and rationally planned crime preventive action is considerably harder than getting it to recognize a business opportunity when it sees one. The growth in crime, and fear of crime, coupled with a perceived lack of resources in policing, a lack of confidence in the criminal justice system, and a crime prevention policy that has sought to privatize some of the responsibility for crime control down to the community, but not through the public sector, has provided an ideal climate in which the private security sector can thrive. Nevertheless, the expansion of the security industry should not only be seen as a recent phenomenon: Shearing & Stenning's (1987) work on private policing makes it clear that the growth in the private sector is an international phenomenon since the end of the Second World War. It is not entirely unconnected to the increase in the amount of public life that now occurs in private space, owned increasingly by very powerful multinational corporations, a point echoed by Reichman (1987).

There are several aspects to the private security sector: it entails variously the design, manufacture, deployment and management of security products, as well as physically guarding and patrolling. It focuses as much as possible on primary prevention, on the basis that the earlier and more broad-based or inclusionary the intervention, the more business opportunities it provides. Hence, the development of the market has moved from more specific forms, such as the guarding of goods in transit, or the provision of an array of locks, bolts and bars that may be bought over the counter, to more general forms, such as the surveillance of massive tracts of public space by CCTV cameras, and the patrolling of both public and private space by security guards.

The Standing Conference on Crime Prevention report on the cost of crime in 1988 reckoned that the public spent £1,600 million on security, two-thirds of which was on security equipment. Reliable figures for this are hard to come by, but it is apparent that there has been a significant expansion in the number of households installing intruder alarms and stronger locks and bolts, often as a condition of gaining household contents insurance. Similarly, the number of independently fitted vehicle alarms has increased sharply. Local authorities have, since the mid-1980s, made greater use of CCTV, and by 1994 there were 200 such schemes around the country, relying on private sector designs, and sometimes also on private sector management. Similar developments have occurred within the private retail sector, and other commercial sites, where new technology has been deployed to bring about an increasingly sophisticated control of access to buildings.

Perhaps the biggest area of concern, however, has been the growth of private security patrols, some of which are contracted to local authorities, but the vast majority of which are employed by private businesses, or by the public. Loveday (1994a) quotes figures suggesting that 180,000 persons are employed within this industry, whereas the House of Commons Home Affairs Committee suggested that by 1995 these figures had reached 300,000. While the employment conditions of these persons are often a cause for concern, a bigger issue has tended to be made about industry regulation. The larger companies are regulated under their own voluntary British Security Industry Association, but far too many small ones are not, and media reports have raised concerns that many of these inappropriately employ former or active criminals, or engage in unethical practices in order to drum up customers – a story that has not been discouraged by the public sector police, who are acutely aware of the potential competition from cheaper alternatives.

Nevertheless, as Stenning (1994) smartly observes, private patrols are not necessarily more unaccountable than public ones, and public regulation is not necessarily any better at securing accountability than market mechanisms. Nor in all cases are the private sector police less well trained. However, Stenning does raise a concern about the powers of the private police: in private space they do wield more powers than the average citizen in terms of such things as surveillance, physical searches, and the denial of access. When these powers are underpinned primarily by the profit motive there is a concern that they might be misused, as private interests take precedence over public ones.

The problem is knowing the full extent of private interests. Obviously profit is paramount, and the removal of the crime problem would threaten this, so there is some concern that too great an effectiveness in crime reductive terms is counter-productive. A stronger and stronger emphasis upon prevention, however, is not, especially as it facilitates the use of sophisticated technology to penetrate ever more deeply into the fabric of social life. Crime prevention technology, like health care technology, is expensive and profitable. This, however, raises a civil libertarian concern about the widening of the net of social control, and what Stenning (1994) refers to as techno-domination. Yet the ambiguity about the advantages and disadvantages of this remain, and are demonstrated to excellent effect in Shearing & Stenning's (1987) article on Disney World, where the control is more Huxley than Orwell, essentially coercing visitors, in time-honoured American fashion, to have a nice day, without spiking the cola.

157

Summary

The intention in this chapter has mainly been the descriptive one of demonstrating the extent of the mixed economy of crime prevention beyond the formal criminal justice system. This mixed economy is thriving in terms of the amount of activity, although it is essentially nothing new. The private and informal sectors' roles and interests in crime prevention preceded the emergence of the modern formal criminal justice system, while many of the local authorities' tasks have historical precedents or parallels in the original meaning of the term "police", which translated simply as administration.

What is new is the current emphasis that is being given to this mixed economy, as part of a more flexible, efficient and deprofession-alized approach to crime control. However, this chapter has also raised a number of concerns that suggest that the promise of the mixed economy might be in danger of exceeding its potential, where beneath the structures and institutional frameworks we find that each sector faces its own difficulties and particular concerns. The partnership approach, moreover, seeks not only to bring these other sectors to the fore, but also together into a corporate approach. The next chapter explores the feasibility of this.

CHAPTER 7

Partnerships in crime prevention

Introduction

Partnership has been a consistent theme throughout the development of crime prevention policy since the 1950s. Initially, it was implicit, both in the urging of private citizens and businesses to have greater regard to the security of person and property, and in the corporate structures that were established in the 1960s and were viewed as an essentially normal part of the corporatist climate in which public policy operated at this time. In the 1980s, the terminology became more explicit, and frequent appeals were made to the multi-agency, inter-agency or co-ordinated approach to crime prevention, while in the 1990s the term partnership has moved to the fore, as it has across a number of different areas of public policy, including urban policy, which is an example of some relevance to crime prevention.

The changing use of names is relevant in so far as they convey subtly different meanings despite ostensibly referring to the same basic thing. In the case of crime prevention, the shift between the 1980s and 1990s, from the multi-agency to the partnership approach, for example, is indicative of a change in emphasis in government policy from an approach that relies on collaboration between, in the main, statutory agencies, to one that relies more on collaboration between different sectors of the mixed economy of crime prevention. The change in emphasis, then, has been from inter-agency to inter-sectoral crime prevention, although both obviously co-exist. The meaning of words, however, lies in the minds of their users, and it may be that the government's intended meaning does not necessarily square with the interpretations of those within the field.

Nevertheless, this discussion does draw attention to the fact that while all crime prevention policy has relied upon some form of collaboration, the nature of that collaboration, both anticipated and actual, has changed over time, as policies have changed. While policy has changed, however, there has tended to be one constant, which is that collaboration has generally proved to be problematic for crime prevention. Collaboration is a much neglected area in the evaluation of crime prevention initiatives, which invariably follows a quasi-experimental pre-test/post-test design that neglects processes in favour of measurable outcomes of crime reduction. Consequently, it is difficult to know what effect collaborative problems have on these outcomes (although collaboration itself can be an outcome (Crawford & Jones 1996)), but in so far as they may be manifested as implementational difficulties, one might anticipate that their effect may be considerable. Indeed, this may be one reason why attempts to replicate "successful" crime prevention projects are so often doomed to failure, as the mechanisms may be faithfully replicated, but the collaborative context may not (Tilley 1993a).

Collaboration is thus an important area of analysis in its own right, and indeed it has received increased academic attention in recent years. Before we can proceed with our analysis, however, we need to be clear about what exactly it is. It means working together, but beyond its literal meaning it implies a number of things. It has an ideology of unity that hints at a common purpose, and a sense of togetherness in an uncertain world. It also implies a level of effectiveness, if only because "two heads are better than one". These broader implications of the term help to account for some of the commonalities in its reception. Sampson et al. (1988), for example, note the tendency for collaboration to be regarded overwhelmingly as a good thing in what they term a benevolent model, although as Crawford & Jones (1995) note, this should be taken less to imply a naïve assumption of consensus among those who regard it as such, than a general desire for unity. Moreover, to be seen to be collaborating is also a good thing, and has much public relations value in itself, assuming it is tied to such a worthy end as crime prevention. Thus, despite the case for it being unproven, it is increasingly becoming necessary, as with the SRB, to demonstrate a collaborative intent and infrastructure before funds for crime prevention will be released.

Beyond the ideology of collaboration lies a more practical concern with the mechanics of collaboration, that uncovers a considerable amount of variation in the intensity of agency relationships. Davidson's (1976) typology is instructive here, identifying a con-tinuum of collaboration that increases in intensity from communica-tion to co-operation, to co-ordination, to federation, to merger. While there are inevitably grey areas in any such classification, its value lies in its demonstration of a simple fact, that the greater the intensity of collaboration, the greater the stakes. Two or more autonomous agents may communicate and co-operate, but the further they move past this point, the more their autonomy is compromised.

Crawford & Jones (1995) express this in a different way. They distin-guish multi-agency from inter-agency collaboration on the basis that the former implies no special arrangements or alteration in core tasks, whereas the latter implies the need for new structures that compro-mise autonomy. This distinction, however, implies an "either or" framework that does not hold true, for the important point is that the nature of collaboration is variable, whatever its infrastructure. Their distinction is intended to highlight a point at which agency autonomy is threatened, but the continuum does this just as well (it comes at some point between co-operation and co-ordination) while still allow-ing for the possibility of agencies flexibly moving up and down this continuum, both between and within themselves, albeit within certain proscribed limits of intensity.

Collaboration and crime prevention policy

There is a considerable amount of routine collaboration within the criminal justice system that, by virtue of its ordinariness (Challis et al. 1988) is unproblematic, although that is not to say that routines are always as efficient and effective as they might be. The exchange of information between the police and Crown Prosecution Service is a case in point here, as is the managerially inspired attempt to get crimi-nal justice machinery to function more like a system, with the smooth-ness of operation that the term implies (Feeney 1985). However, routine implies legitimacy, and the establishment of some kind of equilibrium in collaborative relationships, yet not necessarily in terms of power relations.

Collaborative crime prevention is not at the moment routine, although this is the ideal state that is being aimed for in contemporary crime prevention policy. In Challis et al.'s (1988) terms, it represents "strategic" collaboration, where some new initiative disturbs the equilibrium between agencies, and thus requires some renegotiation of relationships. The details of this strategy have already been covered at some length in Chapter 4, and have broadly entailed a shift through three phases of crime prevention policy, from unfocused, to situational, to community safety. Common to each phase has been a desire to shift the balance of responsibility for the control and reduction of crime away from the formal criminal justice system, but each differs in how this is to be achieved, and so each also differs in its collaborative implications.

The main element of unfocused crime prevention is the publicity campaign, which relies on one-way communication, followed by the hoped-for co-operation of the public in becoming more security conscious. It has not been spectacularly successful. In its early years, the crime prevention message from such communication was rather vague, relying more on slogans than practical action, but while suggestions for practical action have increased, they still have not managed to convincingly penetrate the widespread expectation that the criminal justice system is primarily responsible for crime control. Even where the message has hit its target, the expectation of collaboration has been exposed as unrealistic in a context in which those most at risk appear to have the least available resources to protect themselves. On the question of resources, it is interesting to speculate upon the possibility that the insurance industry has succeeded where the government has failed, by providing a financial incentive to collaboration in joining Neighbourhood Watch schemes, although given that the effectiveness of such schemes is generally unproven, and their coverage is skewed towards the middle classes, the wisdom and equity of such an incentive is questionable. Returning to the theme of the chapter, the key point is that resources have an important bearing upon collaborative responses.

The other element of unfocused crime prevention has been the central and local infrastructure established in the 1960s. However, this lacked a focus in so far as it was not sufficiently problem-oriented, and while there has been some success, for example in terms of the number of crime prevention panels that have been established, a frequent criticism of such groups is that they generally amount to little more than well-intentioned talking shops. In other words, there may be a great deal of communication, but little more in the way of collaborative action, although bearing in mind the public relations value of collaboration, especially for the private sector (Liddle & Gelsthorpe 1994b), communication may be seen as an end in itself by many participants. Since 1988, Crime Concern has taken it upon itself to breathe new life into the crime prevention panel, but in its limited success it has arguably moved the panel from being a vehicle of unfocused policy, to situational crime prevention.

Gladstone (1980) has made it abundantly clear why situational crime prevention requires collaboration: because information about crime is split between a number of interested parties or agencies, and because the resources to do something about it are equally split. The requirement for information in this problem-oriented approach translates as a requirement for communication, while the requirement for resources requires a combination of both co-operation and co-ordination, as the temporal and spatial sequencing of crime prevention measures is often of the utmost importance. The question is how to go about meeting these requirements.

The fact that information and resources are dispersed among a number of agencies implies that some body must bring them all together, and the common approach of centrally funded projects, which has been mimicked outside of them, has been to establish an inter-agency forum. This repeats the model of the unfocused infrastructure, but crucially adds a problem-oriented methodology that offers a logical, rational scientific approach and an unambiguous agenda for action. In many cases, the responsibility for this is placed in the hands of a co-ordinator, who may be drawn from the relevant participating agencies, or from an outside agency, where the role of honest broker may be exploited to enhance the legitimacy of the enterprise (Tilley 1992).

Experience with this approach suggests that it looks much better in theory than in practice. One obvious difficulty, recognized by the interdepartmental working group on crime reduction in the early 1980s, was that of persuading agencies other than the police, whose statutory responsibility makes their attendance obligatory, to take their place at the collaborative table. Once again, expectations about where the responsibility for crime control really lies, and resource limitations, lie behind such a difficulty, which has not been successfully overcome despite the issuing of Home Office circulars and the establishment of a number of demonstration projects and other initiatives in the 1980s. Since then, despite the failure to resolve the question of local leadership, there has been rather more success in terms of getting agencies to the table, although in terms of the distinction established here, this has been more a feature of community safety than situational crime prevention.

Experience with the situational approach has also brought to light a number of other important collaborative difficulties, many of which were identified in the pioneering study by Hope & Murphy (1983) of the Manchester schools vandalism project where the approach was first systematically tested. One difficulty was that despite the intention from policy-makers to restrict the situational approach's purview to opportunity reducing measures, it became apparent that some of the collaborating agencies proffered alternative social solutions to the problem, thus bringing to light the essential conflict between different crime prevention ideologies.

In this particular case, the advocates of the social approach made little headway, in part because this approach was not as easy to grasp, in terms of its crime preventive logic, as the opportunity reducing measures, and because they required ongoing resource commitments beyond the course of a time-limited project. More significantly, however, the research also found a significant power differential between the collaborating agencies: the police and the local authority buildings branch dominated because they were the experts, who routinely had to deal with the vandalism problem or who had information about the nature of the problem, and who shared the ultimate responsibility to do something about it. Consequently, it was their proposals that held sway, although when it came to implementation a series of other practical problems were encountered, from organizational inertia to poor intra-agency communications, and from competing resourcing priorities to unanticipated consequences. Ultimately, and ironically, the only measures that were implemented were those that required no collaboration between agencies. Many of the decisions that had been taken in the inter-agency forum simply were not followed through.

On the basis of their research findings, Hope & Murphy suggested that the situational methodology was too inflexible, and assumed too readily that the whole process would accord with a rational model of decision-making. Indeed, they concluded of the methodology that "its analytic scope needs to be broadened to include the organizational and political arena in which crime prevention is to be pursued" (1983: 48).

Hope & Murphy's research served as a warning to the Home Office as it projected its crime prevention policy on to a much larger screen, although it contained a glimmer of hope in so far as it implied that strong but flexible leadership could surmount many of the barriers uncovered in the research. This was not addressed at the political level, which is why Circular 8/84 was vague on the matter, but in the demonstration projects that the Home Office funded, including the Five Towns Initiative, it ensured that funding was available for an independent co-ordinator to provide the essential ingredient, although Liddle & Bottoms's (1991) retrospective assessment of this initiative indicated that significant collaborative problems remained.

While there are several reasons for the eventual usurpation of the situational approach by community safety, that are explored in detail in Chapter 8, one of them was that it contained the seeds of its own demise. It was devised by Home Office researchers, and associated particularly strongly with Ron Clarke, who had in mind a very rational problem-oriented process that would effectively exclude alternative preventive discourses, which rarely appeared to be problem-oriented, and had a very unimpressive track record as measures of crime prevention. It was assumed, then, that the situational approach would be confined to agencies on a "need to be involved" basis: what was important was the methodology rather than the structure – it was very much a researcher's eye of things.

Inevitably, in practice it had to negotiate the real world in which alternative agendas impinge on rational ideals. Thus the situational approach drew in agencies such as the probation service and the social services that, as Liddle & Gelsthorpe's research (1994b) points out, locate themselves firmly within a social approach to crime prevention, and as Chapter 5 shows, even the police were unclear that their role was supposed to be more in the situational tradition. Consequently, from within the structures that were established to pursue the situational approach an alternative social discourse emerged. Eventually this gained increasing support, until the heavy emphasis on situational "quick fix" solutions that had been so evident in the first half of the 1980s gave way to an official position that was much more accommodating of a more eclectic community safety approach.

Community safety requires collaboration in much the same way as the situational approach does, but a key difference is that it places greater importance upon the local structure, while still seeking, at least according to the Home Office's ideal, a problem-oriented focus. Starting from a position less favourably inclined towards any single approach, community safety is increasingly a corporate approach that requires the representation of all different elements of a coherent crime prevention package, taking in situational and social crime prevention, but also fear prevention and more conventional forms of policing. Moreover, as the magnitude and the differential impact of the crime problem has become apparent, so this, with other factors, has required that this package be located firmly within the community, incorporating private citizens and businesses.

Community safety's requirement for a corporate approach takes it further along Davidson's (1976) continuum of collaboration than either of the other two approaches, touching the point of federation, where the stakes of the collaborative game become much higher. Home Office-sponsored initiatives such as the Safer Cities Programme have tried to manage this by using the independent co-ordinator model alongside a two-tier structure that reflects the distinction between strategic and operational concerns. However, the sheer size of the operation, with its inter-agency and inter-sectoral dimensions, makes this most problematic in the context of finite resources, where priorities have to be identified.

It is here that crime prevention is at its most open-textured and interesting. Many of the difficulties encountered with collaboration in community safety are similar to those encountered with situational crime prevention, but the context has changed, with significant implications (see below). One manifestation of this has been the sensitivity of the leadership question, posed by the Morgan Committee but unsatisfactorily answered by central government, mindful of the distant control that it wishes to retain over the direction of local collaboration, and of the Pandora's Box that community safety has the potential to become.

The opening stages of collaboration

The initial concern in crime prevention policy was that there was not enough collaboration: agencies were unwilling to do it. However, this situation is much improved, and the pressures that have been brought to bear upon agencies, and that have brought them to the collaborative table, provide the starting point for our understanding of collaboration in its broader context.

Hudson (1987) suggests that it is under conditions of interdependence that agencies are most likely to collaborate, where there is a mutual recognition that collaboration is an essential part of the routine of getting the work done. However, as noted above, the collaboration envisaged by crime prevention is not routine. Rather, it has emerged as a result of official recognition that the means of crime prevention is dispersed across a number of different agencies and sectors, in a mixed economy of crime control. This recognition has not, however, traditionally been shared by those within the mixed economy, where there has been a predominant assumption that some agencies are responsible for certain kinds of crime control, while others are not. Consequently, it has been more usual to find other forms of organizational coexistence here beside interdependence – specifically either independence, or even conflict (Hudson 1987).

The emphasis within crime prevention policy has been to attempt an alteration within these conditions of coexistence, so that agencies may effectively be forced together. This has entailed a mixture of voluntarism and coercion, depending upon how willing collaborative partners have been. Davidson (1976) observes that pressure for collaboration comes mainly from the wider environment, where certain changes in economic, political, ideological or social conditions force corresponding changes within agencies. This is not the only source of pressure, for in addition to this macro-level influence we also find significant influences at the mezzo- or agency level, and at the micro- or interpersonal level, although each are interrelated, with the macro-level perhaps ultimately being the most determining one.

The pressure for collaboration is not irresistible, but in the case of crime prevention it has been particularly strong and multidimensional. Examples are numerous. In the case of the probation service, for example, the "invitation" to collaborate has been backed up with a certain sense of "or else", while for reasons that have already been considered in Chapter 5, related to rising crime and declining public confidence, the police have also had little alternative but to participate. The community has been enticed by a powerful ideological crusade for active citizenship, incorporating both individualistic and participative forms, depending upon the source of the pressure. Private businesses have been encouraged to consider the costs of crime for enterprise, and to consider the benefits of collaboration for publicity, while local authorities and the voluntary sector have been enticed by the availability of additional resources through various special central government initiatives, on condition that partnership can be demonstrated.

The pressure has not come only from the government, although through its circulars, publicity and initiatives it has been the main player. McLaughlin (1994), for example, provides an interesting account of how one radical Labour urban local authority was pressurized by electoral concerns to drop its police monitoring and accountability initiatives in favour of victim-friendly community safety strategies that appealed more to the Party's populist concerns in the late 1980s. Finally, pressure has also been more positive: as noted above, collaboration meets a common collective desire for unity, while the promise of greater effectiveness has had considerable appeal in an increasingly managerialist climate.

Overall, then, crime prevention, but particularly the rather vague community safety, which like other community initiatives employs the community tag for ideological effect, has been increasingly successful at attracting collaborative partners, although there are still plenty of areas where it has yet to obtain a foothold. However, while agencies have come to collaborate in crime prevention for a number of reasons, some positive but some negative, it is axiomatic that agencies whose normal relations with one another are either those of conflict or independence will not find it easy to work with one another, for a variety of reasons.

What I have described elsewhere as the definitional elasticity of crime prevention (Gilling 1994), but more particularly community safety, cushions the blow in collaborative encounters. This is because it is an eclectic approach, which eschews any single measure approach to crime control in favour of an approach that incorporates primary, secondary and tertiary prevention, focused upon victims and offenders, both actual and potential. It is thus so wide ranging and multidimensional that in theory there is space for everyone and everything, and so no conflict should ensue. In this way, community safety really only replicates the diversity of crime control that has always been apparent, but presents it in a decentralized and co-ordinated form.

However, in practice, there tends to be a contradiction between the eclecticism and either the methodology that community safety is expected to follow, or the resource context in which it is located, or quite often both. Thus while many preventive measures are plucked out of the air rather than having been based upon strict adherence to a problem-oriented methodology (Liddle & Gelsthorpe 1994c), many do employ this methodology, which explicitly encourages a comparison of different potential measures. Since only the most promising is expected to be selected, this invites competition over what is likely to be so, and quite likely, therefore, conflict.

If the conflict does not come here, it may come because resources make community safety's eclecticism impossible from the start. There are two sorts of resources that community safety is often short of, especially as a new approach that has yet to prove its merit. One of these is money, and the other is time. Limited finances, which are partly in evidence in the very small sum of money devoted to crime prevention from within the criminal justice budget, necessitate the prioritization of one approach over another. Furthermore, many community safety initiatives, and especially those funded from central government, are limited by time: they are short-term projects rather than long-term programmes, or to employ Liddle & Gelsthorpe's (1994c) terminology, they are scheme-focused rather than process-focused. This is a phenomenon that has been noted by other researchers, such as King (1989), and its main significance lies in the fact that it again encourages competition or conflict between measures over their potential to demonstrate short-term results and effectiveness. Indeed, even in longer term projects such a pressure is in evidence, because the demonstration of results is an important element in securing legitimacy for community safety, and thus continued financial support. In effect, this always appears to advantage situational crime prevention measures, since these can promise the short-term results that other approaches cannot.

Research on collaboration in crime prevention

The uncovering of a certain degree of conflict, and the identification of a certain advantaged position for situational approaches, is a common feature of much of the research into collaborative crime prevention that has been conducted since the mid-1980s. This research has drawn attention to the importance of studying the processes of crime prevention initiatives as much as their outcomes: there is clearly a relationship between them, even if it is sometimes a rather ambiguous one.

Hope & Murphy (1983) stumbled over collaborative difficulties in their research, rather than making it the focus of their work, and they incorporated these difficulties within a more general understanding of implementational difficulties with crime prevention initiatives. Since their study, however, collaboration has become more of a focus in its own right, something that links in with the rise of community safety, and increasing attention to multi-agency, partnership or corporate approaches to a wide range of contemporary public policy concerns.

The first most thorough and systematic study of collaboration can be found in the work of a group of researchers writing in different publications under their various names, such as Sampson et al. (1988), Blagg et al. (1988), and Pearson et al. (1992). These studies all refer to the same empirical work, which was conducted across a range of five different sites in the second half of the 1980s, taking in other examples of inter-agency collaboration as well as crime prevention or community safety.

This research identifies a number of important points that serve as a warning to those who might regard this approach to crime control as a panacea. In particular, they contrast a "benevolent" perspective, which consensually regards collaboration as a good thing, with a "conspiratorial" perspective, which portrays things more in terms of the police's colonization of collaborative crime prevention to further their coercive ends. Their own research, while not actually supporting either of these perspectives, certainly stresses the centrality of conflict to collaborative ventures, and leans more towards the conspiratorial perspective in so far as it views the police in particular as the most powerful of all collaborative partners. As a result, it is the police perspective of problem and solution that tends to prevail.

They acknowledge, then, that agencies tend to bring different perspectives with them. These perspectives are employed not only to further a particular ideology, but also to frame problem and solution in such a way that is least demanding upon occupational and organizational workloads. Hence, for example, they note a tendency for the police to off-load unwelcome issues related to minor disorders on to inter-agency groups, to concentrate on those crimes that affect them most, such as burglary or car crime, and to conceive of solutions to these crimes that do not fundamentally challenge their practice, while getting others to do more.

If we turn to the vital question of why it is that agencies such as the police (and also the local housing department) tend to be more powerful than others, we find that it is attributed to the "structured power relations between the state agencies" (Sampson et al. 1988: 479), or more specifically "the deeply rooted structural oppositions between different state agencies, entailing different tasks, preoccupations, responsibilities and powers" (Sampson et al. 1988: 481). It is not entirely clear what the basis of this structural power differentiation is, because in none of the research reports is there a description of the authors' social theory. From Pearson et al. (1992) we do, however, find that gender relations is cited as one of these structural sources, in so far as it is the predominantly male organizations that tend to get their way. This sits uneasily with Liddle & Gelsthorpe's (1994c) research into a greater number of community safety initiatives, which found a dearth of women agency representatives at the level of inter-agency collaboration they were researching. Nevertheless, men and women do not necessarily have to be present for decision-making to have a gendered aspect to it, and Liddle & Gelsthorpe's research focused upon an upper tier of collaboration that involved senior agency management and therefore inevitably came across the glass ceiling phenomenon.

This structured view of power relations has attracted criticism, albeit of a constructive and sympathetic sort, from Crawford & Jones (1995), whose research in two sites in the early 1990s has followed in the wake of those above, and has advanced the debate in a number of key areas. Crawford & Jones object to Sampson et al.'s (1988) distinction between conspiratorial and benevolent perspectives on collaboration, which effectively translate as conflict or consensus structural accounts, and encourage an "either or" view that oversimplifies the complexity of inter-agency relationships.

171

In their place, Crawford & Jones suggest it is important to view collaboration within a neo-corporatist framework that allows for much greater variability in outcome in power relations than the rather deterministic approach of Pearson et al. (1992). Their preferred alternative is to conceive of power in a Foucauldian way, as a creative as well as a constraining force, so that the structuralist script is tempered with a certain flexibility that means that things need not always turn out in such a predictable way. Thus they point out that "The central problematic in multi-agency relations is not merely the existence and recognition of conflict, but the manner in which conflict is subsequently managed" (Crawford & Jones 1995: 25), and they go on to conclude (1995: 31) that

> Our research suggests that when analysing inter-agency relations there is a need to give due emphasis to the creativity of human actions within structural constraints, and for greater specificity of analysis of power relations.

As a manifestation of this creativity, they further distinguish their work from Pearson et al. (who, they argue, tend to focus on visible manifestations of power) by citing examples of collaboration where conflict is avoided (the phenomenon of the non-decision), and where conflict is anticipated and worked around.

In fact, it is possible to argue that Crawford & Jones are prematurely dismissive of Pearson et al.'s work, that despite a rather cumbersome and ultimately self-defeating distinction between benevolent and conspiratorial perspectives actually ends at a similar point, when they argue that "the forms of co-operation and outcomes of multi-agency initiatives are often the result of a complicated set of social relations and interactions that are neither consistent nor directly observable" (Sampson et al. 1988: 491). It appears, on closer examination, that the deterministic model of power and conflict with which these researchers work is somewhat at odds with some of their findings.

This is most apparent when one looks at informal collaboration, which constitutes another point of disagreement between these two groups of researchers. Sampson et al.'s (1988) research uncovers a significant amount of informal collaboration that raises a number of problems regarding such matters as confidentiality and accountability, and yet that paradoxically provides examples of the most effective form of collaboration. Indeed, such informalism is quite often a feature of work between women agency representatives, who find more reward here than in formal contexts where their work and concerns are taken less seriously. This is surely an example of the creativity that Crawford & Jones identify in their own research, yet they fail to see it here.

Crawford & Jones criticize Sampson et al. for celebrating informalism, although they clearly do not, recognizing it as "an unresolved tension" (1988: 491) in their research. Informalism might pose significant difficulties, but it can get things done, as Liddle & Gelsthorpe (1994a) also acknowledge. Crawford & Jones do not suggest going in entirely the opposite direction and demanding formalism at all times, but they do observe that "there is a need for the management of conflicts to be delineated by local community demands within a framework which accords to notions of social justice" (1995: 26). But what does such a framework look like? A framework implies some degree of formalism, but it is this formalism that concentrates the conflict that informal strategies often seek to resolve or avoid, albeit often by setting up other problems, for as Crawford & Jones rightly point out, informalism can sharpen power differentials between those party to the agreements and those excluded.

Formal frameworks, according to Sampson et al. (1988) often work against the interests of women. They contain the most obvious and intractable points of ideological conflict over different visions of crime prevention. They contain representatives who are in fact often only representatives of sectional interests within the agencies they are supposed to represent (including "the community"), and often do not communicate the consequences of their participation within their own agencies. Their goals are often displaced by other motives such as public relations, and when they involve local democratic representatives, these representatives do not necessarily have a constructive role to play, and may indeed demonstrate their own vested interests (Liddle & Gelsthorpe 1994c). The key point is surely that whether arrangements are formal or informal, fundamental difficulties remain, a point that Crawford & Jones acknowledge in their conclusion where they observe that "the manner in which inter-agency and inter-communal conflicts are presently managed in multi-agency forums increasingly resembles neo-corporatist arrangements . . . in which invisible and unaccountable discretion is the order of the day" (1995: 31).

Ultimately, Crawford & Jones and Pearson et al. share a similar conception of power in so far as each identifies structural limits, but each also gives space to human agency to negotiate within these limits. But beyond a reference to gender, they are not entirely specific about how this power manifests itself, although there is an implicit understanding that the privileged position of situational measures derives in part from the political and ideological preferences of central government, expressed through its tight financial control of policy and finance. However, if we take the example of the Safer Cities Programme, then this control appears much weaker than is generally assumed, given that project bids for more than two thousand pounds have to be agreed by the Home Office. As Tilley (1993a) observes, up until April 1991 only 17 ideas out of a total of 1300 schemes were rejected, suggesting more of a permissive than a directive role.

Nevertheless, my own work (Gilling 1992), which was based upon only a single case study and was less extensive than that of those discussed above, does shed some light on how this power is manifested. Hope & Murphy (1983) found that the police and school buildings branch were the most powerful players in the school vandalism project, and Sampson et al. (1988) found that the police and housing department were the most powerful in their research. There are a number of reasons for this. Most obviously, these agencies have the primary responsibility for doing something about the crime problem, since it most affects them. In other words, it is mostly a problem for them. Partly as a consequence of this, they have an expertise to which others cede, for as Barrett & Fudge (1981) observe, the history of policy and practice has an important role in shaping expectations about what is to be done, and by whom.

If we look at the kind of crime prevention pursued by these more powerful agencies, we find that it is overwhelmingly situational in nature. Again, however, there are more mundane reasons why this should be the case. We have already noted, for example, that in a context of limited resources of time and finance, situational crime prevention generally looks the better bet. Yet it is also the case that, as befits crime prevention policy's origins, a strong research focus permeates the whole process. Research depends upon information, and notwithstanding their glaring methodological weaknesses, official crime statistics are commonly regarded as the principal source of hard data about crime. Furthermore, they are in the ownership of the police, who are therefore in the strongest position to identify what is or is not a problem in need of a preventive solution. This is why Sampson et al. (1988) found that areas such as racial harassment and domestic violence are not taken seriously. The groups these problems affect may be lacking in structural power, but the reason why they are excluded from preventive initiatives often has much more to do with the fact that they cannot be proven as problems in the official statistical bible.

Research and evaluation tend to be exceptionally important for crime prevention as means of demonstrating results. But in order to promise results, crime prevention measures must themselves be measurable, which privileges those problems that feature prominently in official statistics. Indeed, Liddle & Gelsthorpe (1994c) note that there is a tendency for agencies that generally lack an evaluative expertise to conceive of evaluation in terms of things that can be expressed through crime statistics: if they cannot be so expressed, they cannot be evaluated.

Not all community safety initiatives place a strong emphasis upon evaluation, but among those that do, the twin pressures of demonstrating results and measurability have the combined effect of prioritizing crimes against property, which are more reliably reported and recorded and regularly account for something like 95 per cent of all recorded crimes. Situational measures are invariably the best way of tackling these, because if they are based upon information, that information says very little about offenders, who mostly remain uncaught and unknown, but a great deal about the circumstances of the offence and the victim, increasingly including such matters as the *modus operandi* and data on repeat victimization. It may well be that certain pieces of information are known about offenders in general, such as that they are unemployed or in debt, but this information is not that useful for crime prevention either because it is speculative, or because crime prevention initiatives are highly localized, yet information about offenders generally is not. Although community safety has a potential to be universal in its coverage, its limitations make it more usually targeted, and this local targeting again tends to privilege situational measures.

The implication of this is that the shape of community safety initiatives is influenced less by structural factors than by factors such as evaluation, resourcing and localism, which mediate and structure the power that the centre holds over the locality. These are the factors that serve to resolve the conflict in one direction rather than another. They are also the factors that constitute core elements of a discourse of managerialism that increasingly informs public policy and provides a backcloth to the neo-corporatism identified by Crawford & Jones (1995). Such a position is not inconsistent with their work, but it is more specific.

Specificity is also a characteristic of the contributions of Liddle & Gelsthorpe (1994a,b,c), who have produced three volumes on inter-agency collaboration within the Home Office Crime Prevention Unit paper series. The fact that three papers have been devoted to this issue, and that the content of these papers provides a good deal more text than is normally the case in this series suggests that the issue of collaboration has been taken quite seriously within the Home Office.

Liddle & Gelsthorpe's work looks at a larger number of crime prevention initiatives than those mentioned above, and it also focuses upon the upper tier of collaboration: that which exists at the strategic rather than the operational level. This is another point of difference with previous research, and not surprisingly it leads to a focus upon some different areas of concern, as well as many similar ones. Their depth of analysis is inevitably limited by the fact that the research is official, conducted for the Home Office in the form of a general audit of collaborative activities in the 1990s, and presented in the customary politically neutral language. Nevertheless, one can glean from their work a number of important observations that help to extend our understanding of collaboration.

For example, their focus upon the difficulties that local authorities encounter when they are not unitary provides another reason why situational crime prevention can dominate local agendas. In this case, there is sometimes a political conflict between district local authorities and county councils that renders collaboration unlikely. As a result, district authorities may often find themselves left to their own devices, which means that there is no input from county-level service such as education or social services, which tend to show a social crime prevention bias. In particular, the onus tends to fall upon housing authorities and the police, and thus the process described above is again likely to unfold.

Even where local authorities are unitary, the increased tendency towards the decentralization of services, and compulsory competitive tendering (CCT) both have the effect of undermining corporate approaches. They do this because decentralization results in agencies being unable to provide representatives with sufficient authority to represent their agencies and commit resources, and because CCT fosters a climate of defensiveness, where there is an unwillingness to countenance devoting resources to new areas. These points demonstrate the importance of considering intra-agency factors alongside inter-agency ones, something acknowledged by all of the researchers considered in this section.

Liddle & Gelsthorpe's work is not placed in a specific theoretical context, but in so far as constraints allow them, they do demonstrate an understanding of the way in which local processes are structured to an extent by central constraints, and particularly the resourcing that encourages a short term scheme-focused approach, from which, it may be implicitly read, a number of the difficulties of collaboration flow. Ultimately, however, they point to the contingent and locally variable nature of collaboration (even agencies such as the police "play the game" differently in different areas), while identifying a number of factors that might bring about a more systematic and effective approach, including higher level agency representation across the board, and the employment of a co-ordinator to provide a more problem-oriented approach.

Summary

This chapter has sought to demonstrate that collaboration has been a consistent theme of crime prevention policy, but that the nature of the requisite collaboration has changed over the years, from a less intensive to a more intensive form, reflecting the wide gap between, say, communication and federation. From the end of the 1970s, the value of crime prevention was recognized largely in terms of its problem-orientation, but as crime prevention has entered its community safety phase this problem-orientation has given way increasingly to a process-orientation, where inter-agency tactics and strategies appear to be as important as the crime prevention measures themselves. This might be regarded as inevitable, as situational crime prevention's implicit scientific rationality underestimated the irrationality, or at least conflicting rationalities, of the implementation process which it had to negotiate.

However, there is also a sense that things have become less easy as inter-agency relationships, and the wider context in which they operate, have become more complicated. In the mid-1980s, the Kirkholt Project, which was a forerunner of much of the community safety we see today, at one stage faltered under the weight of inter-agency difficulties, and sought clarification from the Home Office about whether the priority should be collaboration or crime prevention. The Home Office confirmed that the priority should be crime prevention. Today, however, one wonders whether a different answer might be given. The SRB, for example, is as interested in the demonstration of partnership as it is in what it might achieve, while the Safer Cities Programme's second phase is as interested in ensuring that a crime prevention infrastructure is left in place when the funding period ends as it is in anything else.

Once it was evident that crime prevention policy tended to ignore processes and focus exclusively on outcomes. Now this is less so, as processes have formed an important focus in securing the neo-corporatist objectives to which Crawford & Jones (1995) refer. However, in this process, attention has tended to be diverted from the intrinsic value of what is being aimed for. Consequently, the next chapter switches the focus to the transition from situational crime prevention to community safety, and subjects the latter, as the future of crime prevention, to critical scrutiny.

CHAPTER 8

Community safety and the politics of crime prevention

Introduction

In this final chapter we explore the shift from situational crime prevention to community safety in more detail, and consider the wider implications of this for future crime control. In so doing, we introduce a more structurally informed level of analysis to make sense of the change that has occurred, and to complement and contextualize some of the issues that have been raised in the course of this book.

In essence, earlier chapters have painted a picture of crime prevention as contested terrain, at the levels of both theory and practice. Its usefully imprecise meaning has been employed variously to promote different conceptions of the crime problem, and the interests of different political and occupational groups. This has been obscured to some degree by the scientific aspirations of prevention, especially in the post-war period when the new discourse of crime prevention was accompanied by pragmatism and a technical language that appeared largely apolitical, concerned mainly with the effective management of a crime problem that was increasingly beyond the control of more traditional approaches.

However, the politics was rarely far beneath the surface, and reappeared with a vengeance in the 1980s for a number of reasons. Principal among these was that while situational prevention was largely independent in origin, it held a strong elective affinity with a new right ideology that denied social causation and sought instead a punitive response to individually responsible offenders. This was an essential adjunct to the law and order society that appeared to be heralded in by an ambitious project of restructuring the state's welfare role, and the fall-out that resulted from this. Situational crime prevention was implicated in this. Moreover, the situational approach necessitated a managerial co-ordination of effort between, in the first place, public sector agencies, and at the mezzo-level this soon brought to light a number of territorial disputes and the evident power differentials between agencies.

This "re-politicization" of crime prevention, with its resultant tensions and contradictions, has been intensified by the subsequent supersession of the situational approach by community safety, which has had the effect of bringing in still more agencies from the mixed economy of crime control, including the exceptionally nebulous community itself. These agencies have brought in different conceptions of the crime problem, and an apparent liberalization of policy in so far as questions of causality have once again become legitimate, and crime prevention has moved from its narrower preoccupation with opportunity reduction and victims. Yet this is a very strange change to have occurred, because the restructuring of the state continues, and the situational approach still possesses a much stronger elective affinity with the strong state required as a corollary of the decentring logic of privatization and managerialism elsewhere. In what was once coined the great moving right show, community safety perversely appears to be moving in the opposite direction. The question to ask is why?

In Chapter 4 certain answers suggested themselves. For example, the rise of the discourse of community safety could be presented as an unintended consequence of a poorly judged invitation to agencies such as the probation service to participate in situational crime prevention initiatives, and their subsequent hijacking of such initiatives. However, given the way that such initiatives have been structured to favour opportunity reducing measures, and given the obvious problems that agencies such as the probation service have had in trying to make sense of their crime preventive role, this seems most unlikely.

An alternative explanation might portray situational crime prevention as a victim of its own success. As its impact has spread, especially to local authorities, so the Home Office's hold over its nature and direction has been weakened, and local authorities have increasingly been able to impose their own vision of crime prevention as community safety. There is some evidence of this because it is apparent that, following NACRO, community safety originated within the local authority sector. But in a context of increasing central dominance and control over local authorities and local affairs, the idea that the centre might tolerate this sort of local waywardness, in such a politically important area as law and order, seems most unlikely when it is not tolerated in other areas.

Tilley (1993a) reminds us that the Home Office lacks the enforcement apparatus and administrative machinery of other central departments, but even so this appears most unlikely, especially as the empirical reality is that most local authorities have only belatedly taken to community safety in the 1990s. Circular 8/84 made far less of an impact than 44/90 and the subsequent Morgan Report, yet by this time the community safety discourse had become well established within the Home Office, even if the terminology was not employed. This can be seen in the "hands off" management style that accompanied the Safer Cities Programme from its inception (Tilley 1993a), which allowed considerable scope for the development of community safety and a number of quite innovative projects, perhaps informed by an interdepartmental view of crime prevention that increasingly prevailed within central government from the late 1980s onwards.

It was always apparent that there was no intention that local authorities should be allowed to lead community safety, but it is by no means clear that this was because of a fear that control might be lost over the nature of crime prevention. Hence, even Crime Concern was charged to stimulate the local authority role, and local authorities were well placed to make much use of Safer Cities, even if they were never allowed to be managing agencies.

One last possible explanation for the transition to community safety mentioned briefly in Chapter 4 involves the skilled manipulation of the Home Office minister John Patten by a new guard of researchers and officials, who steered him to take note of what was happening elsewhere in Europe (indeed, community safety is a strong international theme in the 1990s). However, notwithstanding the probable accuracy of "Yes Minister" in its portrayal of a gullible and manipulable minister of government, there has to be some receptiveness to the idea in the first place. In this regard, the above-mentioned interdepartmental focus on crime prevention provided a possible reorientation to a different model of crime prevention, and Patten's introduction to Hope & Shaw's edited collection in 1988 demonstrates a clear incorporation of community safety into an ideological programme that stresses certain themes such as community and active citizenship.

The case remains, none the less, that both these themes are equally well served by situational crime prevention, and there is thus a need to continue our search for other factors that might explain the change to community safety.

The scope of situational crime prevention

One obvious explanation for the shift to community safety might be that situational crime prevention is actually limited in its effectiveness. This notion of its limitations comes through very powerfully from a number of critiques, and notably those that advocate a community safety alternative, under the logic that such an approach offers a more composite and holistic approach to the problem of crime. How valid is this critique?

The principal alleged weakness of situational crime prevention is displacement, which I have referred to elsewhere as its Achilles heel, but which Barr & Pease (1992: 197) more vividly refer to as "an albatross around the neck of purposive crime prevention". This allegation has been made by many commentators to the point at which it has become a taken for granted truth, especially among those who subscribe to a dispositional view of offending, which fails to see how blocking opportunities for crime can dull the deeply entrenched motivation to offend (Trasler 1986).

The possibility of displacement initially put advocates of situational crime prevention on the back foot. Clarke (1980) acknowledged that displacement seemed most likely among professional or highly motivated offenders, and least likely among opportunists, although since there were so many unguarded opportunities available at the time then there were always likely to be rich pickings easily available elsewhere. Moreover, as Clarke (1992) concedes, early research suggested that displacement did result, while Barr & Pease (1992) note that it is impossible to mount an empirical defence against the charge, because research is always limited by time, space and resources, whereas displacement is not, and its potential is ever-present. Consequently, where defences were made, they tended to be limited to examples where whole categories of crime were designed away, therefore putting criminal specialists out of business, but even this might only be for a while.

Through experience, however, confidence grew in the situational approach, and as it became theoretically articulated through rational choice theory so battle was joined with the critics. The new defence stressed that displacement was likely to be only partial. Empirical research evidence (Clarke 1992, Hesseling 1994) showed this to be the case, and was most persuasive where it drew upon interviews with offenders to demonstrate how effective opportunity reduction had been. This defence was accepted by those influential in UK policy-making circles (Heal & Laycock 1986), although even partial displacement could be perceived as a weakness. Nevertheless, supporters of the situational approach began to go on the offensive, shifting the burden of proof by pointing to the need for those measuring crime rate changes to take account of changes in the opportunity structure, offender population and the overall trend in crime rates before displacement could be proven. This effectively called a stalemate to this empirical line of enquiry, for these were as equally indeterminate as the possible forms of displacement.

In the 1990s, it is broadly accepted that displacement depends upon such factors as the relative ease, risk and attractiveness of other targets. However, it is also becoming more clear that while displacement is a potential problem for situational crime prevention, it is also a potential advantage, when what is being displaced is not the crime, but the crime prevention. Clarke (1992, 1995) has referred to this as the diffusion of benefits, where for various reasons small crime prevention initiatives may have a multiplier effect beyond their temporal and spatial confines.

Barr & Pease (1992), meanwhile, have expressed their dissatisfaction with much of the literature on displacement, with its sometimes crude and mechanistic zero-sum conceptualization of the term. They prefer to talk in terms of crime flux, which demonstrates the essentially fluid nature of the distribution of crime. Crime prevention initiatives impact upon this flux in ways that might be benign, malign or neutral. An obvious benign impact would be a quantitative reduction in rates of crime, but more controversially they argue that even without such a quantitative reduction crime can be deflected in qualitatively benign ways. This would occur, for example, where crime was deflected from areas with exceptionally high levels of crime, to areas with much lower levels, thereby effectively spreading the burden of criminal victimization. There is much sense and justice in such an argument, but it is one that is yet to find full favour with the criminal justice policy community, where, via the privatization of crime control, crime preventive effort often flows in the other direction. Nevertheless, it does serve to demonstrate that even where displacement does occur, it may not necessarily be a bad thing. Displacement is not a sound basis on which to reject the situational approach.

Another frequently found criticism is that the situational approach may be well suited to certain types of high visibility property crimes, but it is not applicable to other categories of crime, or to certain categories of offender. Stereotypically, opportunist property crimes may be amenable to opportunity reducing measures, but crimes of violence in particular are characterized by more deeply seated motivations that are less easy to manipulate by practical situational interventions, not least because they are also less static or predictable in their occurrence, and often occur within the private space of the home.

In a similar fashion, it is often claimed that situational crime prevention is inapplicable to the problem of youth crime, and it is noticeable that when different strategies of youth crime prevention are discussed by NACRO (1991) and Bright (1993) the situational approach is barely considered. The apparent inapplicability of the situational approach to youths should be of great concern, since statistics reveal that over half of all recorded crime is committed by youths, and that the peak age of offending for both sexes comes somewhere in the mid-teens. The argument runs that offending behaviour, of an admittedly minor nature, is a relatively normal part of growing up, which most youths grow out of. Rationality for youth, therefore, and particularly in the company of peer pressure, is to test boundaries, rather than to be deterred by the risk of apprehension. Consequently, the focus for intervention should not be opportunity reduction, but intervention in the family, the school and the community so that youths are able to identify the appropriate boundaries, and are given an opportunity to have a stake in society, particularly through the labour market.

These arguments have a similar dispositional feel to them as the one about displacement, and as criticisms of the situational approach *per se* they are misplaced. The concern that situational crime prevention relates only to a narrow range of property offences has more to do with how situational crime prevention has been used, than with where it may be used. Its problem-oriented nature has tended to direct it towards the most obvious and prevalent "problems" (Gilling 1996b), which are clearly most likely to be property crimes, which constitute approximately 95 per cent of all recorded crimes. Since it is most likely that an impact will be made on the overall crime rate by focusing upon these crimes, and since this is the political priority that drives the policy, it is not surprising that property crime about which most public anxiety has been expressed, notably residential burglary and vehicle crime, should form the mainstay of situational efforts.

In the latter half of the 1980s, however, there has been a certain change of emphasis as violent crime has become more intractable, and has become more of a focus of public anxiety. In this period, the versatility of the situational approach has been demonstrated as it has been applied with some success to the crimes of violence which it was assumed it did not fit. Consequently, where Stanko (1990) for example, was quite right to criticize government crime prevention publicity for neglecting domestic violence and indeed increasing the risk by portraying the home as a place of safety that needed to be target hardened from outside threats, the work of Lloyd et al. (1994) has served to demonstrate that this is not because situational technologies cannot be made to work towards the prevention of this kind of crime.

By the same token, the concern of advocates of youth crime prevention is that a narrow reliance on situational prevention will result in a lack of appreciation of why youths offend, and will make a punitive response more likely. But this is not a mark against the effectiveness of situational prevention so much as a concern about its integration within the rest of criminal justice or social policy. Situational prevention is principally about targeted crime reduction, rather than a panacea to the crime problem. Barr & Pease's (1992) idea of crime flux fits this picture well, and it is apparent that its impact can frequently be benign. Indeed, in the case of youth, for example, it is noticeable that the dip in the amount of youth offending in the 1980s and 1990s (Muncie et al. 1995) has corresponded with the rise of situational prevention, although the paucity of research on the decision-making of youth offenders makes any connection entirely speculative. If youth are seeking and probing boundaries, situational prevention makes it unambiguously clear where these boundaries lie.

Overall, then, while criticisms remain about the scope of situational crime prevention, they are not generally well founded, and they do not provide a sound basis on which to reject it as a viable effective crime prevention strategy, although it should be noted that it has not been rejected so much as having been incorporated within a broader approach to crime control. It should also be noted, however, that policy is not rational in the sense that old policies are only replaced because of their practical ineffectiveness, and in this case it is more important that these criticisms have been made, and hold some currency, than that they have a dubious scientific foundation.

The political and moral case against situational crime prevention

As the above section has made clear, the practical concerns about situational crime prevention tend to rest upon shaky foundations; but what, then, of other concerns that are more moral and political in origin? A frequently expressed worry is that situational measures tend to be oriented largely towards social exclusion: strangers or outsiders are the objects of an array of surveillance and security technologies intended to exclude them, but in so doing they generate a mutual suspicion and a profoundly anti-communitarian fortress mentality. This is socially divisive and renders the integration of offenders and other stigmatized and suspect groups increasingly problematic, but it is also extremely inconvenient for the law-abiding, and a potential infringement of their civil liberties (Clarke 1980). It is also assumed that it may contribute to something that has increasingly come to be regarded as a social problem in its own right, namely the fear of crime. Clarke is quite right to put up the defence that many situational measures are unobtrusive and far from being negative, and yet an enduring unease about situational crime prevention remains, in much the same way as the displacement allegation does. What basis does such an unease, or such a fear, have, and what is its wider significance?

Fear of crime is now considered to be an important rationale for preventive intervention in its own right. It is a principal means by which community safety may be distinguished from the situational approach, since the latter at best neglects it, and at worst, as noted above, is alleged to contribute to it. The growing political importance of the crime victim has had as its corollary an official concern with the fear of crime, for reasons that will become apparent in this section, although it should be pointed out that the fear of crime extends beyond the bounds of actual criminal victimization to include also potential victims, so that overall it reaches the status of a quite general social problem.

Fear of crime is, however, exceptionally difficult to measure, because fear is a subjective and nebulous concept. As Sparks (1992) observes, fear may be for one's self or for others, and it merges into other degrees of concern such as worry or anxiety. The main research instrument for measuring fear of crime has been a survey question relating to feelings of safety, especially in public spaces after dark, a measure that Walklate (1995) among others has shown to be woefully inadequate. The paradigm for fear of crime research in the UK has been established by the British Crime Survey, the origins of which lay partly in a conviction that such a survey would provide a more accurate representation of crime than that found in notoriously inaccurate media reporting and representations, which had been perceived to feed a concern completely disproportionate to the risk of criminal victimization. Thus the results of the first such survey were used in a bid to calm these disproportionate fears, especially among some sections of the population, by highlighting the apparent rarity of crime.

The British Crime Survey then, established a conception of fear only in terms of its relation to the risk of criminal victimization: in so far as the latter could be measured, the former could be described as either proportionate, and thus rational, or disproportionate, and thus irrational. This conception has been largely accepted by left realist local survey researchers, who have nevertheless challenged the official empirical portrayal of crime as a rare event. They have sought to demonstrate that in certain localities, and among certain social groups, the risk of crime was so great that an almost debilitating fear, which could significantly constrain the lifestyles of those who experienced it, was really quite rational. National statistical averages concealed a lot more than they revealed, except perhaps about the motive behind their use.

The left realist position has, however, been criticized for failing to move beyond the artificiality of this conception of fear as a response to risk, which is far from being realistic. Sparks (1992) points out that it is theoretically and empirically problematic to seek to attribute a proportionality to the relationship between risk and fear: who is to say what is proportionate and what is not, especially when fear is such a subjective phenomenon? Moreover, while the notion of risk exposes a characteristic desire of modernity to make uncertainty more knowable and actionable (Hollway & Jefferson 1995), it remains extremely difficult to measure accurately in the case of crime anyway.

More importantly, the relationship between risk, fear and behaviour is simply not as rational as the dominant paradigm implies, which is why, after all, there are risks much greater than those of criminal victimization that do not seem to bother us at all, even though they may be equally, if not more, serious in their impact upon our lives. Walklate (1995) makes an important contribution about the gendered nature of this: there is an assumption that risk should be accompanied by strategies of risk avoidance, yet much male behaviour may be governed more by the maxim of risk seeking – something that many young males become particularly adept at in the course of their weekend visits to the local hostelry.

Sparks prefers to conceive of fear as a product of uncertainty, which is itself a product of moral and political intuition, which is why some things bother us while others do not. Crime may be only one of a number of risks that we encounter in our daily lives, but it can elicit a response much greater than may at first appear justified because it can be taken as an indicator of more general concerns. These concerns are an amalgam of environmental cues, for "diffuse anxieties result from social representations of the social and physical environment, whose sources are broader than the risk of victimization as such" (1992: 128). This means that fear of crime and fear of place, which is where these cues are located, are inextricable linked. The disorders and crimes represented in Wilson & Kelling's (1982) "broken windows" thesis form part of these cues, as potentially do situational crime prevention measures, whose deployment signifies an area where trust has been lost.

This is where situational crime prevention measures enter the equation. Rationally, according to the dominant paradigm, situational crime prevention's contribution to the fear of crime debate should lie in its capacity to reduce it: preventive measures should reduce the risk and thus the corresponding fear. If we adopt Sparks' perspective, however, it does not work like this, and indeed a clue to this can be found anyway in the phenomenon of the inverse security law, whereby those least at risk are most likely to take preventive measures. This may partly be a consequence of the differential availability of the resources to purchase and deploy these measures, and there may be correspondingly more lifestyle changes to reduce risk in high crime areas, but it also probably reflects a differential response to uncertainty.

Preventive behaviour may, like fear, be a response or a product of uncertainty, but in a vicious circle it may also contribute to it as an environmental cue. This, as Clarke's (1980) defence implies, may depend upon the obtrusiveness of the measures, but it also depends very much upon individual responses, which as Hollway & Jefferson suggest depends in turn upon psychological factors. They argue, on the strength of some case study research, that

> Fear of crime . . . is an unconscious displacement of other fears which are far more intractable and do not display the modern characteristics of knowability and decisionability (or actionability) which adds up to the belief in one's capacity to control the external world. (1995: 8)

The individually contingent nature of this may perhaps provide a partial explanation for the nature of the debate on the contribution of situational crime prevention measures to fear. This is now played out in the context of the widespread adoption of CCTV in public space, and was formerly played out in differential research findings with respect to Neighbourhood Watch. Yet Hollway & Jefferson do not suggest that fear is entirely a product of individual psychology, and accept that it occurs within a structured context.

The nature of this context is clearly of considerable importance. Smith (1986a) for example, suggests that fear tends to be greatest in areas characterized by high levels of political and economic marginalization, areas where there is presumably much greater cause for uncertainty. But she is referring more to fear generated by crime than by situational crime prevention. Garland (1995), meanwhile, points to an almost pathological mistrust that we all have of surveillance, which is enhanced when it is embodied in technology rather than embedded in social life, and especially when it is perceived as being conducted on behalf of the state. The perception of CCTV certainly fits well into this, with its "Big Brother" connotations, although the majority of situational measures are not associated with the state to anything like the same degree.

The wider context must also include crime prevention policy itself, which has sought to make the risk of crime more knowable, and more actionable at the local or individual level, outside of the formal criminal justice system. Hollway & Jefferson (1995) cite the work of Douglas, who suggests that once risk has been identified in this way, the phenomenon of blaming can come into operation to fulfil certain functions. Thus victim-blaming enhances social control, whereby knowledge of the risk carries a certain obligation to act to prevent it, whereas outsider-blaming enhances loyalty. This is the focus of situational prevention.

This linking of the practice of crime prevention to the phenomenon of blaming is useful, and has a precedent in the work of Walklate (1991), whose analysis of crime prevention policy has charted a move through distinct phases of offender-blaming, victim-blaming, and now community-blaming, under the rubric of community safety. However, this only conceives of a one-way flow of blame, from the state or the criminal justice system to the public.

It is possible that blame may also flow in the opposite direction. Indeed, the policy of off-loading responsibility for crime control on to the community may have served to have generated a considerable amount of uncertainty that in turn feeds fear, as a sense of security, that the criminal justice system was up to the task of crime control, has been undermined. The policy might have been pursued for a number of political and ideological ends, as well as practical ones, but it might have had the unfortunate unintended consequence of contributing to what might be termed system-blaming, where we become conscious that we have to protect ourselves because of the ineffectiveness of the criminal justice system. The more we have to do this, the less we may trust the system. Thus, harking back to Sparks' (1992) point, situational crime prevention indicates lack of trust both in outsiders and in the system itself, with the lack of trust feeding fear. Consequently, fear of crime conceived in this way attains a greater significance than often assumed. It does not criticize the situational approach *per se*, so much as locate a particular criticism of the criminal justice system within its deployment. It is thus not a narrow, particularistic concern, but rather an element of the expression of a more general lack of confidence, and a legitimacy crisis for the state itself. Thus, whatever the inherent strengths and weaknesses of the situational approach, its position becomes untenable.

In a recent account of the situational approach, Clarke (1995: 92) makes the critical observation that "situational prevention conflicts with the mind-sets of criminologists and the vested interests of criminal justice practitioners." The above analysis helps to explain why, for criminal justice practitioners have traditionally been in the business of blaming in the ways identified by Walklate (1991), while Hollway & Jefferson (1995) rightly observe that criminology has traditionally provided an endless supply of scapegoats for them. But situational prevention, while it might certainly contain elements of this, also includes system-blaming, and this makes the system vulnerable, necessitating a defensive response.

If we relate this back to the question posed at the beginning of this chapter, then we can begin to see a possible argument for why the popularity of situational crime prevention declined when it did. It declined because too great a reliance upon it as a strategy of crime control had the effect of undermining confidence in the wider criminal justice system. Community safety thus becomes a means by which this confidence might be restored.

With the benefit of hindsight, it is possible to argue that some within the police were mindful of this at the beginning of the 1980s. Thus while they sought to devolve the responsibility for crime control to others, in the fashion, as some saw it, of discarding a hot potato, they nevertheless sought to ensure that their own position was not undermined by ensuring that the police remained at the hub of the collaborative wheel, and that the form of crime control pursued did not neglect either a social or a community dimension. Consequently, we reach an ironic position where, while many critics argue that the situational approach is the bedfellow of a punitive law and order ideology (although O'Malley (1992) argues this is not inevitably so), in practice it plays an important part in exposing the latter's weaknesses. The responsibility at the heart of the ideology translates into the blame that is a corollary of the identification of risk.

This account broadly fits that offered by Crawford (1995) via a different focus, which suggests that the move to a community orientation in crime prevention is linked to the problem of legitimacy, rather than practical expedience as others such as Hope & Shaw (1988) have argued. Crawford does not distinguish between the situational approach and community safety as we do here, but he does identify a persuasive argument for the attractiveness of community safety nevertheless. He suggests that while critical commentators in the early 1980s predicted a drift to a law and order society, in which a strong state was needed to govern a post-welfare society, in fact this has not happened. This is because the law and order machinery of the criminal justice system has been so ineffective, and hardly an aspect of a strong state. Thus all that has happened is that the legitimacy crisis has been displaced into the law and order arena. Precipitating factors to this crisis were identified in the course of Chapter 4 as contributing to the rise of situational crime prevention, but the implication of the above is that the situational approach has actually contributed to making the crisis more acute, hence its eventual incorporation into a broader community safety approach.

This suggests, then, that far from being a reformist rejoinder to the allegedly harsh situational approach, community safety has been inspired as much by right wing concerns, especially around the notion of active citizenship, but also incorporating the partnership approach. This potentially takes us back towards a position more in line with that adopted by King (1989) in his presentation of a specifically Thatcherite disciplinary version of social crime prevention, which, along with the situational approach, constitute the two main ingredients of community safety. This is similar to the conspiratorial model identified by Sampson et al. (1988), but as Crawford (1994) argues, this essentially instrumentalist account is as inadequate as a benevolent or managerialist account, which sees multi-agency crime prevention as a pragmatic, holistic systems-oriented solution to the problem of crime. As previously noted in Chapter 7, Crawford suggests that it is more accurate to conceive of the changes taking place in terms of the logic of neo-corporatism.

With regard to the account presented in this chapter, the importance of this neo-corporatism lies in its capacity to soften the hard edges of the situational approach, and crucially to regain public confidence. This is why fear of crime is a central focus of community safety, for as it is so difficult to conceive of, it is also difficult to tackle other than by measures that seek to inspire public confidence. Social crime prevention is also an important part of this, for the kinds of social measures that community safety strategies pursue are not the broad-based approaches that Currie (1992) argues are an essential element of a genuine social approach, but rather local, piecemeal efforts that are an important means by which the public, and especially the politically powerful sections thereof, can be convinced that they are not being left to their own devices in the fight against crime. This is why publicity and public relations are also so important to multi-agency crime prevention initiatives, for so much of it is about impression management.

This is not to suggest that community safety is a sham, and merely the expression of the aforementioned conspiratorial approach. Much of it is also genuine, but this genuineness must compete alongside other interests and motives in a neo-corporatist framework in which power is, as Crawford (1994) points out, fragmented. Indeed, it is the fragmentation of power that makes corporatism necessary in the first place. The state is an important player in this context, but its role is fragmented through the conflicting and contradictory ideologies of the different participating professional agencies it supports, and it is joined also by agencies from the voluntary, private and informal sectors, all of which serve to make practical outcomes to a considerable degree locally contingent.

The importance of the desire to inspire public confidence through community safety is further illustrated by the ideological usage of the term community, which as in so many other areas of public policy serves as something of a rallying call. This overlooks all the problems in operationalizing and working with the concept that, as Crawford (1995) describes, soon rise to the surface in practice, in much the same way as they do in the case of the equally ideological usage of the term partnership. These problems and tensions draw attention to the space for negotiation within neo-corporatism, which again demonstrates that outcomes are not conspiratorially structured, although Crawford (1994: 514) is forced to concede that "these new processes of decision-making and implementation, by their nature, tend to silence certain types of offending, forms of social intervention and questions of aetiology". In another article (1995: 120), nevertheless, he suggests that there are pressures against this structuring, embodied, for example, in those seeking more social approaches through alternative discourses of community safety and urban regeneration, both of which "require some [critical] examination of the structures of community".

Here our paths diverge somewhat, for we have previously argued that this structuring occurs within community safety, which is not a radical or reformist rejoinder, at least not in practice. As argued below, the same applies to urban regeneration, again as it is applied in practice. The important point to note, in concurrence with Crawford, is that while there are a number of conflicting pressures that give those promoting community safety an occasionally uncertain and bumpy ride, in general these can be managed in such a way that community safety can be kept on the political and ideological rails built for it. There are a number of mutually reinforcing means by which this may be achieved.

The first of these has already been mentioned, namely the ideological usage of the terms community and partnership. These bring together agencies in such a way that the symbolic purpose of the policy, namely that of legitimacy-building, is fulfilled. However, any attempts to go beyond this are fraught with the difficulties of attempting to operationalize the concepts, which are riddled with contradictions and a lack of appreciation of the power imbalances that exist in the real world. The conflict and stasis that result are potentially self-defeating, which Crawford (1995: 120) effectively acknowledges when he notes that "appeals to community involvement may serve to heighten the politics of crime". Community safety may be a bid for relegitimation, but it is not necessarily wholly effective as such.

A second means has also been previously discussed in the course of this book. Community safety operates in a context where, by virtue of such factors as resource constraint, and the differential distribution of resources, certain conceptions of crime problem and solution are prioritized over others. Thus, while situational prevention has to some extent become overshadowed by the broader community safety, it has not been eclipsed by it, and it still finds itself structurally advantaged within collaborative contexts where there is competition for priorities.

Thirdly, what some perceive optimistically as the liberating potential of community safety, to fully address the social causes of crime, has been significantly undermined by the criminalization of the discourse of social policy (Sampson et al. 1988). The move to a post-welfarist society has by definition reduced the availability of policies to mitigate the worst social consequences of late capitalism, but some have seen in social crime prevention and community safety an opportunity to redress the balance somewhat. However, the opportunity is constrained by the fact that social policy-type measures in pursuit of crime prevention must be justified mainly in terms of their potential to control crime, rather than in terms of social justice or some other equally justifiable end. This implies that the means by which the objective of crime control might be realized is different from the means by which other objectives might be realized. To employ a much abused, but nevertheless useful distinction, it becomes more about control than care, where those "in need" are so by virtue of their being dangerous – at risk of criminality – rather than because they are deserving as citizens.

It is important at this point to be reminded that crime, by its very nature, is a source of conflict more than a source of solidarity, as victim or potential victim is pitched against offender or potential offender. Smith (1987: 63) stresses this point, and although he is referring to community policing, the same holds true of community safety, where "the idea of community does not seem to provide us with a model for dealing with these conflicts". Offenders and potential offenders remain largely unrepresented and unwanted, and things that are done for them, or to them, often end up being more consistent with a right wing version of social crime prevention than with a reformist reclamation of welfare policy. This may entail the betrayal of client confidentialities, and the identification of problem families in localized multi-agency initiatives.

Fourthly, and finally, the linking of community safety to the wider objective of urban regeneration has had a constraining influence on the nature of such an enterprise. This is because the goals of community safety have effectively become subordinated to the goals of urban regeneration, which since the early 1980s has increasingly meant seeking to effect a property-led private sector reinvestment in urban areas. Thus, in such a context, the purpose of community safety is less to attain changes in the social fabric, and more to create an attractive environment (Deakin & Edwards 1993) in which changes in the physical environment become viable, with any social improvements confined to an unconvincing trickle down effect purported to result from the private investment.

The capacity of local areas to resist this has been increasingly undermined by the incentives made available through a competitive bidding process such as the single regeneration budget, which is no longer confined in its applicability to the most depressed urban areas, and is thus a carrot available to all. Moreover, the structure of this bidding process provides a further check, in so far as bids must demonstrate a partnership with the private sector, which Chapter 6 suggested has a limited expertise or interest in crime prevention, as well as the community at large. Also, bids must demonstrate an attempt to maximize leverage of private sector investment.

All of this means, if one adopts a cynical view, that the demonstration of an actual reduction in crime, or of a viable plan to address the long-term causes, is rather less important than the public relations value of showing that something is being done, combined perhaps with an approach that demarcates areas for economic improvement without having much regard to surrounding neighbourhoods. The emphasis may be placed firmly upon social exclusion from areas of improvement, with a concern over potential crime displacement not figuring high on the agenda. Any community safety may then be as much about confining criminogenic communities to their usually depressed neighbourhoods, rather than liberating them from these. In this way, one can see that the legitimacy concerns precipitated by the exclusive focus on the situational approach in the context of rising crime and anxiety were considered most significant when they appeared to touch private sector confidence. The Safer Cities Programme from 1988 sought to restore confidence and legitimacy by tackling the crime and fear that were presented as problems for private sector investment as much as anything else.

This may be a negative reading of the contemporary direction of community safety, but it is one largely justified if the structural constraints of the crime control policy surrounding it are taken into consideration. This calls into question the wider effectiveness of community safety as a strategy of crime control. The situational approach may have often reduced crime at a highly localized level, but at a political cost: might community safety not reduce the crime, but at least not incur the political cost?

The effectiveness of community safety

The implication of the foregoing discussion is that community safety exists more comfortably at the level of rhetoric than at the level of practice, where it is limited by some serious structural constraints. Thus, as a managerial solution to the problem of crime, its rationality is bounded by the political bid for relegitimation by the incumbent government, with which it is closely entwined, and that seemingly guarantees a range of tensions, conflicts and contradictions. In its objective of becoming a meaningful holistic approach against crime, the odds are therefore clearly stacked against it.

The emphasis upon legitimacy within community safety is not in fact confined to a right wing political project. Community safety and its associated theoretical holism is also closely related to the left realist notion of the square of crime (Young 1994). This has a practical application as a model of effective crime control through which the four elements of the square – informal and formal social control, the victim and the offender – must each be addressed. Underpinning this is an emphasis upon localism, expressed as local democratic control through structures of accountability intended to fetter the power of certain statutory agencies such as the police.

We can make an artificial but heuristically useful distinction here and move on from these broader issues to narrower concerns about efficiency and effectiveness. Community safety initially employs the term community in a territorial sense, and is most appropriately suited to residential neighbourhoods that have both high offender and offence rates, and that by their very nature therefore require a holistic approach. This is not only because they are presumed to contain high numbers of offenders and victims, but also because they are presumed to be disorganized in terms of their informal social controls, in a classic Chicagoan sense (Barton & Gilling 1995, Crawford 1995), where community is used more to imply a sense of attachment. Moreover, they are often areas where public services are most problematic. Therefore, all four elements of the square of crime demand attention.

Typically such high crime neighbourhoods are found in areas of municipal housing, in the "difficult to let" or "problem" estates that have appeared across the social landscape in the post-war period, often as a consequence of housing allocation policies and the historical dumping of "problem" families (Bottoms & Wiles 1988). Foster & Hope's (1993) reading of the 1988 British Crime Survey confirms this concentration of high crime rates in areas of municipal housing.

Community safety entails consideration of a range of strategies designed to address the perceived problems of these neighbourhoods, from protecting potential and actual victims (who coincide over the phenomenon of multiple victimization) via situational measures, to helping or controlling offenders, reinvigorating informal social controls, and ensuring a correct fit between these and formal controls. However, the effectiveness of these solutions is inextricably linked to their fitness for the purpose, and in this regard many of the assumptions underpinning community safety may be found wanting.

The assumption, for example, that these high crime neighbourhoods are also disorganized communities in need of organization, may be quite wrong. Thus Bottoms & Wiles's (1988) extensive research in Sheffield has demonstrated that some high crime neighbourhoods are remarkably well organized as "criminal subculture" estates. By contrast, Foster's (1995) valuable ethnographic work has shown that neighbourhoods with relatively high crime rates need not be disorganized or criminal, and in such areas crime may be managed without attaining the status of a problem. She cites Hope (1986: 71) in warning against the "tendency to take the impact of crime as given". The normative assumption of a simple single equilibrium to the square of crime evidently can be deeply misleading, and can lead to community safety presenting itself as a solution in search of an appropriate problem.

Where communities are disorganized and comply to the normative model, community safety initiatives may still have difficulty in locating them, for a number of reasons. Clarke (1987), for example, describes a long-term change in community life in high crime areas where once there was an element of security despite the crime, but now, via sociologically well documented processes of individualization and privatization, and the extension of citizenship rights that has encouraged increased reliance on formal social controls, there is none. This has been exacerbated by high levels of fear, which, as noted above, is a psychological manifestation of individual concerns, situated within a broader context of uncertainty that feeds off other social and economic forces (Currie 1988). The result is both a psychological and physical withdrawal and the erection of barriers to trust between residents (Curtis 1988). In such a situation, to employ Rosenbaum's (1988) typology of methods of community crime prevention, it is much easier to effect personal and household prevention, than neighbourhood prevention.

In these kinds of neighbourhood, it may be difficult to make contact with communities, because there is little in the way of association between members, and there is certainly little in the way of the homogeneity that underpins the community ideology. Consequently, one strategy that may be employed by community safety initiatives is what Graham & Bennett (1995: 74) refer to as community organization, which is "based primarily in the principle that communities can be organized to reduce crime indirectly by strengthening the social processes which regulate behaviour such as informal social control". Foster & Hope (1993: 13) describe this as neighbourhoodism, based upon the idea that "Visible signs of positive investment in the estate may strengthen the community to resist the growth of crime."

This, however, assumes a correlation between improved informal social controls and crime reduction that need not inevitably be the case. It also assumes there is a latent community to be activated, as if there is nothing between organized and disorganized communities. In practice, however, Crawford (1995) describes what may actually happen, as agencies neglect many of these difficulties and are driven forward by the attraction of being seen to be doing something. They are thus too eager to claim they have established contact with the community, and strengthened it in so doing, when in fact they have only established contact with unrepresentative elements of it. These are often the most organized and respectable elements of the neighbourhood. As with participants on police consultative committees (Morgan 1987), the activities and attitudes of these people have little bearing on the activities and attitudes of the greater proportion of non-participants (Skogan 1990). Moreover, the corollary of establishing unrepresentative communities is that others tend to be ghettoized or excluded (Crawford 1995), so that initiatives end up merely reflecting the divisions that exist within them or, worse, reinforcing them and giving them a spurious legitimacy as alternative electoral channels of representation are circumvented.

While there are many forms of social division within these neighbourhoods, the most pertinent and the most problematic for community safety is that which exists between offenders and the rest. Community safety employs an inclusionary ideology of community that overlooks the difficulties when this is applied to offenders: the neat distinction between insider and outsider does not hold in these high crime areas. The community safety solution to this is to engage in what Graham & Bennett (1995: 90) refer to as community development, where much of the focus is upon "the need to reintegrate young people at risk of offending back into the community" by mobilizing families, peers, neighbours, schools, places of employment and other community organizations. But just how likely is this in areas where fear and a lack of trust typically hold sway?

There may be an established tradition of community participation in good deeds associated with youth, but there may be problems if such things are closely associated with crime prevention. In so far as such deeds have social ends beyond crime control ones, then participation may decline with the ebbs and flows of the crime problem so that the social ends may be lost – this is one possible consequence of the criminalization of the discourse of social policy previously discussed above. Moreover, altruistic participation tends to be conditional, with certain groups favoured over others. Children are perceived as a good cause, but older youths and other offenders and suspected offenders are not, and attitudes towards them may be both punitive and discriminatory. Scull (1983) makes a similar point with regard to the communitarian ideology underpinning the decarceration movement, and in the case of community safety, Foster & Hope's assessment of the Priority Estates Project offers a similarly gloomy conclusion:

> In the light of this study, it would seem unrealistic to expect many residents to be able or willing to exert much direct influence over the behaviour of those involved in crime and disorder on the estate. Thus the means to tackle the causes of that criminality which is directed by some residents against others may need to be sought elsewhere. (1993: 92)

The above quote points to the basic fallibility of community safety as a strategy of crime control. It seeks to bring the four elements of the square of crime together into a highly localized managerial infrastructure of community and corporatism, but in so doing encounters a number of hurdles. In particular, high crime communities remain fundamentally divided, so that there is no basis for a reconciliation between victim and offender, even when these are one and the same person. There is also little basis for collective informal social control, and thus the point at which this meets with formal control agencies remains vague and ill-defined, especially as these latter are hardly bound together in a consensual mould.

Despite the goodwill and commitment of those involved, community safety is hardly likely to be effective, but then this may not be its main purpose. Rather, as noted above, it is part of a bid for legitimacy in which, as Reiner & Cross (1991: 10) identify, the government has effectively made a U-turn in criminal justice policy, relying upon the concept of community, "with all its imprecise aura of vacuous virtue". This vacuousness has entailed a consensual ideology that ignores the vital fact that communities work less by consensus than by negotiated compromises variously entailing threats, exchanges and other integrative processes (Weiss 1987). The assumption, then, that consensual communities are the crime control ideal belies the possibility that community is not so much the means to an end as an end in itself (Nelken 1985). The ideal community, thus conceived, represents a premodern vision of certainty and security, in place of the uncertainty and fluidity in social relations that are characteristic of late modernity, and that have been exacerbated by contemporary socio-economic policy (Lacey & Zedner 1995). Ironically, it recalls a capacity for self-policing that to an extent characterized older working-class communities, but that the so-called Fordist project (Lea 1995) broke up because of their assumed criminogenic nature.

Despite the weak foundations of community, community safety nevertheless succeeds in often bringing together an imposing local corporate structure, mixing formal and informal sources of control. Since, however, the informal sources lack a general capacity for self-policing, then in a context of consumerism it may be that community safety provides a means by which the support of "respectable society" may be mobilized for control strategies that reflect their sectional interests (Squires & Measor 1995). In other words, community safety may enhance legitimacy by opening up channels for communication and influence for respectable society, which had increasingly begun to doubt the competence of the criminal justice system elsewhere. But since the communication is confined to respectable society, it is only partial, and the decentralized structures of community safety do not translate as meaningful local accountability.

While those such as Matthews (1992: 39) might argue for "more comprehensive and socialized forms of policing" as an alternative to partial approaches, their faith that these might be delivered through partnership or community approaches seems misplaced. Community interests are partial (Crawford 1995), and where communities are weak the appeal ultimately translates as an appeal to individual interests (Nelken 1985). Weiss (1987: 129) neatly captures the implications of this when he writes that "local community involvement holds out the promise of solidarity on the one hand, and the probability of parochial intolerance on the other". Wilson & Kelling's (1982) solution to the broken windows problem falls into this category (Matthews 1992) since the policing of incivilities inevitably entails acting in the interests of one section of the community against another, thus risking the latter's alienation, to the overall detriment to the goal of crime control.

In such a scenario, community safety plays into the hands of the more articulate and better organized sections of the community, whose rate of victimization may be inversely related to their intolerance of incivility. However, the control of the direction of community safety does not reside wholly within this local "market-place": the decentring/recentring dialectic that Crawford identifies ensures it also exists at the centre (Johnston 1993), where the objective is persuasive governance rather than coercive governance (Lacey & Zedner 1995). To complete the picture, moreover, we must add the organized interests of agency representatives, who seek to pull community safety in yet other directions. Consequently, what tends to get portrayed as administrative or managerial issues in fact raises important political and ethical issues (Johnston 1993).

With so many different interests, at macro-, mezzo- and micro-levels, it is understandable that Matthews (1992: 47) should warn against "strategies . . . which seek to "implant" a solution without influencing the complex matrix of social relations in a particular locality". Strategies need to be moored to such a complex, yet the use of the term community more usually ends up cutting them adrift. The result is that once again outcomes may be locally contingent, something that Nelken (1985) suggests we should not be surprised at, since community approaches may be variously intended as being in, for, or by the community. The choice is often a political one, dependent upon the relative power of different interests, which the ideology of community unhelpfully obscures.

The outcomes that community safety initiatives might have can, however, be over-exaggerated and over-determined. Lacey & Zedner (1995: 308) concede that attempts to recreate communities never work, which raises "a constant danger that the rhetorical postulate of community conceals more important and less politically palatable aspects of the policies at issue". There is a tendency for some to assume this danger is automatically realized, for example in the form of disciplinary dispersal (S. Cohen 1979: 350), in which "The machine might in some respects be getting softer, but it is not getting smaller."

Cohen is deeply critical of moves towards community crime control, in which, in his view, forms of inclusionary and exclusionary control are blended into a totalizing structure of state penetration, organized especially around the principle of bifurcation (Cohen 1985). His accounts have been very influential, portraying a worst case scenario in which the state and its various control technologies comes to consume civil society, thereby realizing our worst fears about a surveillance state (Garland 1995: 3) where "given the routine abuses of power that occur, and the clear divergences of interest between state authorities and those over whom they exercise control, most of us have a lot to be paranoid about".

Others, however, have been critical of Cohen's account of "the punitive city' (S. Cohen 1979), pointing out that patterns of penal policy have in fact demonstrated the relative expansion of things such as fines, which could hardly be described as disciplinary in the Foucauldian sense (Bottoms 1983). Bottoms notes that while Cohen might correctly identify an increased penetration of the state into civil society, the form of this penetration is misread, with all state power being conceived of as disciplinary power. Foucault, who was a strong influence on Cohen's work at this time, actually conceived of forms of power other than just discipline, and Bottoms notes that this has been manifested in other forms, such as bureaucratic-administrative systems to manage the various technologies that order specific aspects of our lives, and welfarism, which generates its own penetrative dynamic when people increasingly look to formal solutions to "social problems". The success of these latter two forms of power, moreover, facilitate the exercise of another, in the form of classical judicial instruments such as the fine.

Bottoms does not suggest that disciplinary strategies do not exist: they are much in evidence for those excluded through the process of bifurcation. Moreover, he concedes that it is possible that policy might move in an increasingly disciplinary direction, and while he is careful to separate words from deeds, he suggests that the Conservative emphasis on law and order and anti-welfarism might presage such a move. Indeed, Lea (1995) points out that things have changed substantially in this direction since Bottoms' chapter was written in the early 1980s, and we have seen a return to a more generalized form of surveillance and discipline as a means of managing the underclass.

It may be, then, that recent developments such as community safety represent the corporatist and managerial interweaving of a number of discrete control strategies. Lowman et al.'s (1987: 10) work across a broader context suggests that "transcarceration" might be a useful term for such a phenomenon:

> Within such a conceptual schema, control comprises and infiltrates many levels of discourse, and many arenas of action. It defies simple encapsulation in the rigid dichotomies of traditional analysis. As a fully reflexive social force it simultaneously serves and constitutes many interests. It is both coercive and benevolent, an instrument of the state and a weapon of resistance, an ideological medium and a counter-hegemonic force.

This notion fits better with Cohen's later work on the subject (1985, 1987), in which, despite a general pessimism about the nature and direction of this decentralized community control, he is prepared to adopt a "moral pragmatist" position that acknowledges certain positive developments, and more preferable outcomes compared to what went before. Indeed, this is a key point about community safety, because while there might be parts to which some people might object, by virtue of its holism there will also be parts to which they will show approval. It has something for everyone, and the fragmented power structure through which it is mediated ensures that whereas some interests might dominate others, this domination is never total. Power is productive as well as negative or repressive, and there is always some scope or arena for its exercise that renders reductionist accounts unwise and inaccurate. Thus, for example, Sutton (1994) warns against dismissing community safety as an extension of state social control, as there is something in it for liberal sensibilities, and the law and order alternative is no better. His position here is identical to that of Cohen's.

The "something for everyone" appeal of community safety demonstrates its value as a strategic bid for legitimation from a government vulnerable on its law and order record. In terms of political economy, given its accompaniment by a fall-back position of enhanced police powers, a disciplinary prison building programme and an increasingly prescriptive and harsh sentencing policy, it also suggests that the crisis it is responding to is more one of legitimacy than fiscal. It can do this, moreover, because it embodies the Foucauldian notion of "governmentality". It incorporates all forms of control, with the balance between them being determined less by questions of effectiveness than by the balance of political programmes (O'Malley 1992).

Hence while the basic preventive approach relies upon a form of actuarialism, its character has generally changed from socialized to privatized, or what O'Malley called prudentialism. But the change is one of degree, rather than being total, and it is managed, for example, by keeping local authorities (until May 1997 of a different political persuasion to central government) in a supporting role. It is also managed by keeping community safety strategies small scale and highly localized (Sutton 1994), so that broader social approaches of the sort advocated by Currie (1992) may be kept off the agenda without this appearing to amount to a political objection. King (1991) is wrong to suggest that social approaches are dissociated from crime prevention policy: rather, they are quite associated, but in a localized and contained fashion. He reads such a policy from the publicity and the rhetoric, which is aimed mostly at enhancing active citizenship, and where the social approach understandably receives less attention.

This is all part of a strategy that Stenson (1995: 11) calls governing at a distance, where "the attempt [is] to harness individual dreams and desires to wider collective goals". This applies equally to supporters of situational or social modes of crime prevention, and the spatial element is important as a symbolic reclamation of territory, as strategies of sovereignty and actuarialism merge.

The great irony in all this is that questions of crime preventive effectiveness take on only a marginal significance, especially as the overall crime rate changes by which governments are judged are more likely to be affected by broader socio-economic forces, than by small-scale initiatives. The attraction of the situational approach, which in retrospect may have been more political than practical, may have temporarily raised the stock of a rational choice criminology and hard-nosed policy-related research, but the rise of community safety has more conspicuously restored the equilibrium. The scientific pursuit of cause and cure is now exposed as useful only in so far as it serves the political pursuit of legitimacy, to govern errant populations and allay the anxiety and uncertainty of the modern condition.

Bibliography

Akers, R. 1990. Rational choice, deterrence, and social learning theory in criminology: the path not taken. *Journal of Criminal Law and Criminology* **81**, 653–76.

Alderson, J. 1983. Community policing. See Bennett (1983).

Andrews, D. & J. Burrows 1988. Key elements in fostering prevention. See Shapland & Wiles (1988).

Association of Chief Officers of Probation. 1985. *ACOP response to Circular 8/84*. Wakefield: Association of Chief Officers of Probation.

Association of Chief Officers of Probation. 1993. *Working with information for crime prevention*. London: Association of Chief Officers of Probation.

Association of District Councils. 1990. *Promoting safer communities – a district council perspective*. London: Association of District Councils.

Association of District Councils. 1994. *Joining forces against crime*. London: Association of District Councils.

Association of Metropolitan Authorities. 1990. *Crime reduction: a framework for the 1990s?* London: Association of Metropolitan Authorities.

Atkinson, C. 1969. *Jeremy Bentham: his life and works*. New York: Augustus Kelly.

Baldwin, J. 1979. Ecological and areal studies in Great Britain and the United States. In *Crime and justice* Volume 1, N. Morris & M. Tonry (eds). Chicago: University of Chicago Press.

Barr, R. & K. Pease 1992. A place for every crime and every crime in its place. An alternative perspective on crime displacement. See Evans, Fyfe, Herbert (1992).

Barrett, S. & C. Fudge (eds) 1981. *Policy and action*. London: Methuen.

Barton, A. & D. Gilling 1995. Community safety and community crime control: exclusion and surveillance, or inclusion and empowerment? Paper presented at Ideas of Community Conference, University of the West of England, Bristol, England.

Bean, P. 1983. Utilitarianism and the welfare state. In *Approaches to welfare*, P. Bean & S. MacPherson (eds). London: Routledge & Kegan Paul.

Becker, G. 1968. Crime and punishment: an economic approach. *Journal of Political Economy* **76**, 169–217.

Bennett, T. (ed.) 1983. *The future of policing*. Cambridge: Institute of Criminology.

Bennett, T. 1989. The neighbourhood watch experiment. In *Coming to terms with policing*, R. Morgan & D. Smith (eds). London: Routledge.

Bennett, T. 1990. *Evaluating neighbourhood watch*. Aldershot: Gower.

Bennett, T. 1992. Themes and variations in neighbourhood watch. See Evans, Fyfe, Herbert (1992).

Bentham, J. 1791. *Panopticon*. London: T. Payne.

Billis, D. 1981. At risk of prevention. *Journal of Social Policy* **10**(3), 367–79.

Blagg, H., A. Sampson, G. Pearson, D. Smith, P. Stubbs 1988. Inter-agency co-operation: rhetoric and reality. See Hope & Shaw (1988).

Bottoms, A. 1974. Review of 'Defensible Space'. *British Journal of Criminology* **14**, 203–6.

Bottoms, A. 1983. Neglected features of contemporary penal systems. In *The power to punish*, D. Garland & P. Young (eds). London: Heinemann.

Bottoms, A. 1990. Crime prevention facing the 1990s. *Policing and Society* **1**, 3–22.

Bottoms, A. 1993. Recent criminological and social theory. The problem of integrating knowledge about individual criminal acts and careers and areal dimensions of crime. In *Integrating individual and ecological aspects of crime*, D. Farrington & P-O. Wikstrom (eds). Stockholm: National Council for Crime Prevention.

Bottoms, A. 1994. Environmental criminology. See Maguire, Morgan, Reiner (1994).

Bottoms, A., R. Mawby, P. Xanthos 1989. A tale of two estates. See Downes (1989).

Bottoms, A. & W. McWilliams 1979. A non-treatment paradigm for probation practice. *British Journal of Social Work* **9**, 159–202.

Bottoms, A. & S. Stevenson 1992. What went wrong? Criminal justice policy in England and Wales, 1945–1970. In *Unravelling criminal justice*, D. Downes (ed.). London: Routledge.

Bottoms, A. & P. Wiles 1988. Crime and housing policy: a framework for crime prevention analysis. See Hope & Shaw (1988).

Braithwaite, J. 1989. *Crime, shame and reintegration*. Cambridge: Cambridge University Press.

Brake, M. & C. Hale 1992. *Public order and private lives*. London: Routledge.

Brantingham, P. 1979. The classical and positive schools of criminology: two ways of thinking about crime. In *Juvenile justice philosophy*, F. Faust & P. Brantingham (eds). St. Paul, Minnesota: West Publishing.

Brantingham. P. & P. Brantingham 1991. *Environmental criminology*, 2nd edn. Prospect heights, Illinois: Waveland Press.

Brantingham, P. & P. Brantingham 1991. Introduction: the dimensions of crime. See Brantingham & Brantingham (1991).

Brantingham, P. & P. Brantingham 1993. Environment, routine, and situation: toward a pattern theory of crime. See Clarke & Felson (1993).

Brantingham, P. & F. Faust 1976. A conceptual model of crime prevention. *Crime & Delinquency* **22**, 284–96.

Brantingham, P. & C. Jeffery 1991. Crime, space and criminological theory. See Brantingham & Brantingham (1991).

Bright, J. 1987. Community safety, crime prevention and the local authority. See Willmott (1987).

Bright, J. 1991. Crime prevention: the British experience. See Stenson & Cowell (1991).

Bright, J. 1993. Youth crime prevention and social policy. In *People in cities*, R. Hambleton & M. Taylor (eds). Bristol: SAUS.

Brody, M. 1976. *The effectiveness of sentencing*. Research study number 35. London: Home Office.

Bryant, M. 1989. *The contribution of ACOP and probation services to crime prevention*. Wakefield: Association of Chief Officers of Probation.

Burrows, J. 1991. *Making crime prevention pay: initiatives from business*. Crime Prevention Unit Paper 27. London: Home Office.

Burton, P. 1995. Urban policy in post-war Britain. In *British social welfare*, D. Gladstone (ed.). London: University of Central London Press.

Central Council of Probation Committees. 1987. *Crime prevention: a role for probation committees*. London: CCPC.

Challis, L., S. Fuller, M. Henwood, R. Klein, W. Plowden, A. Webb, P. Whittingham, G. Wistow (eds) 1988. *Joint approaches to social policy: rationality and practice*. Cambridge: Cambridge University Press.

Clarke, M. 1987. Citizenship, community and the management of crime. *British Journal of Criminology* **27**, 384–400.

Clarke, R. 1980. Situational crime prevention: theory and practice. *British Journal of Criminology* **20**, 136–47.

Clarke, R. 1983. Situational crime prevention: its theoretical basis and practical scope. In *Crime and justice* Volume 4, M. Tonry & N. Morris (eds). Chicago: University of Chicago Press.

Clarke, R. (ed.) 1992. *Situational crime prevention: successful case studies*. New York: Harrow and Heston.

Clarke, R. 1995. Situational crime prevention. See Tonry & Farrington (1995).

Clarke, R. & D. Cornish (eds) 1983. *Crime control in Britain: a review of policy research.* Albany: State University of New York Press.

Clarke, R. & M. Felson 1993. Introduction. See Clarke & Felson (1993).

Clarke, R. & M. Felson (eds) 1993. *Routine activity and rational choice.* New Brunswick: Transaction.

Clarke, R. & M. Hough (eds) 1980. *The effectiveness of policing.* Farnborough: Gower.

Clarke, R. & P. Mayhew (eds) 1980. *Designing out crime.* London: HMSO.

Cleveland County Council. 1991. *Crime prevention, community safety: what tasks? whose responsibility?* Middlesbrough: Cleveland County Council.

Cohen, L. & M. Felson 1979. Social change and crime rate trends: a routine activity approach. *American Sociological Review* 44, 588–608.

Cohen, P. 1979. Policing the working-class city. In *Capitalism and the rule of law: from deviancy theory to marxism,* B. Fine, R. Kinsey, J. Lea, S. Picciotto, J. Young (eds). London: Hutchinson.

Cohen, S. 1979. The punitive city: notes on the dispersal of social control. *Contemporary Crises* 3, 339–63.

Cohen, S. 1981. Footprints on the sand: a further report on criminology and the sociology of deviance in Britain. In *Crime and society,* M. Fitzgerald, G. McLennan, J. Pawson (eds). London: Routledge & Kegan Paul.

Cohen, S. 1985. *Visions of social control.* Cambridge: Polity Press.

Cohen, S. 1987. Taking decentralisation seriously: values, visions and policies. See Lowman, Menzies, Palys (1987).

Cohen, S. 1988. Criminology and the sociology of deviance in Britain: a recent history and a current report. In *A history of British criminology,* P. Rock (ed). Oxford: Oxford University Press.

Coleman, A. 1989. Disposition and situation: two sides of the same crime. See Evans & Herbert (1989).

Coleman, A. 1990. *Utopia on trial,* 2nd edn. London: Hilary Shipman.

Colquhoun, P. 1969. *A treatise on the police of the metropolis.* Montclair: Patterson Smith.

Cornish, D. 1993. Theories of action in criminology: learning theory and rational choice approaches. See Clarke & Felson (1993).

Cornish, D. & R. Clarke (eds) 1986a. *The reasoning criminal.* New York: Springer Verlag.

Cornish, D. & R. Clarke 1986b. Introduction. See Cornish & Clarke (1986).

Cornish, D. & R. Clarke 1986c. Situational prevention, displacement of crime and rational choice theory. See Heal & Laycock (1986).

Cornish, D. & R. Clarke 1987. Understanding crime displacement: an application of rational choice theory. *Criminology* **25**, 933–47.

Crawford, A. 1994. The partnership approach to community crime prevention: corporatism at the local level? *Social and Legal Studies* **3**, 497–519.

Crawford, A. 1995. Appeals to community and crime prevention. *Crime, Law and Social Change* **22**, 97–126.

Crawford, A. & M. Jones 1995. Inter-agency co-operation and community-based crime prevention. *British Journal of Criminology* **35**, 17–33.

Crawford, A. & M. Jones 1996. Kirkholt revisited; some reflections on the transferability of crime prevention initiatives. *Howard Journal*, **35**, 21-39.

Crime Concern 1989. *Looking ahead: 1989 conference report.* Swindon: Crime Concern.

Crime Concern undated. *Tackling crime: a professional approach.* Swindon: Crime Concern.

Croft, J. 1980. Foreword. See Clarke & Mayhew (1980).

Cubbon, B. 1988. Business and crime: the way forward. See Shapland & Wiles (1988).

Currie, E. 1988. Two visions of community crime prevention. See Hope & Shaw (1988).

Currie, E. 1992. International developments in crime and social policy: market and society and social disorder. See NACRO (1992).

Curtis, L. 1988. The march of folly: crime and the underclass. See Hope & Shaw (1988).

Davidson, N. 1993. New directions in environmental criminology. In *Crime and the urban environment*, H. Jones (ed.). Aldershot: Avebury.

Davidson, R. 1981. *Crime and environment.* London: Croom Helm.

Davidson, S. 1976. Planning and co-ordination of social services in multi-organisational contexts. *Social Services Review* **50**, 117–37.

Deakin, N. & J. Edwards 1993. *The enterprise culture and the inner city.* London: Routledge.

van Dijk, J. 1990. Crime prevention policy: current state and prospects. In *Crime and criminal policy in Europe*, G. Kaiser & H. Albrecht (eds). Freiburg: Max Planck Institute.

Dinwiddy, J. 1989. *Bentham.* Oxford: Oxford University Press.

Donnison, H., J. Scola, P. Thomas 1986. *Neighbourhood watch: policing the people.* London: Libertarian Research and Education Trust.

Dowds, L. & P. Mayhew 1994. *Participation in neighbourhood watch: findings from the 1992 British Crime Survey.* London: Home Office Research and Planning Unit.

Downes, D. 1989. Introduction. See Downes (1989).

Downes, D. (ed.) 1989. *Crime and the city.* Basingstoke: MacMillan.

Downes, D. & R. Morgan 1994. Hostages to fortune? The politics of law and order in post-war Britain. See Maguire, Morgan, Reiner (1994).

Downes, D. & P. Rock. 1995. *Understanding deviance*, revised 2nd edn. Oxford: Oxford University Press.

Ekblom, P. 1994. Towards a discipline of crime prevention: a systematic approach to its nature, range and concepts. Paper presented at 22nd Cropwood Conference, Cambridge, England.

Emsley, C. 1983. *Policing and its context 1750–1870*. London: Macmillan.

Evans, D., N. Fyfe, D. Herbert (eds) 1992. *Crime, policing and place*. London: Routledge.

Evans, D. & D. Herbert (eds) 1989. *The geography of crime*. London: Routledge.

Eysenck, H. 1977. *Crime and personality*, 3rd edn. London: Routledge & Kegan Paul.

Farrell, G. & K. Pease 1993. *Once bitten, twice bitten: repeat victimisation and its implications for crime prevention*. Crime Prevention Unit Paper 46. London: Home Office.

Farrington, D. 1992. Criminal career research: lessons for crime prevention. *Studies on Crime and Crime Prevention* 1, 7–29.

Feeney, F. 1985. Interdependence as a working concept. In *Managing criminal justice*, D. Moxon (ed.). London: HMSO.

Felson, M. 1986. Linking criminal choices, routine activities, informal control, and criminal outcomes. See Cornish & Clarke (1986a).

Felson, M. 1987. Routine activities and crime prevention in the developing metropolis. *Criminology* 25, 911–31.

Felson, M. 1992. Routine activities and crime prevention: armchair concepts and practical action. *Studies on Crime and Crime Prevention* 1, 30–34.

Felson, M. 1994. *Crime and everyday life*. Thousand Oaks, California: Pine Forge Press.

Fielding, N. 1984. *Probation practice*. Aldershot: Gower.

Forrester, D., M. Chatterton, K. Pease 1988. *The Kirkholt burglary prevention project, Rochdale*. Crime Prevention Unit Paper 13. London: Home Office.

Forrester, D., S. Frenz, M. O'Connell, K. Pease 1990. *The Kirkholt burglary prevention project, phase II*. Crime Prevention Unit Paper 23. London: Home Office.

Foster, J. 1990. Villains: crime and community in the inner city. London: Routledge.

Foster, J. 1995. Informal social control and community crime prevention. *British Journal of Criminology* 35, 563–83.

Foster, J. & T. Hope 1993. *Housing, community and crime: the impact of the Priority Estates Project*. Research Study 131. London: Home Office.

Foucault, M. 1977. *Discipline and punish*. Harmondsworth: Penguin.

Foucault, M. 1991. Governmentality. In *The Foucault effect*, G. Burchell, C.

Gordon, P. Miller (eds). Hemel Hempstead: Harvester Wheatsheaf.

Freeman, R. 1992. The idea of prevention: a critical review. In *Private risks and public dangers*, S. Scott, G. Williams, S. Platt, H. Thomas (eds). Aldershot: Avebury.

Gamble, A. 1981. *An introduction to modern social and political thought.* Basingstoke: Macmillan.

Garland, D. 1985. *Punishment and welfare: a history of penal strategies.* Aldershot: Gower.

Garland, D. 1994. Of crimes and criminals. The development of criminology in Britain. See Maguire, Morgan, Reiner (1994).

Garland, D. 1995. Surveillance and society. *Criminal Justice Matters* **20**, 3–4.

Geraghty, J. 1991. *Probation practice in crime prevention.* Crime Prevention Unit Paper 24. London: Home Office.

Gilling, D. 1992. *The evolution and implementation of the multi-agency approach to crime prevention.* Doctoral dissertation. University of Manchester.

Gilling, D. 1993. Crime prevention discourses and the multi-agency approach. *Howard Journal* **21**, 145–7.

Gilling, D. 1994. Multi-agency crime prevention in Britain: the problem of combining situational and social strategies. *Crime Prevention Studies* **3**, 231–48.

Gilling, D. 1996a. Policing, crime prevention and partnerships. In *Core issues in policing*, F. Leishman, B. Loveday, S. Savage (eds). Harlow: Longman.

Gilling, D. 1996b. Problems with the problem-oriented approach. *Crime Prevention Studies* **5**, 9–23.

Gladstone, F. 1980. *Co-ordinating crime prevention efforts.* London: HMSO.

Glaser, D. 1979. A review of crime-causation theory and its application. In *Crime and justice*, Volume 1, N. Morris & M. Tonry (eds). Chicago: University of Chicago Press.

Gordon, P. 1984. Community policing: towards the local police state? *Critical Social Policy* **10**, 39–58.

Gottfredson, M. & T. Hirschi 1990. *A general theory of crime.* Palo Alto, California: Stanford University Press.

Graham, J. (ed.) 1987. *Home Office Research Bulletin 24: special European edition.* London: HMSO.

Graham, J. 1990. *Crime prevention strategies in Europe and North America.* Helsinki: HEUNI.

Graham, J. & T. Bennett 1995. *Crime prevention strategies in Europe and North America.* Helsinki: European Institute for Crime Prevention and Control.

Greater London Council 1986. *Policing London: collected reports of the GLC police committee.* London: GLC.

Hale, C. 1992. Crime and penal policy. In *Social policy review 4*, N. Manning & R. Page (eds). London: Social Policy Association.

Hall-Williams, J. 1981. *Criminology and criminal justice.* London: Butterworths.

Harding, J. (ed.) 1987. *Probation and the community.* London: Tavistock.

Harding, J. 1987. Introduction. See Harding (1987).

Harris, R. 1992. *Crime, criminal justice and the probation service.* London: Routledge.

Harvey, L., P. Grimshaw & K. Pease 1989. Crime prevention delivery: the work of CPOs. In *Coming to terms with policing*, R. Morgan & D. Smith (eds). London: Routledge.

Hay, D. (ed.) 1975. *Albion's fatal tree.* Harmondsworth: Penguin.

Heal, K. 1983. The police, the public and the prevention of crime. *Howard Journal* **22**, 91–100.

Heal, K. 1987. Crime prevention in the United Kingdom: from start to go. See Graham (1987).

Heal, K. 1992. Changing perspectives on crime prevention: the role of information and structure. See Evans, Fyfe, Herbert (1992).

Heal, K. & J. Burrows (eds) 1983. *Crime prevention: a co-ordinated approach.* London: HMSO.

Heal, K. & G. Laycock 1986. Principles, issues and further action. See Heal & Laycock (1986).

Heal, K. & G. Laycock (eds) 1986. *Situational crime prevention: from theory into practice.* London: HMSO.

Heal, K. & G. Laycock 1988. The development of crime prevention: issues and limitations. See Hope & Shaw (1988).

Henderson, P. 1986a. Community work and the probation service. *HORPU Research Bulletin* **20**, 13–16.

Henderson, P. 1986b. *Community work and the probation service.* London: NISW.

Henderson, P. 1988. Community as a resource. *Justice of the Peace* **152**, 21–5.

Her Majesty's Chief Inspector of Constabulary. Annual Report 1965. London: HMSO.

Her Majesty's Chief Inspector of Constabulary. Annual Report 1970. London: HMSO.

Her Majesty's Chief Inspector of Constabulary. Annual Report 1972. London: HMSO.

Hesseling, R. 1994. Displacement: a review of the empirical literature. *Crime Prevention Studies* **3**, 197–230.

Hirschi, T. 1986. On the compatibility of rational choice and social control theories of crime. See Cornish & Clarke (1986).

Holdaway, S. 1983. *Inside the British police.* Oxford: Basil Blackwell.

Hollway, W. & T. Jefferson 1995. The risk society in an age of anxiety. Paper presented at British Criminology Conference, Loughborough, England.

Home Office 1977. *Review of Criminal Justice Policy 1976*. London: HMSO.

Home Office 1983. *Crime reduction: report of an inter-departmental group on crime*.

Home Office 1984. *Circular 8/84: crime prevention*.

Home Office. 1991. *Safer communities: the local delivery of crime prevention through the partnership approach*. London: Home Office.

Home Office 1993a. *A practical guide to crime prevention for local partnerships*. London: Home Office.

Home Office 1993b. *Police reform: a police service for the twenty-first century*. London: HMSO.

Home Office 1995. *Review of the police core and ancillary tasks: final report*. London: HMSO.

Home Office Crime Prevention Centre 1991. *Inter-agency co-operation for the 1990s: the way forward*. London: Home Office Crime Prevention Centre.

Home Office Crime Prevention Unit 1985. *Crime prevention initiatives in England and Wales*.

Home Office Crime Prevention Unit 1986. *Crime prevention and the community programme*.

Home Office Crime Prevention Unit 1988. *The five towns initiative*.

Hope, T. 1986. Crime, community and environment. *Journal of Environmental Psychology* **6**, 65–78.

Hope, T. 1987. Crime prevention, housing policy and research in England. See Graham (1987).

Hope, T. 1995. Community crime prevention. See Tonry & Farrington (1995).

Hope T. & D. Murphy 1983. Problems of implementing crime prevention. *Howard Journal* **22**, 38–50.

Hope, T. & M. Shaw 1988. Community approaches to reducing crime. See Hope & Shaw (1988).

Hope, T. & M. Shaw (eds) 1988. *Communities and crime reduction*. London: HMSO.

Hostettler, J. 1992. *The politics of punishment*. Chichester: Barry Rose.

Hough, J., R. Clarke, P. Mayhew 1980. Introduction. See Clarke & Mayhew (1980).

Hudson, B. 1987. Collaboration in social welfare: a framework for analysis. *Policy & Politics* **15**, 175–82.

Hugman, R. 1992. *Power in caring professions*. Basingstoke: Macmillan.

Husain, S. 1988. *Neighbourhood watch in England and Wales*. Home Office Crime Prevention Unit Paper 12. London: Home Office.

Husain, S. 1994. Neighbourhood Watch. See Association of District Councils (1994).

Illich, I. 1977. *Disabling professions*. London: Marion Boyars.

Jacobs, J. 1961. *The death and life of great American cities*. London: Cape.

Jeffery, C. 1971. *Crime prevention through environmental design*. Beverly Hills: Sage.

Jeffery, C. 1990. *Criminology: an interdisciplinary approach*. Englewood Cliffs, New Jersey: Prentice Hall.

Jeffery, C. & D. Zahn 1993. Crime prevention through environmental design, opportunity theory and rational choice models. See Clarke & Felson (1993).

Johnson, E. (ed.) 1987. *A handbook of crime and delinquency prevention*. Westport: Greenwood Press.

Johnson, T. 1972. *Professions and power*. Basingstoke: Macmillan.

Johnston, L. 1992. *The rebirth of private policing*. London: Routledge.

Johnston, L. 1993. Privatisation and protection: spatial and sectoral ideologies in British policing and crime prevention. *Modern Law Review* **56**, 771–92.

Johnston, V., M. Leitner, J. Shapland, P. Wiles 1994. *Crime on industrial estates*. Crime Prevention Unit Paper 54. London: Home Office.

Johnston, V., J. Shapland, P. Wiles 1993. *Developing police crime prevention: management and organisational change*. Crime Prevention Unit Paper 41. London: Home Office.

Jones, T., T. Newburn, D. Smith 1994. *Democracy and policing*. London: Policy Studies Institute.

King, M. 1989. Social crime prevention à la Thatcher. *Howard Journal* **28**, 291–312.

King, M. 1991. The political construction of crime prevention: a contrast between the French and British experience. See Stenson & Cowell (1991).

Kinsey, R., J. Lea, J. Young 1986. *Losing the fight against crime*. Oxford: Basil Blackwell.

Lacey, N. & L. Zedner 1995. Discourses of community in criminal justice. *Journal of Law and Society* **22**, 301–25.

Laycock, G. & K. Heal 1989. Crime prevention: the British experience. See Evans & Herbert (1989).

Laycock, G. & K. Pease 1985. Crime prevention within the probation service. *Probation Journal* **32**, 43–7.

Lea, J. 1995. Fragmentation, crime and justice. Paper presented at British Sociological Association Conference, Leicester, England.

Lebeau, J. 1987. Environmental design as a rationale for prevention. See Johnson (1987).

Lefevre, C., C. Rowan, E. Chadwick 1839. *First Report of the Constabulary*

Force Commissioners. London: Charles Knight.

Levi, M., P. Bissell, T. Richardson 1991. *The prevention of cheque and credit card fraud*. Crime Prevention Unit Paper 26. London: Home Office.

Liddle, M. & A. Bottoms 1991. *Implementing circular 8/84: a retrospective assessment of the Five Towns Crime Prevention Initiative*. Cambridge: Institute of Criminology.

Liddle, M. & L. Gelsthorpe 1994a. *Inter-agency crime prevention: organising local delivery*. Crime Prevention Unit Paper 52. London: Home Office.

Liddle, M. & L. Gelsthorpe 1994b. *Crime prevention and inter-agency co-operation*. Crime Prevention Unit Paper 53. London: Home Office.

Liddle, M. & L. Gelsthorpe 1994c. *Inter-agency crime prevention: further issues*. Supplementary paper to Crime Prevention Unit Papers 52 and 53. London: Home Office.

Lilly, J., F. Cullen, R. Ball 1995. *Criminological theory: context and consequences*, 2nd edn. Thousand Oaks, California: Sage.

Lloyd, C. 1986. *Response to SNOP*. Cambridge: Institute of Criminology.

Lloyd, S., G. Farrell, K. Pease 1994. *Preventing repeated domestic violence: a demonstration project on Merseyside*. Crime Prevention Unit Paper 49. London: Home Office.

Loveday, B. 1994a. The competing role of central and local agencies in crime prevention strategies. *Local Government Studies* **20**, 361–73.

Loveday, B. 1994b. Government strategies for community crime prevention. *International Journal of the Sociology of Law* **22**, 181–202.

Loveday, B. 1995. The Police and Magistrates' Courts Act. *Policing* **10**, 221–33.

Lowman, J., R. Menzies, T. Palys (eds) 1987. *Transcarceration: essays in the sociology of social control*. Aldershot: Gower.

Maguire, M., R. Morgan, R. Reiner (eds) 1994. *The Oxford handbook of criminology*. Oxford: Clarendon Press.

Manning, N. 1985. Constructing social problems. In *Social problems and welfare ideology*, N. Manning (ed.). Aldershot: Gower.

Matthews, R. 1992. Replacing "broken windows": crime, incivilities and urban change. In *Issues in realist criminology*, R. Matthews & J. Young (eds). London: Sage.

Matza, D. 1964. *Delinquency and drift*. New York: John Wiley.

Mawby, R. 1977. Defensible space: a theoretical and empirical appraisal. *Urban Studies* **14**, 169–79.

May, T. 1991. *Probation: politics, policy and practice*. Milton Keynes: Open University Press.

Mayhew, P. 1979. Defensible space: the current status of a crime prevention theory. *Howard Journal* **18**, 150–59.

Mayhew, P. 1991. Crime in public view: surveillance and crime prevention. See Brantingham & Brantingham (1991).

Mayhew, P., R. Clarke, A. Sturman, J. Hough 1976. *Crime as opportunity.* Research Study Number 34. London: Home Office.

McConville, S. & D. Shepherd 1992. *Watching police, watching communities.* London: Routledge.

McLaughlin, E. 1994. *Community, policing and accountability.* Avebury: Aldershot.

Merry, S. 1981. Defensible space undefended: social factors in crime control through environmental design. *Urban Affairs Quarterly* **16**, 397–422.

Michaelson, P. 1991. The Association of Metropolitan Authorities' perspective. See Home Office Crime Prevention Centre (1991).

Miller, M. & D. Brown 1994. Corporate involvement in community safety programs. In *Private sector and community involvement in the criminal justice system*, D. Biles & J. Vernon (eds). Canberra: Australian Institute of Criminology.

Morgan, R. 1987. The local determinants of policing policy. See Willmott (1987).

Morris, T. 1983. Crime and the welfare state. In *Approaches to welfare*, P. Bean & S. MacPherson (eds). London: Routledge & Kegan Paul.

Muncie, J., G. Coventry, R. Walters 1995. The politics of youth crime prevention: developments in Australia and in England and Wales. In *Contemporary issues in criminology*, L. Noaks, M. Levi, M. Maguire (eds). Cardiff: University of Wales Press.

Nash, M. & S. Savage 1994. A criminal record? Law, order and Conservative policy. In *Public policy in Britain*, S. Savage, R. Atkinson, L. Robins (eds). Basingstoke: Macmillan.

National Association for the Care and Rehabilitation of Offenders. 1988. *Policing housing estates.* London: NACRO.

National Association for the Care and Rehabilitation of Offenders. 1989. *Crime prevention and community safety.* London: NACRO.

National Association for the Care and Rehabilitation of Offenders. 1991. *Preventing youth crime.* London: NACRO.

National Association for the Care and Resettlement of Offenders. 1992. *Crime and social policy: international seminar at Edinburgh 1991.* London: NACRO.

National Association of Probation Officers. 1984. *Draft policy statement; crime prevention and reduction strategies.*

National Board for Crime Prevention. 1994. *Wise after the event: tackling repeat victimisation.* London: Home Office.

National Crime Prevention Institute. 1986. *Understanding crime prevention.* Boston: Butterworths.

Nelken, D. 1985. Community involvement in crime control. *Current legal problems*, 239–67.

Nellis, M. 1992. Criminology, crime prevention and the future of probation training. In *Criminal justice: theory and practice*, K. Bottomley, T. Fowles, R. Reiner (eds). London: British Society of Criminology.

Nellis, M. 1995. Probation values for the 1990s. *Howard Journal* **34**, 19–44.

Newman, K. 1983. *Report of the Commissioner for the Metropolis 1982*. London: HMSO.

Newman, O. 1973. *Defensible space*. London: Architectural Press.

Newman, O. & K. Franck 1980. *Factors influencing crime and instability in urban housing developments*. Washington, D.C.: Government Printing Office.

O'Malley, P. 1992. Risk, power and crime prevention. *Economy and Society* **21**, 252–75.

O'Malley, P. 1993. Neo-liberal crime control – political agendas and the future of crime prevention in Australia. In *The Australian criminal justice system*, D. Chappell & P. Wilson (eds). Sydney: Butterworths.

O'Malley, P. 1994. Responsibility and crime prevention: a response to Adam Sutton. *Australian and New Zealand Journal of Criminology* **27**, 21–4.

Owen, D. 1994 Making the links. See Association of District Councils (1994).

Palmer, S. 1988. *Police and protest in England and Ireland 1780–1950*. Cambridge: Cambridge University Press.

Partridge, M. 1984. Developing the role of crime prevention. See Proceedings of a national conference of crime prevention panels (1984).

Pasquino. P. 1991. Criminology: the birth of a special knowledge. In *The Foucault effect*, G. Burchell, C. Gordon, P. Miller (eds). Hemel Hempstead: Harvester Wheatsheaf.

Patten, J. 1988. Crime watch. *The Guardian*, 8 April 1988.

Patten, J. 1989. Be a local hero. *The Guardian*, 12 July 1989.

Pearson, G., H. Blagg, D. Smith, A. Sampson, P. Stubbs 1992. Crime, community and conflict. In *Unravelling criminal justice*, D. Downes (ed.). London: Routledge.

Pease, K. 1994. Crime prevention. See Maguire, Morgan, Reiner (1994).

Power, A. 1989. Housing, community and crime. See Downes (1989).

Poyner, B. 1986. *Crime reduction on housing estates: an evaluation of NACRO's crime prevention programme*. London: Tavistock Institute.

Proceedings of a national conference of crime prevention panels 1984.

Radzinowicz, L. 1966. *Ideology and crime*. London: Heinemann.

Raynor, P., D. Smith, M. Vanstone 1994. *Effective probation practice*. Basingstoke: Macmillan.

Reichman, N. 1987. The widening webs of surveillance: private police unraveling deceptive claims. See Shearing & Stenning (1987).

Reiner, R. 1992. *The politics of the police*, 2nd edn. Hemel Hempstead: Harvester Wheatsheaf.

Reiner, R. & M. Cross 1991. Introduction: beyond law and order – crime and criminology into the 1990s. In *Beyond law & order*, R. Reiner & M. Cross (eds). Basingstoke: Macmillan.

Reiss, A. 1988. Why are communities important in understanding crime? In *Communities and crime*, A. Reiss & M. Tonry (eds). Chicago: University of Chicago Press.

Reiss, A. 1993. Key issues in the integration of individual and community explanations of crime and criminality. In *Integrating individual and ecological aspects of crime*, D. Farrington & P-O. Wikstrom (eds). Stockholm: National Council for Crime Prevention.

Reith, C. 1956. *A new study of police history.* Edinburgh: Oliver and Boyd.

Reppetto, T. 1976. Crime prevention through environmental policy: a critique. *American Behavioural Scientist* **20**, 275–88.

Roberts, D. 1982. Jeremy Bentham and the Victorian administrative state. In *Jeremy Bentham – ten critical essays*, B. Parekh (ed.). London: Frank Cass.

Rock, P. 1988. Crime reduction initiatives on problem estates. See Hope & Shaw (1988).

Rosenbaum, D. 1986. *Community crime prevention.* Beverly Hills: Sage.

Rosenbaum, D. 1988. Community crime prevention: a review and synthesis of the literature. *Justice Quarterly* **5**, 323–95.

Roshier, B. 1989. *Controlling crime.* Milton Keynes: Open University Press.

Ryan, M. 1983. *The politics of penal reform.* Harlow: Longman.

Sampson, A. & D. Smith 1992. Probation and community crime prevention. *Howard Journal* **31**, 105–19.

Sampson, A., P. Stubbs, D. Smith, H. Blagg, G. Pearson 1988. Crime, localities and the multi-agency approach. *British Journal of Criminology* **28**, 478–93.

Scull, A. 1983. Community corrections: panacea, progress or pretence? In *The power to punish*, D. Garland & P. Young (eds). London: Heinemann.

Sen, A. & B. Williams 1982. Introduction. In *Utilitarianism and beyond*, A. Sen & B. Williams (eds). Cambridge: Cambridge University Press.

Shapland, J. & J. Vagg 1988. *Policing by the public.* London: Routledge.

Shapland, J. & P. Wiles 1988. *Business and crime.* Swindon: Crime Concern.

Shearing, C. & P. Stenning 1987. Say "cheese"! The Disney order that is not so Mickey Mouse. See Shearing & Stenning (1987).

Shearing, C. & P. Stenning (eds) 1987. *Private policing.* Beverly Hills: Sage.

Skogan, W. 1988. Disorder, crime and community decline. See Hope & Shaw (1988).

Skogan, W. 1990. *Disorder and decline: crime and the spiral of decay in American neighbourhoods.* New York: Free Press.

Smith, D. 1987. Policing and the idea of community. See Willmott (1987).

Smith, L. & G. Laycock 1985. *Reducing crime: developing the role of crime prevention panels*. Home Office Crime Prevention Unit Paper 2. London: Home Office.

Smith, S. 1986a. *Crime, space and society*. Cambridge: Cambridge University Press.

Smith, S. 1986b. Review of "Utopia on Trial". *Urban Studies* **23**, 244–6.

South, N. 1987. *The security and surveillance of the environment*. See Lowman, Menzies, Palys (1987).

Sparks, R. 1992. Reason and unreason in "left realism": some problems in the constitution of the fear of crime. In *Issues in realist criminology*, R. Matthews & J. Young (eds). London: Sage.

Squires, P. 1990. *Anti-social policy*. Hemel Hempstead: Harvester Wheatsheaf.

Squires, P. & L. Measor 1995. Community, ambiguity and the languages of crime prevention. Paper presented at Ideas of Community Conference, University of the West of England, Bristol, England.

Stanko, B. 1990. When precaution is normal: a feminist critique of crime prevention. In *Feminist perspectives in criminology*, L. Gelsthorpe & A. Morris (eds). Milton Keynes: Open University Press.

Stenning, P. 1988. Corporate policing: some recent trends. See Shapland & Wiles (1988).

Stenning, P. 1994. Private policing – some recent myths, developments and trends. In *Private sector and community involvement in the criminal justice system*, D. Biles & J. Vernon (eds). Canberra: Australian Institute of Criminology.

Stenson, K. 1991. Making sense of crime control. See Stenson & Cowell (1991).

Stenson, K. 1994. Youth work, risk and crime prevention. *Youth and Policy* **45**, 1–15.

Stenson, K. 1995. Communal security as government – the British experience. In *Jahrbuch für Rechts- und Kriminalsoziologie 1995: die sichere Stadt – Prävention und kommunale Sicherheitspolitik*, W. Hammerschick, I Karazman-Morawetz, W. Stangl (eds). Baden-Baden: Nomos.

Stenson, K. & D. Cowell (eds) 1991. *The politics of crime control*. London: Sage.

Stern, V. 1987. Crime prevention: the inter-organisational approach. See Harding (1987).

Sumner, C. 1994. *The sociology of deviance: an obituary*. Buckingham: Open University Press.

Sutton, A. 1994. Crime prevention: promise or threat? *Australian and New Zealand Journal of Criminology* **27**, 5–20.

Symes, R. 1984. Working with a crime prevention panel: successes and difficulties. See Proceedings of a national conference of crime prevention panels (1984).

Tallack, W. 1889. *Penological and preventive principles*. London: Wertheimer.

Taylor, I. 1993. Driving the vermin off the streets. *New Statesman and Society* (8 October), 16–18.

Taylor, I., P. Walton, J. Young 1973. *The new criminology*. London: Routledge & Kegan Paul.

Taylor, R. & S. Gottfredson 1986. Environmental design, crime, and prevention: an examination of community dynamics. In *Communities and crime*, A. Reiss & M. Tonry (eds). Chicago: University of Chicago Press.

Tilley, N. 1992. *Safer Cities and community safety strategies*. Crime Prevention Unit Paper 38. London: Home Office.

Tilley, N. 1993a. Crime prevention and the safer cities story. *Howard Journal* **32**, 40–57.

Tilley, N. 1993b. *The prevention of crime against small businesses: the Safer Cities experience*. Crime Prevention Unit Paper 45. London: Home Office.

Tobias, J. 1979. *Crime and police in England 1700–1900*. Dublin: Gill & Macmillan.

Tonry, M. & D. Farrington 1995. Strategic approaches to crime prevention. See Tonry & Farrington (1995).

Tonry, M. & D. Farrington (eds) 1995. *Building a safer society*. Chicago: Chicago University Press.

Trasler, G. 1986. Situational crime control and rational choice: a critique. See Heal & Laycock (1986).

Trasler, G. 1993. Conscience, opportunity, rational choice and crime. See Clarke & Felson (1993).

Tuck, M. 1987. Crime prevention: a shift in concept. See Graham (1987).

Walklate, S. 1991. Victims, crime prevention and social control. In *Beyond law & order*, R. Reiner & M. Cross (eds). Basingstoke: Macmillan.

Walklate, S. 1995. *Gender and crime*. Hemel Hempstead: Prentice Hall.

Weatheritt, M. 1983. Community policing: does it work and how do we know? See Bennett (1983).

Weatheritt, M. 1986. *Innovations in policing*. Beckenham: Croom Helm.

Weatheritt, M. 1987. Community policing now. See Willmott (1987).

Webb, B., B. Brown, K. Bennett 1992. *Preventing car crime in car parks*. Crime Prevention Unit Paper 34. London: Home Office.

Webb. B. & G. Laycock 1992. *Tackling car crime*. Crime Prevention Unit Paper 32. London: Home Office.

Weiss, R. 1987. The community and prevention. See Johnson (1987).

Whiskin, N. 1989. Conference address. See Crime Concern (1989).

Whiskin, N. 1991. Crime Concern: what has been achieved? See Home Office Crime Prevention Centre (1991).

Wilding, P. 1982. *Professional power and social welfare*. London: Routledge & Kegan Paul.

Wilkins, L. 1964. *Social deviance*. London: Tavistock.

Willmott, P. (ed.) 1987. *Policing and the community*. London: Policy Studies Institute.

Wilson, J. & G. Kelling 1982. Broken windows. *Atlantic Monthly* (March), 29-38.

Wilson, S. 1980. Vandalism and "defensible space" on London housing estates. See Clarke & Mayhew (1980).

Wilson-Croome, 1990. *Report to the working group on partnership in crime prevention*. Wakefield: Association of Chief Officers of Probation.

Windlesham, Lord 1987. *Responses to crime*. Oxford: Clarendon Press.

Windlesham, Lord 1993. *Responses to crime*, Volume 2. Oxford: Clarendon Press.

Young, J. 1981. Thinking seriously about crime: some models of criminology. In *Crime and society*, M. Fitzgerald, G. McLennan, J. Pawson (eds). London: Routledge & Kegan Paul.

Young, J. 1986. The failure of criminology: the need for a radical realism. In *Confronting crime*, R. Matthews & J. Young (eds). London: Sage.

Young, J. 1994. Incessant chatter: recent paradigms in criminology. See Maguire, Morgan, Reiner (1994).

Index

225